Scrivener™ FOR DUMMIES®

by Gwen Hernandez

WILEY

A John Wiley and Sons, Ltd, Publication

Scrivener™ For Dummies®

Published by
John Wiley & Sons, Ltd.
The Atrium
Southern Gate
Chichester
West Sussex
PO19 8SQ
England

Email (for orders and customer service enquires): cs-books@wiley.co.uk

Visit our home page on www.wiley.com

Copyright © 2012 John Wiley & Sons, Ltd, Chichester, West Sussex, England

Published by John Wiley & Sons Ltd, Chichester, West Sussex

For general information on our other products and services, please contact our Customer Care Department within the U.S. at 877-762-2974, outside the U.S. at 317-572-3993, or fax 317-572-4002.

For technical support, please visit www.wiley.com/techsupport.

Wiley publishes in a variety of print and electronic formats and by print-on-demand. Some material included with standard print versions of this book may not be included in e-books or in print-on-demand. If this book refers to media such as a CD or DVD that is not included in the version you purchased, you may download this material at http://booksupport.wiley.com. For more information about Wiley products, visit www.wiley.com.

British Library Cataloguing in Publication Data: A catalogue record for this book is available from the British Library.

ISBN: 978-1-118-31247-6 (pbk); ISBN 978-1-118-31244-5 (ebk); ISBN 978-1-118-31245-2 (ebk); ISBN 978-1-118-31246-9 (ebk)

Printed and bound in the United States by Bind-Rite

10 9 8 7 6 5 4 3 2 1

About the Author

Gwen Hernandez began working with Scrivener in 2009 and created a series of blog posts to share its lesser-known features with her writing friends. Encouraged by her growing community of followers, she developed a popular Scrivener online class that's offered several times a year.

With a degree in Management Information Systems, Gwen started her professional life as a programmer and then transitioned to teaching technology and business courses. She changed tack with an advanced degree, working as a manufacturing engineer in a semiconductor plant — yes, she wore a "bunny suit" — before rediscovering her childhood passion for writing.

When Gwen's not teaching classes about Scrivener, she uses it to spin tales of romance and suspense, and every once in a while, someone actually likes reading them. In 2011, she was a finalist in the Romance Writers of America's Golden Heart® contest.

As a military brat and Air Force spouse, Gwen isn't sure she'll ever be able to settle down, but she currently resides in northern Virginia with her husband, two boys, and a lazy golden retriever. She loves to travel, run, explore, learn, and relax in her favorite recliner with a good book. Find her online at www.gwenhernandez.com.

Dedication

For my mom, who would have smiled proudly and bought me a houseplant.

Author's Acknowledgments

Many hugs to my husband and boys for their unwavering — though not without some eye rolling — support. I love you guys!

Thanks to Christine Glover for introducing me to Scrivener. Bet you didn't think your first mention from me would be in a technical book.

I'd be remiss if I didn't add my appreciation for the blog readers and students who've encouraged me along the way. Your support and enthusiasm mean the world to me.

I owe Keith, Ioa, Jennifer, and Lee at Literature & Latte a huge debt of gratitude for pointing out technical errors, providing examples and suggestions, and keeping me up to date on what's coming next. Any mistakes or omissions are not for their lack of effort. Their help with this book was invaluable.

To Keith Blount and the whole Literature & Latte crew, thanks for your dedication to making — and keeping — Scrivener so fabulous. And to David who's always generous in spreading the word.

Finally, I have to add my thanks to the entire Wiley team who worked so hard on this book, especially Laura Miller, who tweaked and questioned and clarified, and made this book so much better than I could have on my own, and Chris Webb who believed in me enough to let me tackle this project.

Publisher's Acknowledgments

We're proud of this book; please send us your comments at http://dummies.custhelp.com. For other comments, please contact our Customer Care Department within the U.S. at 877-762-2974, outside the U.S. at 317-572-3993, or fax 317-572-4002.

Some of the people who helped bring this book to market include the following:

Acquisitions and Editorial

Project Editor: Laura K. Miller

Acquisitions Editor: Chris Webb

Assistant Editor: Ellie Scott

Copy Editor: Laura K. Miller

Technical Editors: Keith Blount, Ioa Petra'ka

Editorial Manager: Jodi Jensen

Senior Project Editor: Sara Shlaer

Editorial Assistant: Leslie Saxman

Cover image: © Literature & Latte

Cartoons: Rich Tennant (www.the5thwave.com)

Composition Services

Sr. Project Coordinator: Kristie Rees

Layout and Graphics: Jennifer Creasey

Proofreaders: The Well-Chosen Word

Indexer: Valerie Haynes Perry

UK Tech Publishing

Michelle Leete, VP Consumer and Technology Publishing Director

Martin Tribe, Associate Director–Book Content Management

Chris Webb, Associate Publisher

Marketing

Louise Breinholt, Associate Marketing Director

Lorna Mein, Marketing Manager

Kate Parrett, Senior Marketing Executive

Publishing and Editorial for Technology Dummies

Richard Swadley, Vice President and Executive Group Publisher

Andy Cummings, Vice President and Publisher

Mary Bednarek, Executive Acquisitions Director

Mary C. Corder, Editorial Director

Publishing for Consumer Dummies

Kathleen Nebenhaus, Vice President and Executive Publisher

Composition Services

Debbie Stailey, Director of Composition Services

Contents at a Glance

Table of Contents

Introduction

*I*f writing tools were teachers, your word processor would be the one who admonishes you to color within the lines and always use green for grass. Scrivener would be the cool teacher who encourages you to draw your own picture and praises your purple sun.

Don't get me wrong: Word processors have their place. But although they provide the tools to make your manuscript look pretty, they force you to write in a linear fashion that just doesn't match the way many writers work.

Scrivener, on the other hand, is so flexible, it could teach yoga. The program bends over backwards to accommodate your writing needs. Want to write the ending first? Go for it! Want to look only at scenes from one character or storyline? No problem.

Scrivener's flexibility makes it powerful — but sometimes a bit overwhelming, which is where this book comes in. In these pages, you can figure out many of Scrivener's jaw-dropping moves so that, before long, you too can bend like a pretzel in pursuit of writerly nirvana.

Conventions Used in This Book

This book is not a philosophical work on the theory and value of writing software. In my house, that kind of book would be a doorstop.

No, this book is a hands-on, get-to-work teacher on the page. So, to try out any of the actions described, you have to get your hands on the keyboard and mouse (or trackpad).

With that in mind, you need to have a few skills:

- ✔ **Clicking:** You need to know how to click, double-click, and right-click with your mouse or trackpad. Right-clicking opens up a whole new world of contextual menus that apply to whatever you're working on. Also called a *secondary click,* you can Control-click on the Mac if your mouse isn't set up to right-click.

- ✔ **Drag and drop:** You'll be dragging things around a lot in this book — but I promise nothing heavy. Dragging is accomplished by clicking an object and holding the mouse button down while moving the pointer on the screen. You drop by letting go of the mouse button.

> Don't know how to drag with a trackpad? While hovering the pointer over the selected items, click the trackpad and hold it down while using another finger to drag the items where you want them to go. (I usually click with my thumb and drag with my index finger, but use whatever feels comfortable to you.)

To make reading easier, you'll see some of the following conventions used throughout the book:

- ✓ A keyboard shortcut is represented like this: ⌘+V. This text means that you press and hold the ⌘ key and type the letter V, then release both keys.

    Some keyboard shortcuts are combinations of more than two keys, such as Shift+⌘+S. For this one, press and hold Shift and ⌘, and then type the letter S. Then release all three keys.

- ✓ Menu commands are written like Project⇨New Text, which tells you to click Project to open the Project menu and choose New Text from that menu.

- ✓ Web addresses appear like `www.literatureandlatte.com`.

- ✓ When I want to show you a message or text that appears in the editing portion of Scrivener, it looks like this: `Bob didn't know what to do next. Should he buy a gun or a beer?`

- ✓ When I'm directing you to type specific text, it appears in bold. For example, I might tell you to type **Bob didn't know what to do next**.

Windows users, have no fear. Although Scrivener was originally created for the Mac — and at this time, the Mac version is still the most advanced — much of this book still applies to the Windows version, too.

For more on the key differences between Scrivener for Mac and Scrivener for Windows, check out Chapter 1.

What You're Not to Read

Unless you really, really want to, you don't have to read this book from cover to cover. Each section and chapter is designed as a freestanding module so that you can dip in anywhere and get right to work.

Foolish Assumptions

We all know what assumptions do, but in order to write this book, I had to make a few anyway. For starters, I assumed that you have some fundamental skills with your computer, such as turning it on, starting a program, using a mouse, and accessing and saving files.

In addition, I assumed you've at least used a word processor before — whether Microsoft Word, Corel WordPerfect, Apple Pages, or something else — so you have some familiarity with selecting text, basic formatting (such as font, font size, justification, and spacing), and keyboard use.

Not only that, but because this book is about a piece of writing software, I figured you *write something.* I know, dangerous, right? Really, I don't care if it's a 1,000-page futuristic mystery about flying snakes or weekly letters to your grandmother. It's all writing. Academic papers, news articles, recipes, and diaries count, too.

Finally, I reasoned that you actually want to find out Scrivener's secrets. Whether you've been playing with it for years without digging into what it can really do, or you just heard from a friend that Scrivener was the best thing to happen to writers since the ballpoint pen and you want to know what all of the fuss is about, there's a reason you picked up this book.

When I use the word *Scrivener,* I'm referring to Scrivener 2 for Mac — and specifically for Mac OS X Lion — but much of the information I provide applies to the Windows version, as well. And if it doesn't now, it will eventually. Those fabulous guys over at Literature & Latte are working like an army of ants to get the Windows version all caught up.

How This Book Is Organized

This book is organized into seven major parts that have two or more chapters each. The chapters are split up into even smaller sections. If you're a complete Scrivener newbie, don't worry, each section is written as a stand-alone piece that takes you step-by-step through the topic.

No need to read in order. You can jump right to the section about project templates without wading through corkboards and outlines, if you so desire. So, pick a topic, flip — literally or virtually — to the appropriate page, and try something new.

Part I: Getting to Know Scrivener

This part introduces Scrivener and its unique parts. You can find out how to create a new project, find your way around, and work with documents inside your project. Newbies: Start here!

Part II: Meeting the Inspector

This part walks you through the Scrivener Inspector pane's many features, from the Synopsis, to metadata, to all those buttons at the bottom. You can get the scoop on notes, references, keywords, and snapshots.

Part III: Starting to Write

The chapters in this part deal with getting the words down on virtual paper. They cover the Editor, working in Split Screen mode, Composition (Full Screen) mode, the Corkboard, the Outliner, annotations, and footnotes.

Part IV: Getting Your Manuscript Out There

This part talks about exporting your work from Scrivener. Whether you just need to get a few chapters into Word or the whole book into EPUB format, this part's for you.

Part V: Customizing Your Scrivener Experience

This part digs into some of the fun and cool features that really make Scrivener shine, such as tracking your progress, custom layouts, creating project templates, and document templates.

Part VI: Getting the Most Out of Scrivener

The chapters in this part introduce you to functions that can make your writing life easier: searching, creating collections, working with revisions, and backing up your work.

Part VII: The Part of Tens

This traditional final part of any *For Dummies* book contains chapters that introduce you to cool features that didn't fit anywhere else and gives you ideas on how to find more Scrivener help.

Icons Used in This Book

Tips alert you to helpful information or timesaving shortcuts.

The Remember icon calls your attention to important ideas to keep in mind while performing a task.

This icon points out extra tidbits for your inner computer geek. Helpful, but not strictly necessary to know, you can skip these if they make your eyes cross.

I use the Warning icon sparingly, but when you see it, take notice. It calls your attention to potential pitfalls.

Where to Go From Here

Dig in! Unless you're new to Scrivener — and even then — you don't have to start at page one. I won't be offended if you don't read every word I wrote. Well, not *too* offended.

Go on. Peruse the Table of Contents or the handy index at the back of the book, and find a topic that interests you.

In need of a distraction-free desktop? Chapter 7 can help you find your Zen. Been dying to unravel the mystery of project templates? Investigate Chapter 15. Stumped by exporting and compiling? Part IV can enlighten you.

If, for some reason, you want to know more about me — or contact me — visit my website at www.gwenhernandez.com. I'd love to know what your favorite Scrivener feature is or how the program helped your writing process.

I hope you enjoy this book. If it helps you use Scrivener to support your unique approach to writing, then I've done my job.

Good luck, and write on!

Part I
Getting to Know Scrivener

The 5th Wave   By Rich Tennant

"Oddly enough, he keeps his story elements well organized in the Binder."

In this part . . .

When a friend first told me about Scrivener —
"gushed enthusiastically" might be a better
description — I wondered what writing software could
possibly offer that a word processor can't. So I downloaded the free trial, and three days later, I paid for it, not
even waiting for the trial to expire.

I knew I had to have Scrivener in my life.

Word processors are wonderful pieces of software, and
they definitely have an important place in a writer's tool-
box, but Scrivener opens up a whole new way of putting
together your story, poem, screenplay, dissertation, epic
novel, or blog post.

Simply put, Scrivener puts you in charge of how you write.
This part of the book introduces you to the fundamentals
of this amazing program.

Chapter 1

Getting Started in Scrivener

*P*arts of Scrivener probably look very familiar to you. The Editor pane, for example, is essentially the built-in word processor. If you've been using a computer to write — and not, say, carving stone tablets or working in crayon — then the act of putting down words will be a piece of cake in Scrivener, too. At least, Scrivener makes writing easy from a technical standpoint. It can't do anything about your muse.

Outside the Editor, however, things look a little different, maybe even a bit confusing. If you're not already familiar with the Scrivener interface — and maybe even if you think you are — you can use this chapter to make sure you understand the basic terminology fundamental to using Scrivener and get to know Scrivener's many wonderful parts.

Understanding What Scrivener Is (and Isn't)

Scrivener's core purpose is to help you write. It's not intended to tell you *how* to write or force you to get the work done. Instead, Scrivener provides an environment in which you can keep your writing, research, character sketches, synopses, outlines, and images in one project file.

You can export your work into many formats and document combinations without affecting the original manuscript. So you can export three chapters to a word processor one minute, and then create an e-book file the next, all without modifying the format in Scrivener. You can write in green, Comic Sans text but export in black, Times New Roman text.

Writing software is all about the experience of writing, not the format of the final text. You can write without distraction in Composition (Full Screen) mode, view multiple scenes at the same time, storyboard by using electronic index cards, or view your work as an outline.

Scrivener was created to support all aspects of the creative process of writing, from inception to final revision, not just the period when you actually lay down the words.

Understanding the Differences between Mac and Windows Versions

Scrivener was originally created for the Mac, but in November 2011, Literature & Latte — the company behind the software — released a much-anticipated version for Windows. At some point, the Windows version is expected to match the capabilities of the Mac version, but at the time of this book's publication, some features still aren't available to Windows users.

Take heart, Windows users, because those features will come in time, and the Windows programmers have done a fabulous job of incorporating the most beloved functions of Scrivener. I make note of differences between the two versions whenever I can.

I'm not going to talk about all the functional differences because program updates are frequent and the list would quickly be out of date. The best resource is provided by the Literature & Latte folks at `http://literatureandlatte.com/forum`. From this page, click Scrivener for Windows; click Technical Support (Windows) on the Scrivener for Windows page that appears; and on the Technical Support (Windows) page that appears, click Differences between the Mac and Windows Versions.

Although the programmers strive to put menu commands in the same location on both versions, there will always be some disparity because Windows and Mac each have their own rules and standards. For example, Mac software always has a program menu — in this case, the Scrivener menu — whereas Windows doesn't.

Mac also has a standard menu called Window. Its commands can often be found in the Tools menu on the Windows version. Table 1-1 provides a list of commands that have different locations in the Mac and Windows versions and where to find those commands.

Table 1-1	Menu Locations of Scrivener Commands	
Command	*Mac Menu*	*Windows Menu*
Preferences	Scrivener⇨Preferences	Tools⇨Options
Customize Toolbar	Edit	Tools
Layouts	Window	View
Scratch Pad	Window	Tools

Looking at Scrivener Keyboard Conventions

Scrivener has a lot of keyboard *shortcuts,* combinations of keys that activate a menu command when pressed simultaneously. If you're a mouse hater (but they're so cute!) or just dread taking your fingers off the keyboard, you'll love keyboard shortcuts.

Any command that has a keyboard shortcut lists the shortcut next to the item on the menu, as shown in Figure 1-1.

New Text	⌘N
New Folder	⌥⌘N
New From Template	▶
New Media File	▶
Show Project Targets	⇧⌘T
Project Statistics...	⌥⇧⌘S
Text Statistics...	^⌥⌘S
Project Notes...	⌥⌘P
Show Project Keywords	⌥⇧⌘H
Meta–Data Settings...	⌥⌘,
Auto–Complete List...	
Text Preferences...	
Set Selection As Templates Folder	
Empty Trash...	

Figure 1-1:
Keyboard
shortcuts
are listed
next to their
menu items.

The shortcut might look like a lot of gobbledygook, but it's just a series of keys that can get the job done. Table 1-2 shows the common shortcut characters and their equivalent key.

Table 1-2	Keyboard Shortcut Characters	
Character	*Key*	*Operating System*
⌘	Command	Mac
⇧	Shift	Mac/Windows
⌃	Control/Ctrl	Mac/Windows
⌥	Option	Mac
⌥	Alt	Windows
⎋	Esc	Mac/Windows

In Windows, the Return key is called Enter.

Creating a Project

Scrivener files are called *projects*. A Scrivener project is a collection of documents, some of which contain the text of your manuscript; others hold reference materials, photos, notes, and so on. Think of a project like a virtual three-ring binder: You can break up your writing into multiple documents, as well as include supporting notes, documentation, images, and website content, all under the umbrella of a single project file.

In order to get started in Scrivener, you must first create a project, in part because the program saves while you write (two seconds after every pause, by default!). To save your work automatically, it must already know the name of the file and where the file is stored on your computer.

If you've never used Scrivener before, or you closed all open projects last time you used it, Scrivener brings up the Project Templates window when you open it. You can also open the Project Templates window by choosing File⇨New Project.

Choosing the right template

A template is kind of like a new house purchased from a builder. You and your neighbor might buy the same model, but then you add your own paint colors, window dressing, flooring, fixtures, and landscaping. The neighbors might prefer antique furnishings, but your house is full of glass and steel. They might choose white siding, where you choose brick. They have garden gnomes, and you have a gazing ball. They . . . well, you get the idea.

Same template, different results.

The same is true in Scrivener. Each project template gives you a starting point from which to customize the project for your needs so that you don't have to start from scratch. In fact, in Part V of this book, you can find out how to create and save your own templates for use with future projects.

The Project Templates window is organized into tabs for each template type, as shown in Figure 1-2.

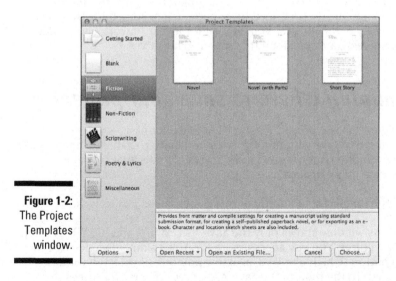

Figure 1-2: The Project Templates window.

Click a tab to see the templates associated with that type. A pane at the bottom of the Project Templates window displays a short description of any template when you select it. Choose the template that most closely matches the type of project you're working on. Then, you can mold that template to meet your needs, with the help of this book.

For the examples in this book, I use a project based on the Novel template. For those working in non-fiction, the General Non-Fiction template provides a close match to the figures in this book.

Naming your project

After you select a template, click the Choose button. Scrivener opens the Save As window and prompts you to enter a filename. (Windows users: The Save As section is in the New Project window. Select a filename, click Browse to choose a location, and then click Create.)

Consider these facts when naming your file:

- ✔ **Scrivener uses the filename as the project name.** If you select certain templates, the project name is automatically inserted into the title page and into the header when you export the project (to print the manuscript, convert it to an e-book, and so on). However, you can change the project name manually or rename the project file at a later time.

- ✔ **Be sure to give the project a name that you can easily find again later.** If your manuscript is a novel about a man who shape-shifts into a rabbit when he visits the planet Lotharia, you might not want to call it Project1. The working title doesn't need to be perfect, just something that makes the file easy to locate after you let it sit for a year to work on that zombie private-investigator mash-up that was nagging at you.

Determining where to save your project

After you figure out the project's name — at least, for now — you need to determine where to save your project. Because I'm excruciatingly organized — well, on my computer, anyway — I have a writing folder that contains sub-folders for each major project.

Of course, the Documents folder may serve your needs just as well.

If your Save As window shows only the Save As text box and the Where drop-down list, don't fret. You can access more locations simply by clicking the Expansion button (which displays an arrow pointing down if the window isn't expanded) to the right of the Save As text box. Figure 1-3 shows the Expansion button after the window expands (with the arrow now pointing up). Windows users, click the Browse button in the New Project window to choose a location.

Click to hide/expand location options

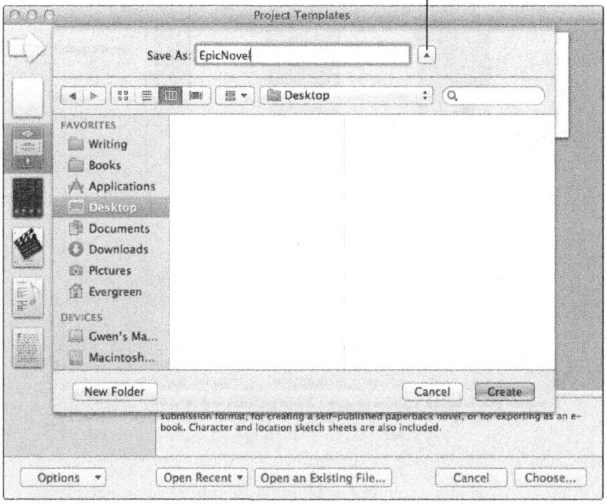

Figure 1-3:
Clicking the
Expansion
button
provides
more
options for
locations to
save your
file.

Now, simply select a location by clicking the desired folder in the list on the left. If needed, choose subsequent subfolders until you reach your destination folder. Then click Create.

Understanding the Scrivener Interface

When Scrivener first opens your new project, you can immediately see that this program is more than a word processor. Don't be alarmed by all the stuff that appears. Hopefully, after you understand what all these pieces and parts can do for you, you think of them merely as more to love.

The following sections provide an overview of the major elements of the Scrivener workspace, and the remaining chapters in this part and all the chapters in Part II are devoted to explaining each element in more detail.

Figure 1-4 names the major components for you. Don't worry about what they all mean. Unless you have a photographic memory, just keep a thumb, or maybe a sticky note, tucked into this page so that you can refer to it, as needed.

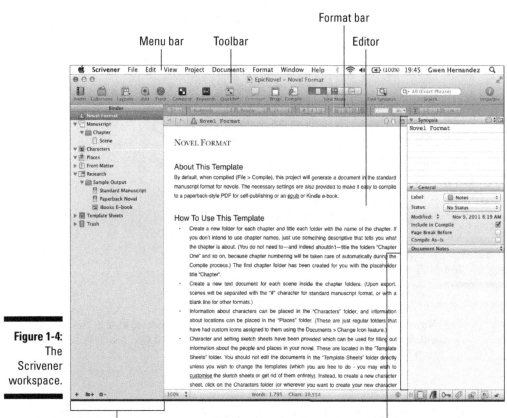

Format bar

Menu bar   Toolbar   Editor

Figure 1-4:
The
Scrivener
workspace.

Binder   Inspector

Menu bar

Across the top of your window is the menu bar. The menu bar, aptly named as it is, provides an organized menu of the program's commands. Although many of the menu commands have shortcuts, via keyboard or button, almost anything you need to do is available in one of the menus.

If you're using the Windows version, the menu bar looks a bit different, but most commands are still there somewhere. And if they're not now, they will be.

Each menu is organized into groups of menus and submenus that, mostly, make sense. So, commands that relate to working with a project file in a generic sense — such as opening a new project or saving the current one — are listed in the File menu.

Toolbar

The toolbar lives below the menu bar. At the top-center of the toolbar, Scrivener displays the project title followed by the active document name. (The Windows version doesn't display the project name in the toolbar, only the project title in the title bar, which appears above the menu bar.) Beneath the title, you find a row of colorful buttons for some of the most commonly used menu commands. To see the name of each button, hover your pointer over it for a second. A small tooltip pops up with the button name.

If you find hovering tiresome, Mac users can turn on text for the button icons by going to View⇨Customize Toolbar. At the bottom-left of the Customize Toolbar window that appears, select Icons and Text from the Show drop-down list, as shown in Figure 1-5. In this window, you can also decide which buttons to display in the toolbar by dragging them from the field of buttons into the toolbar.

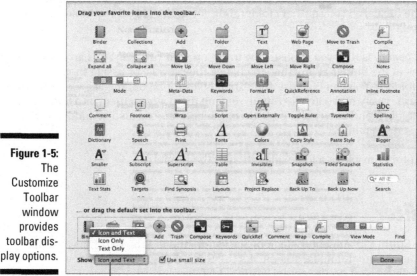

Figure 1-5: The Customize Toolbar window provides toolbar display options.

Change toolbar display options

Binder

The purpose of the Binder is to help you navigate and organize your documents. If it's not visible, go to View⇨Layout⇨Show Binder or click the Binder button in the toolbar.

Much like Finder (or Windows Explorer) does for your computer, the Binder provides access to all the files located within your project and keeps those files organized in an easy-to-see, hierarchical fashion. But even more, the Binder gives you an outline view of your manuscript.

Documents can be organized into folders (which may have a folder icon or some other icon) and multiple levels of subfolders, if desired.

For example, in the Manuscript folder (which is called Draft in the Scrivener User Manual and goes by other names, depending on which template you choose), you store all the documents you want to include in your final manuscript. If you want, you can break up your project into four parts in the Manuscript folder, with chapter folders within each part that contain the scene documents for each chapter. Try finding an easy way to do that in a word processor!

Or, within the Research folder, you might add subfolders to help further classify your research by type (for example, firearms, weather, period costumes, police procedure, plants). You can store photos, PDFs, and website archives in the Research (or another) folder, but not in the Manuscript folder, which is for text only.

The beauty is that *you* choose how to set up your project. You can rearrange items in the Binder at any time to change their levels, or assign them to different folders. You can collapse and expand files for an outline-like view of your project, easily move items around, rename them, group them into folders and subfolders, and even color-code them. The Binder can also be hidden if you find it distracting.

Chapter 2 provides a full explanation of the Binder.

Editor

The Editor sits at center stage in Scrivener, and it's the part that probably seems the most familiar to you. It's the text-editing part of Scrivener — the part where you do the actual writing. Just like a word processor, it contains a formatting bar at the top, a ruler (which may or may not be visible initially), and a blank space for adding your words.

If you chose a template other than Blank, your new project displays a description of the template and how it's set up. This is a handy reference that sits at the top of the Binder unless you delete it, so you may want to keep it until you get the hang of things.

If the Editor looks like a corkboard or a series of horizontal lines, choose View➪Document (called Scrivenings when multiple files — or a container — are selected).

Within the Editor pane, you have access to several views: Document/ Scrivenings (which displays the text editor), Corkboard (index cards), and Outliner.

The Editor has plenty of tricks up its virtual sleeve, which are covered in Part III of this book.

Inspector

The Inspector isn't a police detective — but for many new users, it's a bit of a mystery. Located at the far-right of the Scrivener window, the Inspector is a common feature in Mac-based programs, but exists in the Windows version, as well. If it's not visible, choose View➪Layout➪Show Inspector or click the Inspector button in the toolbar.

The Inspector displays all sorts of extra information — known as metadata — about the items in your Binder and allows you to modify a lot of that information. If each scene, chapter, or section within your project were a cereal box, your written text would be the chocolaty rice puffs inside, and the Inspector would be all the information on the outside of the box. (Anyone else hungry?)

When you first start Scrivener, the Inspector displays the Synopsis, general metadata, and notes for whichever document is selected in the Binder:

- ✔ **Synopsis:** The top portion of the pane. You can type a brief summary or outline of that scene, chapter, part, image, or whatever can help remind you what it's about. When you work with the Corkboard (which I describe in Chapter 8), you can see that the index card contents are pulled from the Synopsis section.

- ✔ **General:** Located in the middle of the Inspector pane, you store other information about the file here.

- ✔ **Document/Project Notes:** This bottom section of the Inspector pane lets you record notes or reminders about the document.

If you want more room to write, or just less clutter in general, you can hide the Inspector by clicking the Inspector button in the toolbar or choosing View➪Layout➪Hide Inspector.

Want to investigate the Inspector's many secrets? Part II of this book is devoted entirely to solving the puzzle of the Inspector.

Determining Your Writing Style

Whether you sit down in front of a blank piece of paper with only the spark of an idea or you create an 80-page outline complete with a storyboard and photos of all your characters before you write, Scrivener accommodates you.

The aforementioned people who write by the seat of their pants — so-called pantsers — might start writing, get to the logical end of the scene, and then start a new document for another scene, whether next in order or not.

Plotters, on the other hand — those who live and die by the outline — might start their process in the Corkboard (Chapter 8) or Outliner (Chapter 9), creating a title and brief synopsis for each scene, moving the scenes around until the order is just right, and then, after setting the storyline, begin filling in the actual text of the story.

Perhaps, like me, you're somewhere in between. It might even change from one manuscript or type of project to the next. The real beauty here is that you don't have to stick with one style. Pantsing your way through and got stuck? Try playing with your scenes in the Corkboard. Had a perfect outline, but your characters protested your "all is lost" moment in the plot? Try opening a blank document and free-writing your way through it.

There's no right or wrong style, only your style. And no matter what style works for you, Scrivener has your back.

Chapter 2

Organizing Your Work with the Binder

. . . .

In This Chapter

▶ Looking at Scrivener documents and folders

▶ Branching off from the root folders

▶ Putting the elements of your project in place

▶ Adjusting items in Scrivener

. . . .

*T*hrough the Binder, Scrivener gives you total control over how you organize your manuscript. By using folders to separate it into chapters or parts — or anything else you can think of — you can quickly and easily navigate through your work.

When I write, I like to get all the scenes down without worrying about dividing them into chapters until later. Because I've recently started doing some basic outlining before I start, I now set up four folders — one for each of the book's parts — and add the newest scene to whichever part it belongs. At the end, I go back and group the scenes into chapter folders.

Scrivener gives you the flexibility to write (or, at least, synopsize) out of order, if desired. And unlike in a word processor, where you might have to create a separate file for those scenes you weren't ready for, or keep pushing the out-of-order scenes to the bottom of the word processor document, you can keep them all within your Scrivener project without creating a mess.

This chapter shows you how to organize and manipulate your files and folders to set up the best structure for your writing process.

Understanding Files and Folders in Scrivener

Before you dig into working in the Binder, a couple of things require clarification: The concept of folders and files is less rigid in Scrivener than you're probably used to. A Scrivener folder can contain text, just like a document, and can be converted back to a document at any time.

Document files can contain sub-files, making them a container much like a folder — called a *file group* — and can be converted to a folder at any time.

Folders and files are essentially the same, except for their icons and default view modes. Files open in Document view, but folders open in the last-used group view (Scrivenings, Corkboard, or Outliner). The distinction can help you organize your documents.

The difference between files and folders as containers really becomes significant only when you compile (export) your manuscript, which I cover in Part IV.

The following are definitions for the terms I use throughout this book when discussing the Binder:

- **Item:** Any file or folder within the Binder, regardless of type.

- **Document:** An item that contains text. A document could be a new file created within the Scrivener project or a file that's been imported from outside the project (for example, a Word, RTF, or plain text file). You can use an empty document as a placeholder for a future scene, with or without a Synopsis.

- **Folder:** A container for documents and other folders. Designated by the folder icon — or another icon of your choosing (see the section "Changing folder and file icons," later in this chapter) — folders can also contain text, such as a chapter introduction or a chapter title.

  Folders can be converted to a file or file group without losing any text or data. They are mainly used to visually organize your documents and to create chapter headings and divisions when you export the manuscript.

- **File group:** Much like a folder, but designated as a file, rather than a folder. Represented by a paper stack icon, a file group is still a container, but it can also act like a document.

- **Container:** Any Binder item that contains other files or folders, or is designated as a folder.

Figure 2-1 breaks down the Binder, using an example project created with the Novel template. Each type of item has its own icon, and some folders have specialty icons.

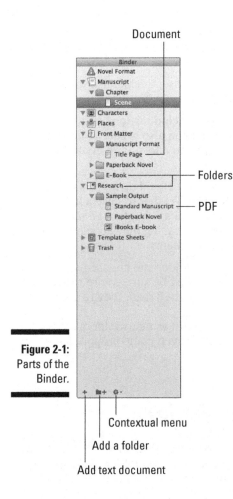

Figure 2-1:
Parts of the
Binder.

Working with the Root Folders

Despite the fact that roots are low on a plant, a *root folder* is a folder at the highest level. Think of a plant's roots in the ground. They start from one central point and then branch out from there. Your files are organized in the same way.

Root folders are the top of the root ball. You can't delete them, but you can change their names and icons.

Every Scrivener project starts out with three root folders:

   ✔ **Manuscript (Draft):** Where you store the files that you want included in your final manuscript. No matter how you have it organized, when you export your manuscript, Scrivener combines the files from this folder into one long document. (You do have options for exporting a partial draft, which I cover in Part IV.)

Only text and folder files can be contained within the Manuscript folder; however, images can be inserted into text within a document, just like in a word processor.

Depending on the project template you chose, the Manuscript folder may have a different name, such as Draft or Screenplay.

✔ **Research:** Holds all your, well, research, including non-text files, such as PDFs, image files, and web archives. You can also create or import text files that aren't part of your manuscript and add subfolders to further organize your research files.

✔ **Trash:** Items that you delete from your project end up in the Trash folder. When the Trash contains files, the icon for Trash looks like a full trash bin. Files in the Trash appear in search results (Chapters 17 and 18 cover searching), but their icons are *ghosted* — meaning they appear faded — so that you can easily tell that they're deleted items.

To empty the Trash, right-click the Trash folder and choose Empty Trash from the contextual menu that appears. Just be sure you're ready to get rid of those files because after you empty the Trash, they're gone!

In addition to the three root folders, you can add as many folders as you want at the root level. Some project templates even come prepopulated with additional root-level folders.

Building Your Scrivener Project

Before you can start writing, you need a document to write in. The following sections show you how to create new documents, add folders to keep them organized, and import existing writing and documentation into your project.

Adding a text document

So, you're sick of staring at a blank screen, and you're ready to start writing? First, you need to add a text document to your Scrivener project (see Chapter 1 for more on creating a project). Just follow these steps:

1. **In the Binder, select the folder to which you want to add the document.**

   The folder can be at any level, in or out of the Manuscript root folder.

   If you want the document included in the final exported manuscript, put it in the Manuscript folder.

2. **Click the Add button in the toolbar.**

   A new file displaying the text document icon and the word Untitled appears below the folder, as shown in Figure 2-2.

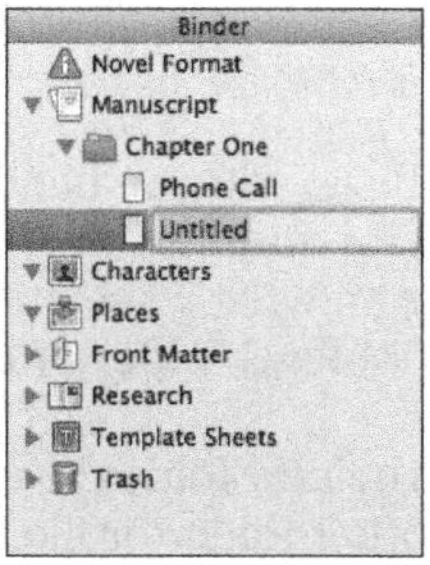

Figure 2-2:
A new text
document in
the Chapter
One folder,
ready to be
named.

3. **Type the name of the document and press Return.**

   Your new document has been added to the selected folder.

You can add a new text document in a number of ways, in addition to the method in the preceding step list. Select the folder to which you want to add a document, and then do one of the following:

✔ Click the Create New Document button (the plus sign [+]) at the bottom-left of the Binder (refer to Figure 2-1).

✔ Choose Project⇨New Text.

✔ Right-click the folder and select Add⇨New Text from the contextual menu that appears.

When selecting the location for a new document, you don't have to choose a folder. You can instead select another document within the folder. In fact, you can select an existing document and simply press Return to create a new one, which appears below the existing one.

Understanding document icons

The Binder icons aren't there just to look pretty. They actually give you a lot of information. Scrivener uses at least three variations of the text document icon:

✔ **Blank sheet of paper:** Text has not been added to this document.

✔ **Paper with lines of text:** The document contains text.

✔ **Index card:** The document has no text, but it does have a Synopsis. You see this

icon a lot if you start your manuscript by storyboarding in the Corkboard or Outliner. Synopses are covered in Chapter 3.

✔ **Other icons:** You may also encounter other icons for specialty file types, such as PDFs.

If a text document has a folded upper-right corner, that means it has an associated snapshot (Chapter 19 covers snapshots in detail).

Adding a folder

You can organize your folders into as many levels as you can handle. The methods for adding a folder are similar to those for adding a file (as discussed in the preceding section), but depending on what's selected in the Binder, the new folder may end up as either a root-level folder or a subfolder.

If you select the Manuscript or Research folder, the new folder is added as a subfolder (child) of the root. If you select any other folder or file, the new folder is added at the same level (making it a sibling) of the selected item.

Creating a subfolder

To create a subfolder — a child-level folder — follow these steps:

1. **In the Binder, right-click either Manuscript or Research.**

2. **From the contextual menu that appears, select Add⇨New Folder.**

   A new folder appears with the words New Folder highlighted, as shown in Figure 2-3.

3. **Type the name of the folder and press Return.**

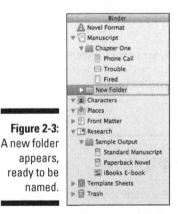

Figure 2-3:
A new folder appears, ready to be named.

Creating a sibling folder

To add a folder at the same level as another item in the Binder — except for the Manuscript or Research folders — follow these steps:

1. **Select the Binder item, either folder or document, that's at the same hierarchy level as the folder you want to add.**

If you want to place the new folder at a lower level than anything existing in your Binder, you can create it and then drag it into another container, as outlined in the section "Moving Binder items," later in this chapter.

2. **Click and hold the Add button in the toolbar to make the Add submenu appear.**

3. **Choose New Folder from the submenu.**

   A new folder appears with the words New Folder highlighted.

4. **Type the name of the folder and press Return.**

Creating a folder at the root level

Although the Manuscript, Research, and Trash folders can't be deleted or moved from the root level, there's nothing to stop you from adding your own folders at the root level. In fact, several templates include additional top-level folders, such as Characters, Places, Front Matter, and Template Sheets.

I also like to add a few folders of my own. Some folders that pop up regularly in my work include

- ✔ **Unused Scenes:** Stores all scenes that I removed from the manuscript. I frequently rummage through this folder for snippets of text or dialogue to add to a scene I'm writing or revising. You can also use such a folder to store unwritten scenes that are only in the idea stage, or those that have been written but don't have a place yet. You may have to kill your darlings, but you never have to delete them.

- ✔ **Outlines:** Holds the various incarnations of my attempts to herd my ideas into something resembling a story.

- ✔ **Ideas:** A place to add notes about storyline changes, future scene ideas, and so on.

I sometimes keep a file in the Ideas folder called a Change Log, in which I list any revisions I think I need to make to the manuscript. Instead of making the edits as I'm writing, I just make a note and continue writing as if I'd already made the change. This keeps me in the writing frame of mind, and saves me time in case I change my mind again or come up with an even better idea down the road.

Follow these steps to actually create one of these root-level folders:

1. **Click in the empty area of the Binder below the Trash.**

   If you have so many items that you can't see the empty space, try collapsing some folders first.

   At this point, nothing in the Binder should be highlighted (selected).

2. **Right-click and, in the contextual menu that appears, select Add⇨New Folder.**

   A new folder appears with the words New Folder highlighted.

3. **Type the name of the folder and press Return.**

Importing files

In Scrivener, you can store your research right within your project. Importing is one of the best ways to bring it in.

You can import text files, web pages, photos, and even videos. Not only that, you can also import work done in another Scrivener project — handy if you want to move a project from one template to another or transfer relevant research and notes from another project.

And, of course, if you started — or even completed — a manuscript in a word processor, you can import that file into Scrivener, as well.

Imported files, especially media files, add to your project file size. If you have a lot of research to keep track of but don't need to view it regularly, consider creating references, instead (covered in Chapter 5).

When you import, Scrivener makes a copy of the file so that the original remains untouched. It doesn't create a link between the original and the imported copy, so changes in one don't affect the other.

Supported file types

Scrivener supports the following text-type file types for import:

- ✔ **RTF (Rich Text Format):** RTF is usually the best format for importing from a word processor because Scrivener can convert the footnotes, comments, and images from this file type. Most common word processors can save a file as RTF.

- ✔ **RTFD (Rich Text Format Directory):** A proprietary Apple format used for Mac Cocoa applications such as Pages and TextEdit. (Not to be confused with the chocolate stuff, Mac Cocoa is a programming tool for Mac OS X and iOS software developers.)

- ✔ **DOC/DOCX:** Microsoft Word format. If you have any format issues when importing a Word document that contains footnotes, comments, or images, try saving it as an RTF file before importing. (In Word, choose File⇨Save As, and then select Rich Text Format from the Format As drop-down list of the Save As dialog box that appears.)

   DOCX is compatible only with Mac OS X Leopard or newer.

- ✔ **ODT (Open Document Text):** File created in Writer, the word processor component of OpenOffice (formerly knows as StarOffice). Supported by Mac OS X Leopard and newer.

- ✔ **TXT:** Plain text format. This type of file contains little to no formatting and is compatible with even the most basic word processors.

- ✔ **FDX:** A file created in Final Draft screenwriting software version 8 or newer.

- ✔ **FCF:** A file created in Final Draft screenwriting software versions 5 to 7.

- ✔ **OPML (Outline Processor Markup Language):** Used by outlining applications. Scrivener can import the outline tree into the Binder, with attached notes added to the main text of each item.

- ✔ **.indexcard:** Index Card for iPad format. If you're using Index Card but not keeping it synced with Scrivener, you can import cards directly into the Binder.

- ✔ **Other text-type extensions:** Files with no extension, or with the XML, TEX, MMD, MD, or .markdown extensions, are imported as text files.

You can also import other types of files:

- ✔ **Images:** TIF, JPG, JPEG, GIF, PNG, BMP

- ✔ **Videos:** MOV, MPG, WAV, MP3

- ✔ **Web pages:** HTML, .webarchive

- ✔ **PDF:** Portable Document Format. Created by Adobe to produce a file that's consistent in appearance, regardless of the operating system or application used to view it.

If Scrivener doesn't support a file type, you can still import that file type by disabling Import Supported File Types Only in the Import & Export Preferences tab. When you select the item in the Binder, the file appears in the Editor as an icon, which you can click to open the file's native program.

For Mac OS X Lion or newer, if the file type supports Quick Look, the Editor displays a read-only version of the file. To view the file in its native software program, right-click the file, and then select Open➪In External Editor from the contextual menu that appears.

How to import files

You can import a file in several ways. The File menu provides some extra import tricks, but for a super quick import, dragging and dropping is king.

The File⇨Import submenu lets you bring in not only research, media, and web pages, but also existing work from Scrivener or other sources. Here's a quick overview of each submenu option:

- ✔ **File:** Allows you to import most file types straight into the Binder.

- ✔ **Web Page:** Lets you enter the web address (URL) of the web page you want to import. You can type it in, copy from the address bar and paste it in, or drag the URL from the address bar to the Address text box on the Import window.

  This option is disabled if the selected folder is the Manuscript (Draft) folder.

  Pages that require a login don't work with Import. You have to copy and paste the content or save to your computer as a PDF or other file type before importing.

- ✔ **Research Files as Aliases:** Imports a file while retaining a link to the original file so that you always have the most up-to-date version.

  This option works only for non-text files (PDF, multimedia, and web pages), and the link works only when both the Scrivener project and the research file are located on the same computer.

  This option is disabled if the selected folder is the Manuscript (Draft) folder.

- ✔ **MultiMarkdown File:** Imports a MultiMarkdown file into the project and splits it into files based on its structure.

  Scrivener creates a document from the metadata block, and then uses subsequent headers to create each new document at the appropriate hierarchy level.

- ✔ **Plain Text Formatted Screenplay:** Works for importing screenplays from programs that export plain-text scripts.

  Scrivener converts the file automatically to script format. If you're using Final Draft, you should use the Import and Split option outlined in the "Splitting and merging documents" section, later in this chapter.

- ✔ **Scrivener Project:** Imports another Scrivener project, grouping it all into one folder called Imported Project and placing it at the bottom of the Binder.

  Using this option also imports keywords and project references from the original project, and creates a separate document at the top of the Imported Project folder for all project notes.

  If you have a project that has been corrupted and no longer opens in Scrivener, you can use this feature to retrieve whatever remains of the file. Text, Synopses, notes, and snapshots will be imported, but not the original structure.

✔ **Import and Split:** For regular text files (DOC, RTF, TXT), you can specify the separator at which to divide the file into separate documents in the Binder. See the "Splitting and merging documents" section, later in this chapter, for more on splitting text files.

This option also works when you want to import files from Final Draft. You can choose a separator and format the files with Scrivener's script formatting.

If you're trying to import into the Manuscript folder, not all options in the Import submenu are available. For non-text-based files, choose a location outside the Manuscript folder.

When importing, you may get a warning message about how Scrivener will handle the incoming file. If you don't want to see the message every time you import, you can select the Do Not Show This Warning Again check box.

So that you can see how importing works, I explain how to import a web page. Just follow these steps:

1. **Select the Research folder.**

2. **Choose File⇨Import⇨Web Page.**

   A window appears, as shown in Figure 2-4, prompting you to enter the web address.

3. **In the Address box, type the address of the web page (its URL).**

   Be sure to include the http://.

   You can also very easily copy the URL from the address bar of your Internet browser and paste it in this text box.

4. **Type a title in the Title text box.**

5. **Click OK.**

   The imported page shows up in the Research folder with a web icon next to it. It may take a minute or two to import the page.

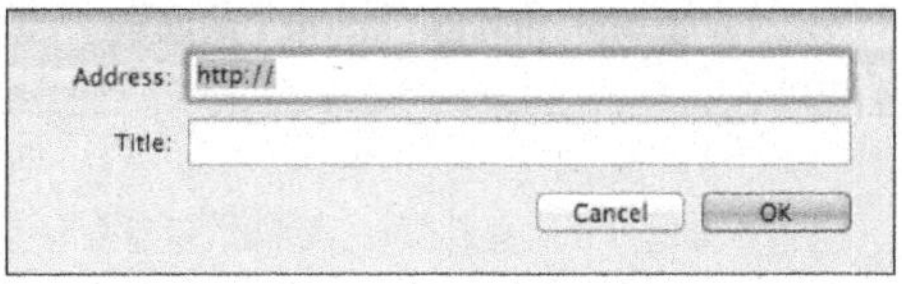

Figure 2-4:
Import
a web
page into
Scrivener.

Address: | http://
Title: |
Cancel   OK

If you have trouble getting a website to import, try opening the page in your browser first, and then follow the steps in the preceding list.

When you import, all ties to the original file or website are severed, so even if the original web page is updated, your imported page isn't.

Another way to import a file is to simply drag it from Finder (or Windows Explorer) into the Binder. And if you have another Scrivener project open, you can drag items from one to the other.

You can also import directly from the Binder by right-clicking to open the contextual menu and then selecting Add⇨Existing Files or Add⇨Existing Web Page.

Selecting multiple items

Why bother with *multiple selection* (selecting more than one file at a time)? Because you can apply many commands to a group of items all at the same time. Instead of spending your time performing the same operation repeatedly, you can be busy writing.

Contiguous is just a fancy word for objects that are next to each other in a sequence. For example, in the alphabet, ABCDE is a contiguous group; ADLRY isn't. To select a contiguous group of items, follow these steps:

1. **Select the first item of the desired sequence in the Binder.**

   For the ABCDE example, you click A.

2. **Press and hold the Shift key, and then click the last item.**

   The first and last item — and all items in between — are now selected.

   If you click E in the example, all the letters A through E are highlighted.

3. **Release the Shift key.**

A *noncontiguous* group of items is made up of those that aren't next to each other in sequence, such as ADLRY in the alphabet. Follow these steps to select noncontiguous files:

1. **Select one of the items from the desired group in the Binder.**

   Sticking with the alphabet theme — too much *Sesame Street* in my youth, maybe? — you'd click A.

2. **Press and hold ⌘ (Ctrl for Windows users), and then click the remaining items individually.**

   Every time you click an additional item while still holding the ⌘ key, that item is added to the selection.

   So, for the example, you'd click D, L, R, and Y in turn.

3. **Release the ⌘ (or Ctrl) key.**

Working with Scrivener Items

After you populate your project with documents and folders (as discussed in the preceding sections), you may eventually want to change things: names, locations, and the organizational hierarchy. This section shows you how to rename, move, group, split, and merge items, as well as change their icons.

Renaming an item

Anything in the Binder can be renamed, regardless of level or type. You have three simple options for renaming an item:

- ✔ Right-click the item and select Rename from the contextual menu that appears. Type the desired name when the current name is highlighted.

- ✔ Select the item to rename, and then press the Esc key (on a Mac) or the F2 key (for Windows). The current name is highlighted, ready for you to type over it.

- ✔ Double-click the item to select the title, and then type the desired name.

Moving Binder items

Part of the power of Scrivener is that it gives you the ability to easily rearrange your documents and folders. You can either drag and drop an item or use the contextual menu to choose a new location.

Dragging and dropping

Dragging and dropping is probably the quickest and most common method for moving items in the Binder. Simply click and hold the item, and then drag it to the new location, releasing the mouse button to drop the item.

Watch for the blue line that tells you where the item will drop and the blue box that shows which container it'll end up in. Figure 2-5 shows the target line and box, which designate where the item will drop.

When moving a container, you can collapse it first so that you don't have to deal with all its files. Collapsing subfolders of other containers in the Binder can also prevent you from dropping the item at the wrong level.

Collapse or expand a container in the Binder by clicking the triangle next to its icon. When the triangle points down, the container is *expanded*, meaning its contents are fully visible.

When the triangle points to the right, the container is *collapsed,* so its contents are hidden.

To expand or collapse all containers in the Binder, go to View⇨Outline⇨ Expand All/Collapse All.

To expand or collapse all the subfolders within a container, Option-click (Alt-click in Windows) the triangle next to the item.

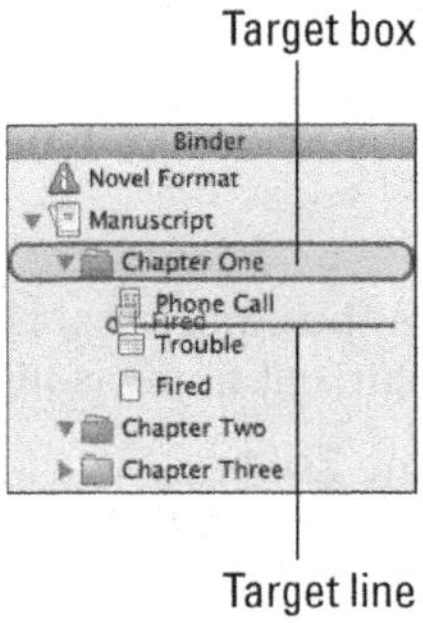

Target box

Figure 2-5:
When dragging and dropping an item in the Binder, look for the target line and box.

Target line

Using the contextual menu

If the drag-and-drop method is dragging you down (see the preceding section), or you have more levels and subfolders than you want to wade through, you can move your item by using the contextual menu. The catch is that you have to know your destination. After you know where you want to place your item, follow these steps:

1. **Right-click the item you want to move.**

   The contextual menu appears.

2. **Select Move To, and then select the location from the submenus.**

   Just follow the subfolders path until you get to the container you're looking for. Figure 2-6 shows a file being moved several levels deep in the Manuscript.

   The item moves to the new location. If you choose a text document, the selected document becomes a file group, and the moved item appears in that file group.

Figure 2-6:
You can move Binder items via the contextual menu.

Grouping items

What if you have all your scenes written and you want to organize them into chapters after the fact? Or maybe you have all your chapter folders but want to organize them into parts of the book.

You don't have to create the folders first and then drag the documents or subfolders into those folders. Instead, you can use grouping, which organizes the selected items into a new folder.

Whatever organizational strategy you use, follow these simple steps to get it done:

1. **Select the items that you want to group.**

   Shift-click for contiguous items and ⌘-click (Ctrl-click in Windows) for noncontiguous items.

2. **Right-click any of the selected items to open the contextual menu.**

3. **Select Group.**

   A new folder appears, ready to be named, and the selected items are moved into the folder.

4. **Type the name for the folder and press Return.**

5. **If the items in your new folder aren't visible (meaning they're not expanded), click the triangle next to the folder icon to display the items inside.**

Changing folder and file icons

You can change the icon of any folder, even a root folder. In fact, the same method works to change a file icon, as well.

I love picking icons that convey the purpose of the item. For example, my Productivity file sports a chart icon. My Ideas folder icon is a light bulb. Very original, right?

Procrastinate the day away playing with icons by following these steps for all the items you want to personalize:

1. **Right-click the desired item.**

   The contextual menu appears.

2. **Point to Change Icon, and then choose the desired icon from the submenu that appears.**

   Figure 2-7 shows the submenu.

   The icon changes to reflect your choice.

Splitting and merging documents

Working with a bunch of individual documents in Scrivener is great, right? But what if you were on a roll and you just kept writing without giving thought to scenes or chapters? Or you imported that 90,000-word tome you wrote in another program, and now it's one long document just sitting in your Binder like a useless lump?

No worries. Splitting a document is dead easy by using either of the methods in the following sections.

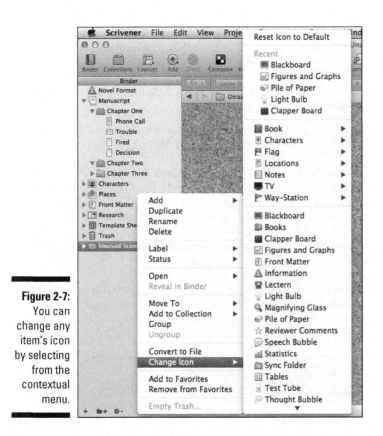

Figure 2-7:
You can
change any
item's icon
by selecting
from the
contextual
menu.

Splitting manually

Splitting a document manually gives you total control over how you break it up, but can also be time consuming if the document requires a lot of divisions. Follow these steps to split a document manually:

1. **Select the document to be split.**

   The text appears in the Editor pane. If it doesn't, choose View⇨ Document.

2. **Click to insert your cursor at the exact spot where you want to break up the file.**

   For example, you can create a split at the beginning of a new paragraph.

3. **Choose Documents⇨Split⇨At Selection.**

   A new document that has the original name with a number added is created, as shown in Figure 2-8. The new file contains everything after the point at which you chose to split.

The keyboard shortcut for this menu item might be worth memorizing if you have a lot of splits to make: ⌘+K (Ctrl+K in Windows).

4. Type the new name and press Return.

5. Select the new document and follow Steps 2 through 4 for each split you need to make.

You can keep splitting the most recently created document until you've broken the work into the desired number of files.

If you select a few words of text and choose Documents➪Split➪With Selection as Title, the file splits at the beginning of the selection and uses the selected text as the document title. This option is especially handy if you have headings already entered in your document but no separators. By using the Find by Format feature (covered in Chapter 17), you can search for a heading, and then split the document with the selection as the title, find the next heading, and so on.

When you split a document, all metadata is retained by both documents, but any snapshots (covered in Chapter 19) stay only with the original document (the one that contains all text prior to the split).

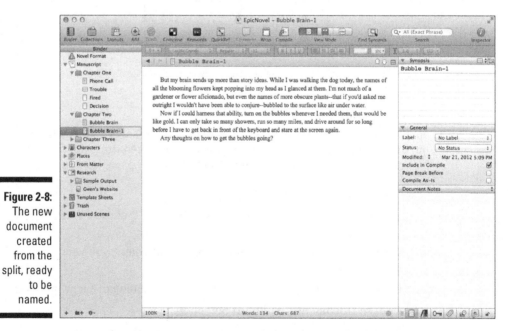

Figure 2-8: The new document created from the split, ready to be named.

Using the Import and Split feature

The Import and Split feature lets you import a file and split it automatically. What's the catch? The file already has to have a separator character — on its own line — to designate the division between each document. Every time Scrivener encounters the separator character, it removes the character and the blank line, and then splits the file at that point to create a new document.

Follow these steps to import and split a file:

1. **Select the desired location for the imported file.**

2. **Choose File⇨Import⇨Import and Split.**

   The Import and Split window opens.

3. **Navigate to the desired file to import.**

4. **(Optional) Change the scene divider, if necessary, by entering the divider you used in the file into the Sections Are Separated By text box.**

   The # is a common scene divider in the publishing world. Figure 2-9 shows the # as the separator character. But if you used another character or set of characters to separate the file, such as * or ###, enter it in this text box.

5. **Click Import.**

   The imported file is split into individual text documents at each separator and added to the Binder.

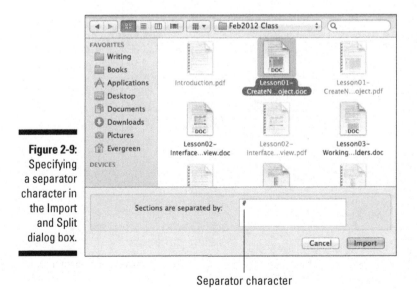

Figure 2-9: Specifying a separator character in the Import and Split dialog box.

Separator character

Merging documents

Like a deadbeat boyfriend, you're an expert at splitting if you've read the preceding sections, but what about when you want to join two or more files together? Scrivener's got you covered.

Follow these steps to get your files on their way to wedded bliss:

1. **In the Binder, select the files that you want to merge.**

   Press Shift-click to select contiguous files. ⌘-click (Ctrl-click in Windows) for noncontiguous files.

2. **Choose Documents➪Merge.**

   All the selected files merge into one document, retaining the name of the topmost file, as shown in Figure 2-10.

When you merge files, the Synopses, notes, keywords, references, and snapshots also combine, but the resulting document has the Label, Status, and other metadata settings of the topmost file.

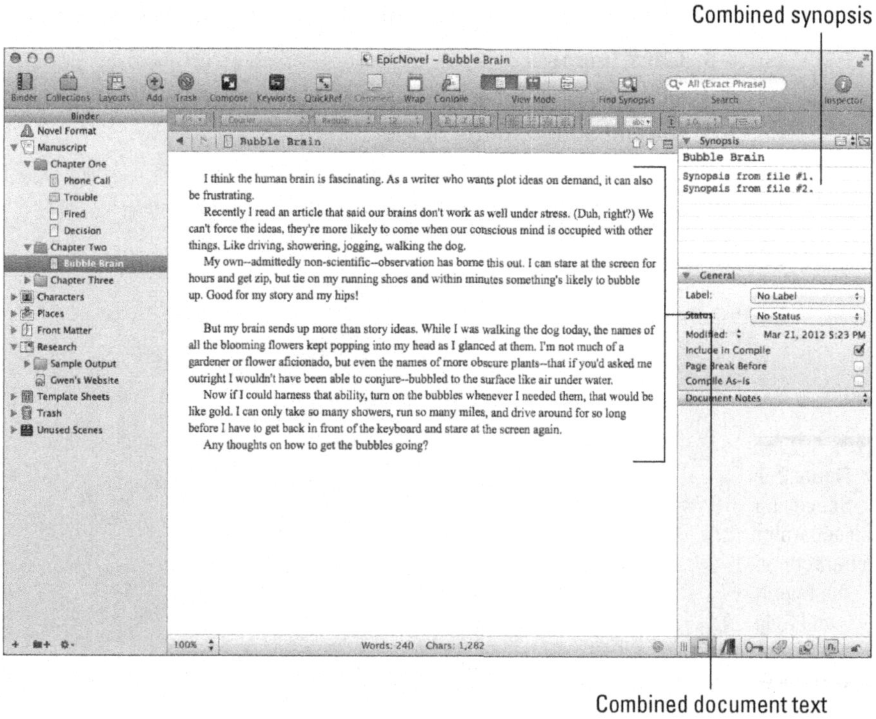

Combined synopsis

Combined document text

Figure 2-10:
The original two files merged into one, with a combined Synopsis.

By default, Scrivener inserts an empty line between the text of merged documents. To change the merged documents separator, follow these steps:

1. **Choose Scrivener⊅Preferences.**

   Windows users, choose Tools⊅Options.

   The Preferences (or Options) window appears.

2. **Select General.**

3. **In the Separators section, select the desired separator from the Merged Documents drop-down list.**

Deleting files and folders

I never delete any of my words, even if they won't end up in the final manuscript. I've pillaged old scenes for text and ideas too many times to risk permanent deletion. That said, you may really want to delete an item at one time or another.

Maybe you created a file or folder by mistake. Or you made a copy. Or you've decided to store links to your research, rather than the research text. For any number of reasons, you might choose to delete an item from the Binder.

If you want to go that route, follow these steps to wield the axe of death:

1. **Select the offending item(s) in the Binder.**

   Press Shift-click to select contiguous files; ⌘-click (Ctrl-click in Windows) for noncontiguous files.

2. **Right-click, and then select Delete from the contextual menu that appears.**

   As a last-ditch effort to save you from yourself, the selected items move to the Trash folder.

   You can also select and drag items directly to the Trash.

3. **If you're really, really sure that you don't want the items anymore, right-click the Trash folder and select Empty Trash from the contextual menu that appears.**

   A warning window appears.

4. **Click OK.**

   The files are permanently removed from the project. This step can't be undone.

Part II
Meeting the Inspector

The 5th Wave   By Rich Tennant

In this part . . .

*T*his part covers each section of the Inspector pane —
located on the right side of the Scrivener window. The
Inspector displays a collection of data about whichever
item last had the focus in the Editor (or Corkboard or
Outliner). The contents of the Inspector pane change
depending on the type or number of items selected.

Chapter 3

Working with the Synopsis

In This Chapter

▶ Figuring out how to use the Synopsis

▶ Working with text and images in the Synopsis

*T*he Synopsis is the virtual index card at the top of the Scrivener Inspector pane. It shows the title and optional description of the item displayed in the Editor pane.

Think of the Synopsis just like a real index card that you might use to write down scene notes or for storyboarding. The Synopsis text isn't the actual words for your manuscript, but rather an overview or other thoughts to help you keep track of which part of your story or paper you're working with.

This chapter can help you understand what a Synopsis is and how to add a Synopsis to your items.

Understanding the Synopsis

The Synopsis resides at the top of the Inspector pane and looks a lot like an index card. In the Synopsis, you can enter a brief description of your scene, chapter, part, or whatever type of item you're working with.

But don't think of this section as simply the three-sentence recap. You can enter all sorts of things in the Synopsis. You might use it to track your time-line, point of view (POV), setting, subplot, scene purpose, or questions you need to answer.

Save longer notes for the Document Notes (covered in Chapter 5), but for an at-a-glance view of what your document is about, the Synopsis is perfect.

When you view your project in the Corkboard (more on the Corkboard in Chapter 8), the index cards show whatever's written in the Synopsis section. So, if you're storyboarding, think about what you need to see for each document.

Figure 3-1 provides an overview of the parts of the Synopsis.

Collapse/Expand Synopsis

Text/Image toggle

Figure 3-1: The key parts of the Synopsis.

Title —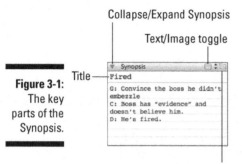

Auto-Generate Synopsis

If the Inspector isn't visible, click the Inspector button in the toolbar. If the Synopsis isn't displayed in the Inspector pane, choose View➪Inspect➪Synopsis.

What appears in the Editor and what's selected in the Binder may not always match, but the Inspector pane always applies to the file displayed in the Editor. If you're viewing files in the Corkboard or Outliner, the Inspector applies to the selected item, or to the container if no item is selected.

Populating the Synopsis

Two parts of the Synopsis are editable:

✔ **Title:** The Synopsis title is the same as the item's title in the Binder. If you rename an item, the title is updated in both places.

✔ **Text:** Below the title is the text area, where you enter whatever text you want to appear in the Synopsis.

In addition to text, the Synopsis can also hold an image.

Renaming an item

Just as you can rename items from the Binder (demonstrated in Chapter 2), you can also rename them from the Synopsis pane. Follow these quick and easy steps:

1. **Select the title in the Synopsis pane.**

2. **Type the new item name.**

3. **Press Return.**

   The new name of the item appears in the Synopsis, the header of the Editor, and in the Binder.

Adding text

The main value of the Synopsis lies in the text you enter into it — especially if you plan to use the Corkboard feature, covered in Chapter 8, or the Outliner, addressed in Chapter 9. You can add text in several ways.

Manually adding text

If you have a very specific idea of what you want in the Synopsis, it's best to add it yourself. For example, I like to use the Synopsis to track the POV character's scene goal, the conflict that's blocking him, and the outcome of the scene.

To add your own text to the Synopsis, follow these steps:

1. **Click in the text area of the Synopsis, below the title.**

   Your cursor appears in the text area. If the Synopsis already contains text, you can either delete and replace it, or click at the end of the existing text to add to it.

2. **Type the desired text.**

   You can add, insert, delete, and select text in this area; however, the Synopsis section doesn't support text formatting, such as italics, bold, or highlighting.

Auto-generating the synopsis

If you want just a few lines of text in the Synopsis to remind you of what the document is about when you're in the Corkboard or Outliner, you can let Scrivener automatically populate the Synopsis for you.

The Auto-Generate option overwrites any existing Synopsis text, so be sure you don't want to save anything that already appears there.

The Synopsis section has an auto-fill feature that gives you one of two choices:

- ✔ If no text is selected in the Editor and you click the Auto-Generate Synopsis button (as shown in Figure 3-1), Scrivener overwrites whatever currently appears in the card with the first few lines of the document, as shown in Figure 3-2.

- ✔ If you select lines of text from your document in the Editor before you click the Auto-Generate Synopsis button, Scrivener fills the card with the selected lines when you click the button.

Figure 3-2:
A synopsis created by the Auto-Generate Synopsis button, with no text selected in the Editor.

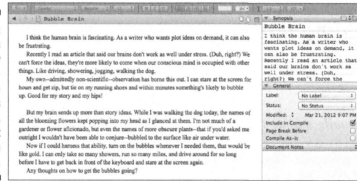

Adding an image

In the Synopsis section, you can add a graphical synopsis of the document. You know how "a picture is worth a thousand words"? Well, if you have a photo that perfectly represents what that document is about, then no typing is necessary.

Does the car blow up? Do the lovers kiss? If you like to storyboard in visual mode, this feature is for you. You can use an image rather than text or as a supplement to the text.

A photographic synopsis can also help you reference a photo while writing a visual description. You could even add a character photo based on whose POV the scene is in. Again, it's up to you.

Follow these steps to add a photo to the Synopsis:

1. **Click the Text/Image toggle button (refer to Figure 3-1).**

2. **Select the Image icon from the small menu that pops up.**

   The synopsis text area turns black and displays the message Drag in an Image File.

3. **Drag the desired image from the Binder and drop it onto the black space in the Synopsis pane.**

   Alternatively, you can drag an image from Finder (on the Mac) or Windows Explorer (in Windows).

   A small version of the photo appears in the black space, as shown in Figure 3-3.

Click the Text/Image toggle button (refer to Figure 3-1) to switch between viewing the image and the text in the Synopsis pane. This button affects the Synopsis view in the Inspector and the Corkboard, as well.

Figure 3-3:
A photo-
graphic
synopsis.

Deleting an image

To remove an image from the Synopsis, follow these steps:

1. **If the image doesn't appear in the Synopsis pane, click the Text/Image toggle button (see Figure 3-1) to display it.**

2. **Click the Clear Picture button in the upper-right corner of the pane.**

   The image disappears, and the Synopsis changes back to a black space, as it appeared before you originally added the image.

3. **(Optional) To view the text rather than the black space, click the Text/ Image toggle button.**

Chapter 4

Tracking Scene Elements with Metadata

*M*etadata might sound like a character out of *Star Trek,* but in Scrivener, it's the set of data associated with each item you add to your project, whether the item is a document, a folder, an image, or a web archive.

Metadata can be anything. For example, if you were an item in your project's Binder, some of your metadata might include your birthdate, your phone number, mailing address, hair color, shoe size, or favorite cartoon character.

At the most basic level, metadata includes the title of an item, its Synopsis text, and the associated image, if any. It even includes the word count and word count target (which you can find out how to set in Chapter 14).

In the Inspector, Scrivener provides a default set of fields, of which the first two — Label and Status — can be customized. Beyond that, Scrivener also allows you to create additional fields through custom metadata and keywords (boldly go to Chapter 5 for more on creating fields).

Want to track the revision status for each document in your project? Metadata is the answer. Or maybe you want to track the character's point of view in which each scene is written. You guessed it: Metadata works for that task, too. In this chapter, you can find out what you need to know to make metadata work for you.

Navigating the General Meta-Data Section

Scrivener comes pre-populated with several metadata fields. You can find them in the General Meta-Data section of the Inspector pane, as shown in Figure 4-1.

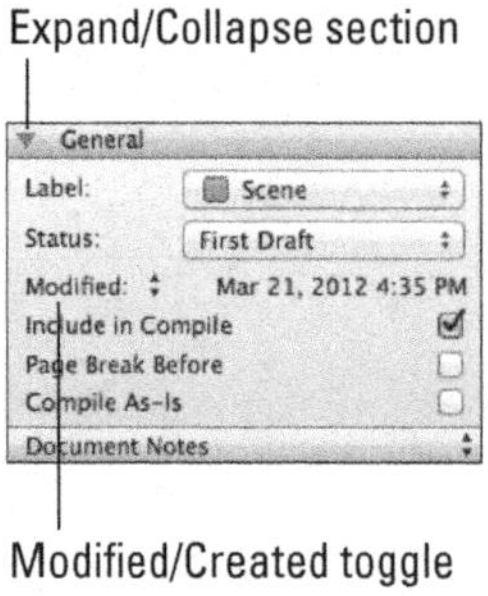

Expand/Collapse section

Figure 4-1:
The General
Meta-Data
section in the
Inspector
pane.

Modified/Created toggle

In the Novel template, the first field, Label, is set up so that you can tag an item with one of the following values: Idea, Notes, Research, Chapter, or Subsection.

Below Label, the Status field has a value list that lets you assign a status — see how brilliantly these fields are named? — to an item: To Do, First Draft, Revised Draft, Final Draft, Title Page, or Done. (The Title Page Status lets you mark your title page so that it doesn't show up when you search by Status — covered in Chapter 17 — or filter by Status when compiling — see Chapter 12.)

The default values in the Label and Status fields vary, depending on which template you choose.

You can click the up-and-down arrow button next to Modified to toggle between the date the item was last changed and its creation date.

The last three fields — Include in Compile, Page Break Before, and Compile As-Is — apply to compiling (exporting) your project, which is covered in Part IV of this book.

Working with the Label and Status Fields

The Label and Status fields are the treasure in the General section. You can customize them to suit your needs by changing their names and their values. For the Label values, you can even change the colors.

Not only that, but other than the item's title, the Label and Status fields are the most visible pieces of metadata in your project.

The Label field is the most powerful piece of metadata because you can apply its associated color to icons in the Binder, index cards in the Corkboard (see Chapter 8), and Outliner rows (covered in Chapter 9). So save it for something that you want to be able to discern at a quick glance — for example, character point of view.

The Status field can appear in the Corkboard as a stamp — similar to a watermark — across the index cards, but you can't use it for color-based identification. It's also available as a column in the Outliner.

Both the Label and Status fields also show up at the top of every QuickReference pane.

Two parts of the Label and Status fields are customizable: the name of the field itself and the set of values available in the Label and Status drop-down lists.

Why would you want to customize Label and Status? Great question. Here are just a few of the ways you might want to use them:

- ✔ **Point of view (POV):** If you limit each scene/chapter to one POV, you can use the Label field to color-code your scenes by POV.

- ✔ **Location:** Specify the setting of the scene, or the blog or journal for which a piece was written.

- ✔ **Day:** Use Mon-1 for Monday of week 1, Tue-1 for Tuesday of that week, and so on, so that you can track your timeline in a story. Instructors writing lessons in Scrivener might use Day to keep track of when a lecture will be posted.

✔ **Species:** Say what? Well, I know this paranormal author who writes about shape-shifters and uses Species to keep track of the animal that the character can shift into. This option could also work for science fiction and fantasy writers who have aliens or otherworldly races to keep straight.

✔ **Storyline:** If you have a complicated plot with several story lines to keep track of, the Label field makes it a cinch.

✔ **Author:** If you're co-writing a book or academic paper with other authors, you can track which chapters or documents each person is working on.

✔ **Purpose:** Group scenes by their purpose (to advance the plot, expand on a character, and so on).

You're limited only by your imagination and one important constraint: You can assign only one Label value and one Status value to each Binder item. For example, if Bob, Fabiana, and Nigel all get a viewpoint in the same document, POV isn't a good field choice because you can't assign multiple values to the document.

Never fear — if you want to apply multiple values, you can use keywords, which you get to play with in Chapter 5.

Changing the field name

The procedure for changing a field's name is the same for both the Label and Status fields:

1. **In the General section, click to open the Label (or Status) drop-down list and select Edit.**

   The Meta-Data Settings window opens, as shown in Figure 4-2.

   You can also access the Meta-Data Settings window by choosing Project⇨Meta-Data Settings.

2. **Select Label (or Status) in the Custom Title text box, and then type the desired field name.**

3. **Click OK to close the window.**

Your new field name replaces the Label (or Status) field in the General pane of the Inspector, as shown in Figure 4-3, where the Label field is renamed POV.

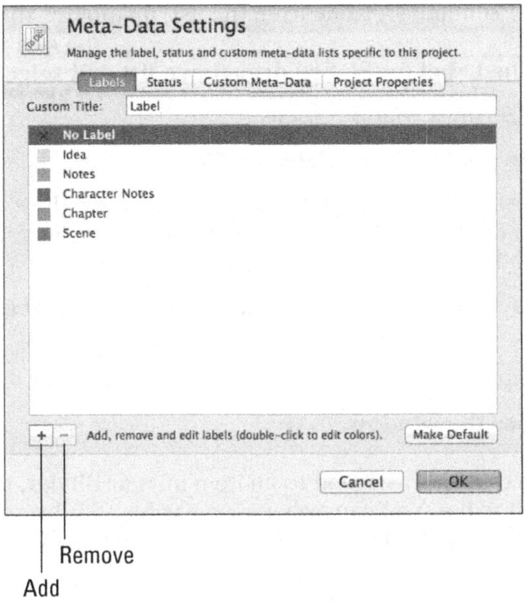

Figure 4-2:
The Meta-
Data
Settings
window.

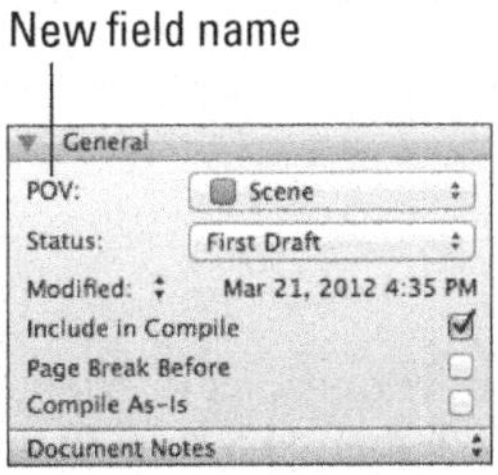

Remove

Add

New field name

Figure 4-3:
The Label
field
renamed to
POV.

Deleting existing values

Just like Mom always said, it's what's on the inside that counts. In the case of the Label and Status fields, that's the values in the drop-down lists. Even if you choose to keep the Label and Status fields as-is, you might not want all the values to appear in the lists.

One of your co-authors could back out of the project, your characters might never actually take that trip to Iceland you initially planned, or your editor could force you to leave Nina on the cutting room floor (metaphorically speaking, of course).

Anytime you want to eliminate a value from the list, just follow these steps:

1. **Click to open the Label (or Status) drop-down list and select Edit.**

   The Meta-Data Settings window opens.

2. **Select the value you want to delete.**

   To save time, use multiple-selection to choose all the values you want to remove from the list. Shift-click to select contiguous files, ⌘-click (or Ctrl-click in Windows) for noncontiguous files.

3. **Click the Remove button at the bottom-left of the window (refer to Figure 4-2).**

   The selected value — or values — is removed from the list.

4. **Click OK to close the window.**

If you delete a value that was assigned to an item in your Binder, that item reverts to the default value. You can assign a new value to it by using the procedures outlined in the section "Assigning Label and Status Values," later in this chapter.

You can't delete the No Label and No Status values. However, you can rename them, as demonstrated in the "Editing existing values" section, later in this chapter.

Adding new values

Just as you can remove values, you can add new ones, as needed. You know, when Mindy strolls onstage unexpectedly and demands a role, your characters hop a plane to Morocco without telling you in advance, or you meet a new author who's a perfect fit for the book on kindergarten classroom politics you and a friend are writing.

Follow these steps to add a value to the Label (or Status) drop-down list:

1. **Click to open the Label (or Status) drop-down list and select Edit.**

   The Meta-Data Settings window opens.

2. **Click the Add button (refer to Figure 4-2) at the bottom-left of the Meta-Data Settings window.**

   A colored square appears next to a blank text box if you're working with Label values. When you add new Status values, no colored square appears.

3. **Type the desired name of the new value.**

4. **Click OK to close the window.**

Figure 4-4 shows the Label field changed to POV, with a new list of values.

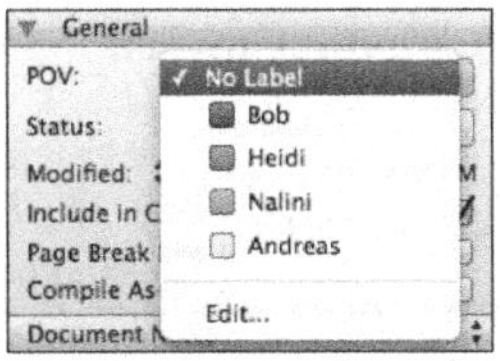

Figure 4-4:
A modified
Label field
name and
values.

▼ General	
POV:	✓ No Label
Status:	🔲 Bob
Modified:	🔲 Heidi
Include in C	🔲 Nalini
Page Break	☐ Andreas
Compile As	Edit...
Document N	

Editing existing values

At some point during your writing, you're going to change your mind about the values you chose. Well, maybe not — because writers never change their minds, right?

But just in case Bob gets renamed to Peter, your Regency-London historical relocates to India, or your editor declares that your family of shape-shifting wolves must now be panthers — who knew wolves were on the not-so-hot list? — follow these steps to edit existing list values:

1. **Click to open the Label (or Status) drop-down list and select Edit.**

   The Meta-Data Settings window opens.

2. **In the list, double-click the value that you want to change.**

   Be sure to choose the text, not the colored square, if you're editing a Label value. If you accidentally double-click the colored square, just close the Colors window that appears and try again.

3. **Type the new value.**

4. **Click OK to close the window.**

Changing value colors

The Label and Status fields differ when it comes to value colors. Unlike in Status, which doesn't use value colors, each Label field value has a color associated with it by default. If you don't like the auto-assigned colors, you can change them by following these steps:

1. **Click to open the Label drop-down list and select Edit.**

   The Meta-Data Settings window opens.

2. **Double-click the colored square next to the value you want to change.**

   The Colors window appears, as shown in Figure 4-5.

3. **Mac users, click the button at the top of the window to open the color selection tool that you want to use.**

   You can choose from the color wheel, color sliders, color palettes, image palettes, or crayons. I'm partial to crayons, myself.

4. **Choose a new color by clicking on it.**

   The colored square changes to the selected color.

5. **Click the red X button (Mac) to close the Colors window.**

   Windows users, click OK.

6. **Click OK to close the Meta-Data Settings window.**

Color selection tools

Figure 4-5:
Crayon
choices in
the color
window.

Rearranging the list of values

If you use some values more often than others, you can rearrange the list for quicker selection. Just follow these steps:

1. **Click to open the Label (or Status) drop-down list and select Edit.**

   The Meta-Data Settings window opens.

2. **Click and drag the list item to the desired spot.**

   The blue line shows where the value will end up when you drop it (see Figure 4-6).

3. **After you have your list arranged the way you want it, click OK to close the window.**

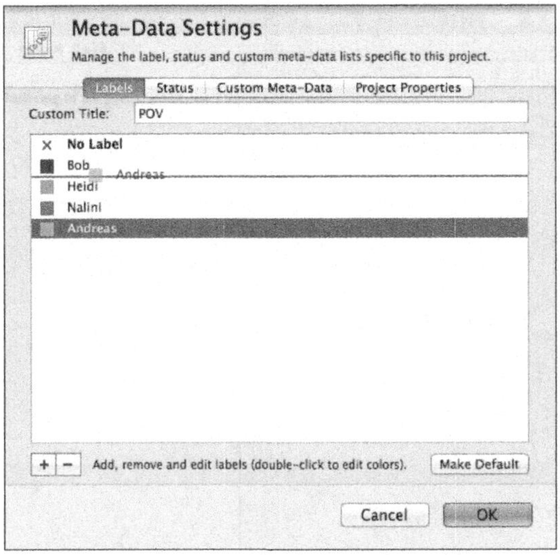

Meta-Data Settings

Manage the label, status and custom meta-data lists specific to this project.

| Labels | Status | Custom Meta-Data | Project Properties |

Custom Title: POV

X **No Label**
   Bob
   Andreas
   Heidi
   Nalini
   Andreas

[+][−] Add, remove and edit labels (double-click to edit colors). [Make Default]

[Cancel] [OK]

Figure 4-6:
You can
move list
values.

Setting a default value

The default values for the Label and Status fields appear in bold text for easy identification. Initially, the default value for the Label field is No Label. Unless you change it, every time you create a new item in your project, the Label value is automatically set to No Label. The default value for Status is No Status.

But suppose you change Label to POV, and you expect your studly hero Bob to have the most scenes. Then you can make Bob the default value. After he's the default, even if Bob and his curvy love interest, Fabiana, have an equal number of scenes, you need to change the value of a new scene only 50 percent of the time, rather than every time.

Hey, I'm all about efficiency. Follow these steps to increase your own by changing the default value for the Label (or Status) field:

1. **Click to open the Label (or Status) drop-down list and select Edit.**

   The Meta-Data Settings window opens.

2. **Select the value that you want to set as the default.**

3. **Click the Make Default button at the bottom-right of the window.**

   The value turns bold, as you can see in Figure 4-7. (I do like a bold hero.)

4. **Click OK to accept the change and close the window.**

Default value

Figure 4-7:
Bob as the
default POV
value.

Assigning Label and Status Values

After you set up your Label and Status fields exactly the way you want them (as discussed in the preceding sections), you can assign values to your documents and folders.

Assigning a value from the Inspector

You can choose the Label or Status value that you want to assign to an item in the General pane of the Inspector by following these steps:

1. **Select the item in the Binder to which you want to apply the Label (or Status) value.**

2. **In the Inspector, click to open the Label (or Status) drop-down list.**

The list of value options appears.

3. **Click the value in the list that you want to apply to the selected item.**

   If you use Label colors in the Binder or icons (which I describe how to do in the section "Using Label Colors to Distinguish Items," later in this chapter), the color changes to match the new value, as shown in Figure 4-8. The new value also appears in the Inspector.

Assigning a value with the contextual menu

You can also change the Label (or Status) value of a Binder item by using the contextual menu. Follow these steps:

1. **Right-click the item(s) in the Binder to which you want to assign a Label (or Status) value.**

   The contextual menu appears, as seen in Figure 4-9.

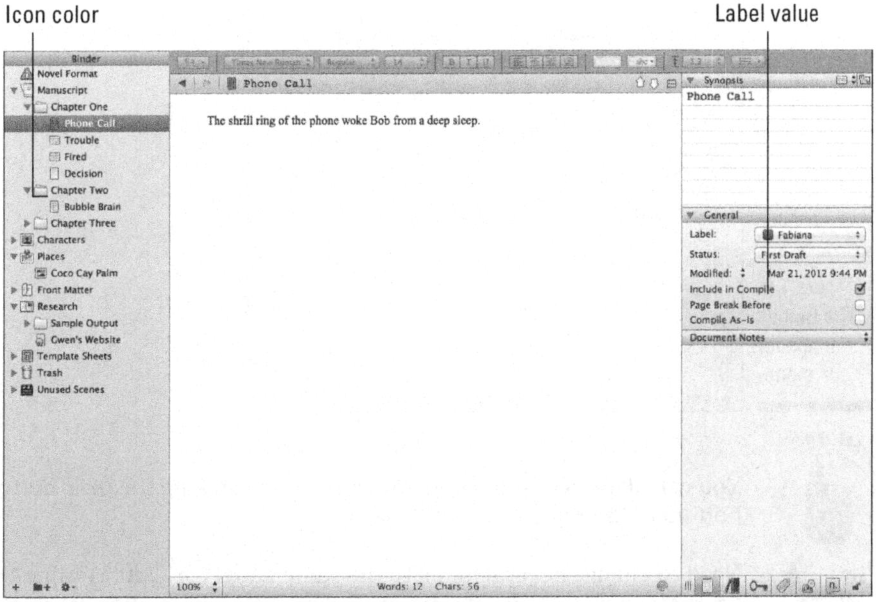

Icon color   Label value

Figure 4-8:
The icon changes color to match the new value.

2. **Select Label (or Status).**

   A submenu opens, listing the values.

3. **Select the desired value from the submenu.**

   The new value appears in the Inspector, and the color changes in the Binder. (See the "Using Label Colors to Distinguish Items" section, later in this chapter, to turn on Label colors in the Binder.)

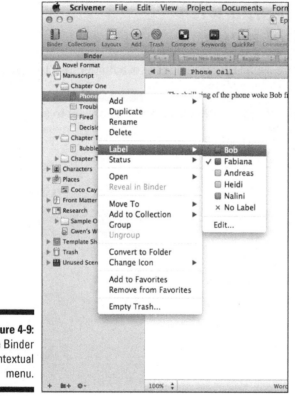

Figure 4-9:
The Binder
contextual
menu.

You can also access the contextual menu by clicking the gear button at the bottom of the Binder.

Need to change several items to the same Label (or Status) value? Select the desired items in the Binder before following the preceding steps. (Shift-click to select contiguous files, ⌘-click [Mac] or Ctrl-click [Windows] for noncontiguous files.)

Using Label Colors to Distinguish Items

The real power of the Label field lies in the fact that you can tint the icon of an item according to its Label value, giving you an instant visual reminder of its value and a way to quickly compare an item's value to other items. You can also view the Label color of an item in the Binder, the Corkboard, the Outliner, and the QuickReference panel.

Say you're working on that masterpiece about Bob and Fabiana. If you make Bob's POV color blue and Fabiana's POV color pink — yeah, it's cliché, but helpful — it takes just a quick glance at the Binder to see in which POV a scene is written or to notice that the hero is getting too many scenes in a row. (Sometimes Bob gets pushy like that.)

Take charge by choosing View➪Use Label Color In, as shown in Figure 4-10.

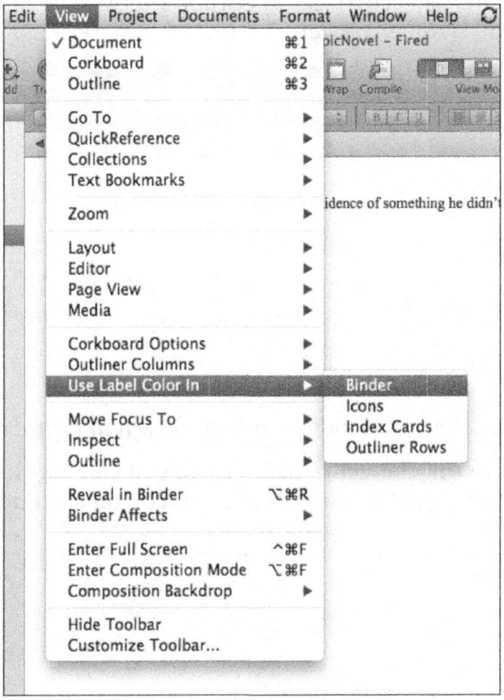

Figure 4-10:
The Use
Label Color
In options.

The Use Label Color In submenu provides four options:

🗸 **Binder:** Adds a color block around the item name in the Binder, as shown in Figure 4-11.

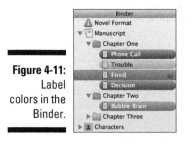

Figure 4-11:
Label
colors in the
Binder.

🗸 **Icons:** Tints the icon in the Binder and anywhere else the icon appears in the Scrivener interface, such as the Corkboard (which I pin down in Chapter 8) and the Outliner (covered in Chapter 9). See Figure 4-12.

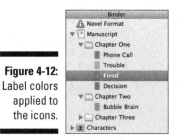

Figure 4-12:
Label colors
applied to
the icons.

🗸 **Index Cards:** Tints the entire index card, as shown in Figure 4-13.

If you don't want to tint the entire index card, you can use the Label color as a pushpin or shaded card corner, which you can find out how to do in Chapter 8.

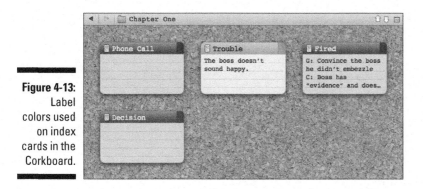

Figure 4-13:
Label
colors used
on index
cards in the
Corkboard.

✓ **Outliner Row:** Tints the item's row in the Outliner (which is outlined in Chapter 9). See Figure 4-14.

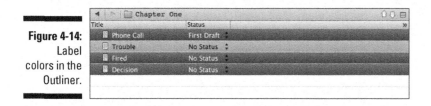

Figure 4-14:
Label
colors in the
Outliner.

The four options in the Use Label Color In submenu aren't mutually exclusive: You can choose one or more of them. However, you have to choose them from the submenu one at a time.

You can tell which options are turned on because they have a check mark next to them.

To turn off an option, choose View⇨Use Label Color In and select the option in the submenu to remove the checkmark.

Chapter 5

Working with Document Support Panes

*T*he document support panes are like one of those magical expanding bags that holds more than it appears. That row of buttons at the bottom of the Inspector has a surprising number of tricks.

The document support panes let you take notes, create links to reference material, tag items with keywords, create custom metadata, take a snapshot of a document to preserve its current version, and add comments and footnotes.

This chapter covers notes, references, keywords, and custom metadata, so read on to learn a few tricks of your own.

Looking at the Document Support Panes

Six different options are available in the document support panes: Notes, References, Keywords, Custom Meta-Data, Snapshots, and Comments & Footnotes. Each of them has a corresponding button at the base of the Inspector, as noted in Figure 5-1.

The first four options take up the lower half of the Inspector when selected, and the last two commandeer the entire panel when selected.

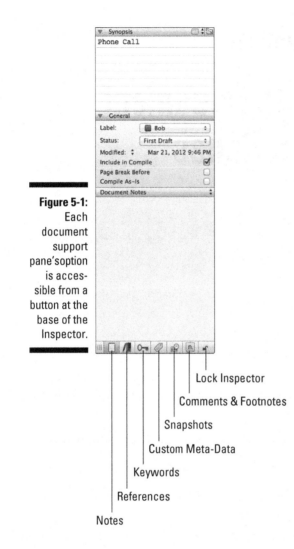

Figure 5-1:
Each
document
support
pane'soption
is acces-
sible from a
button at the
base of the
Inspector.

Lock Inspector

Comments & Footnotes

Snapshots

Custom Meta-Data

Keywords

References

Notes

Which options are available, and the types of information they can display, depends on what type of item is selected. When multiple items, or a container, are selected in the Binder, Corkboard, or Outliner, only those options that apply to the entire project — such as project notes and project references — appear in the Inspector.

Taking Notes

The Notes section is a place to jot down thoughts, ideas, items you want to reference quickly, or anything else you can imagine. Think of it like the notepad on your desk where you scribble random items to deal with later so that you don't have to get out of the writing flow.

You can add, insert, delete, and select text in this area and — unlike the Synopsis pane — even format the text by using the Format bar (see Chapter 6 for more on the Format bar).

Comparing project and document notes

The Inspector offers two types of notes:

 ✔ **Project notes:** Apply to the entire project and are visible regardless of which item is selected in the Editor, Corkboard, or Outliner.

 ✔ **Document notes:** Apply only to the document selected in the Editor, Corkboard, or Outliner.

If the Notes section isn't visible in the Inspector, click the Notes button (refer to Figure 5-1). You can toggle between the two types of notes by clicking the Notes header and selecting from the drop-down list that appears, as shown in Figure 5-2.

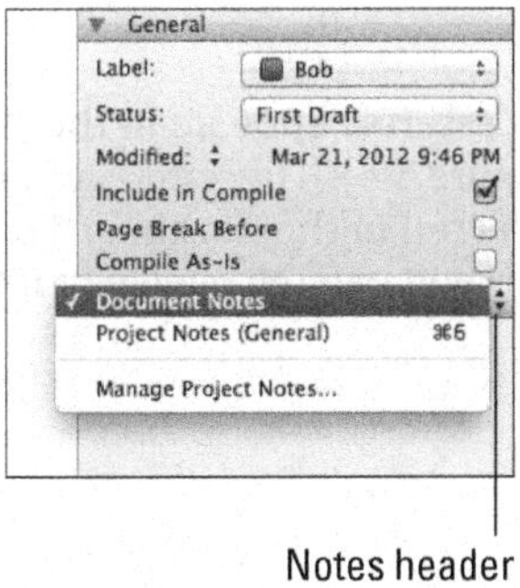

Figure 5-2:
Click the Notes header to toggle between project and document notes.

Notes header

Entering notes

The Project Notes pane lets you capture your thoughts on the whole project: from something as simple as `Look up reference to man-eating sharks`, to a list of each character's name and occupation, to ideas for plot changes.

In the Document Notes pane, you can record information that applies to one specific file, such as ideas for revisions, red herrings, or alternate endings.

Whatever you use them for, follow these steps to add notes:

1. **Click the Notes header, and then select either Project Notes (General) or Document Notes from the drop-down list that appears, depending on the kind of notes you want to add.**

   If you select Project Notes (General), the header changes to Project Notes (General). If you select Document Notes, the header changes to Document Notes.

2. **Click in the text area and type.**

   That's it! Figure 5-3 shows an example of a project note.

Figure 5-3:
Project notes are visible regardless of which item has the focus.

If you add a document note to an item, an asterisk appears in the Notes button at the bottom of the Inspector (refer to Figure 5-4). The asterisk denotes that the document you're viewing (or have selected in the Corkboard or Outliner) has a document note associated with it, so you can tell even when the Notes pane isn't displayed in the Inspector.

Figure 5-4:
The asterisk lets you know that a document has associated document notes.

Asterisk in Notes button

Modifying notes

If you want to change or remove a project or document note, make sure the Notes pane you want to modify is visible in the Inspector. (See the preceding section for more.)

You can modify notes just like text in the Editor. Simply click in the text section of the note that you want to modify to make it editable. Now, you can delete text, insert your cursor to add text, or format text by using the Format bar's buttons (Chapter 6 has the scoop on the Format bar).

Adding an image to notes

Not only can you add text to your notes, but you can insert an image. Why would you want to do that? Well, maybe you want to have a quick, easy reference to a photo of your character or setting. Or maybe you just want a soothing image of a waterfall to keep you happy while you type.

Either way, this ability is handy if your Synopsis image pane (covered in Chapter 3) is occupied with a visual synopsis but you want to refer to another photo.

Follow these steps to add an image to a note:

1. **Make sure the Notes pane to which you want to add the image is visible in the Inspector.**

   You can work with either document or project notes. See the "Entering notes" section, earlier in this chapter, for more.

2. **Drag the photo from the Binder and drop it in the Notes pane.**

   Alternatively, you can drag the photo from Finder (or Windows Explorer on a PC).

   The image lands wherever you dropped it, as shown in Figure 5-5. It can be inserted above or below existing notes text.

If you need to delete a photo from a note, just click in the Notes pane to insert the cursor after the photo, and then press the Delete key (the Backspace key in Windows).

Figure 5-5:
You can add
an image to
either the
project or
document
Notes pane.

Managing project notes

Find yourself running out of room, but want to add more project notes? Or maybe you wish the project Notes pane was larger and easier to move around in. No worries.

You can create additional project notes, and easily edit them, by following these steps:

1. **Click the Notes button in the Inspector to view the Notes pane.**

2. **Click the Notes header and select Manage Project Notes from the drop-down list that appears.**

   A small window that looks like a notepad appears.

3. **If desired, drag the edges of the window to resize it.**

4. **Click the plus sign (+) button.**

5. **Enter the desired title of the new notepad in the Notepad tab.**

   A new tab appears with the title you provided, as shown in Figure 5-6.

To move between the notepads, click the tab of the notes that you want to work in. From the Project Notes window, you can edit, format, delete, or add text and images, just like in the Notes pane.

You can rename any project notepad — even Project Notes (General) — by double-clicking the tab to get a Note Title text box and entering the new name.

After closing the Project Notes window, you can navigate between notepads by clicking the Notes header and choosing the desired notepad from the drop-down list that appears.

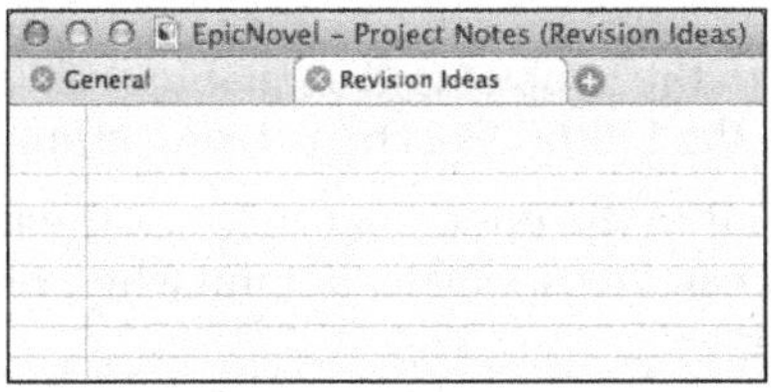

Figure 5-6:
Work with
project
notepads in
the Project
Notes
window.

Figure 5-6:
Work with project notepads in the Project Notes window.

Getting the Skinny on References

Back in the old days — when I was, uh, five — I had to trudge to the library to do my research. And if the books I needed were part of the reference section that couldn't be checked out, or my sources were on microfiche, I had to make copies to lug home, where I might or might not be able to find them again when I needed them.

Now, so much is available online or in electronic format, the lugging part is easy — but that doesn't always mean you can find a resource again when you need it.

Scrivener solves this problem with references. References provide you with quick access to research files or websites that you want to associate with your project or document, but don't want to import into the project.

Unlike importing (covered in Chapter 2), when you add a reference, all that's stored in Scrivener is the link to it. When you open a reference, you always get the most up-to-date version. However, if the file or website is moved — or the filename changes — the link doesn't work anymore.

References are also great for files that can't be viewed within Scrivener, such as spreadsheets, presentations, or other files created with specialty software.

Access references by clicking the References button at the bottom of the Inspector (refer to Figure 5-1).

Linking to a reference is incredibly handy, but before you start, consider a couple of things:

- Do you want the reference linked to the project as a whole or a particular document?
- Is the reference an existing file within your project, or is it on your hard drive or a website?

References can either be linked to the whole project or a single document:

✔ **Project references:** Linked to the project and available regardless of which item has the focus in the Editor, Corkboard, or Outliner.

✔ **Document references:** Linked to the document that has the focus. Using document references can be especially helpful when preparing a bibliography.

To switch between project and document references, click the References header and select Document References or Project References from the drop-down list that appears, as shown in Figure 5-7.

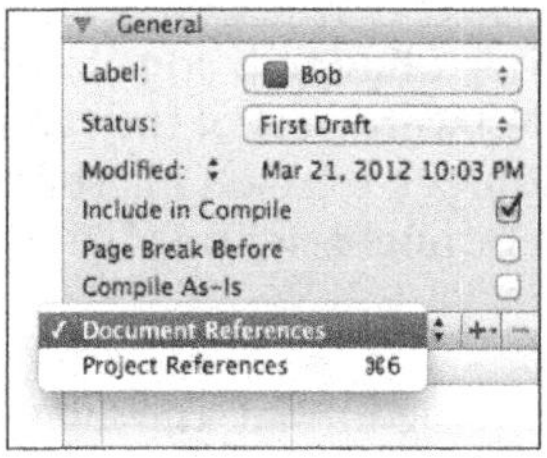

Figure 5-7:
Choose
between
project and
document
references.

References (whether they're project or document references) can either be internal or external, depending on where the original file resides:

✔ **Internal references:** Links to items within the same Scrivener project.

Why bother if they're already in the project? Well, if you have a lot of files in your Research folder, internal references save you time by letting you link to those files that are relevant to the document you're working on so that you don't have to wade through them all.

✔ **External references:** Links to items outside the project.

Linking to Reference Material

Do you keep referring to a file in your project while writing a certain scene? Instead of hunting for it in the Binder each time you need it, you can create an internal reference.

Or maybe you've been scouring the Internet and finally found the elusive website that has everything you ever needed to know about green sea turtles. It's far more information than you could possibly store, and you want to save the link for future reference and for your bibliography. What to do? Create an external reference!

If the References pane isn't visible, click the References button at the bottom of the Inspector. The References pane appears in the lower half of the Inspector.

Adding an internal reference

Internal references link to files stored within your project. Follow these steps to create one:

1. **Click the References header to open a drop-down list, and then choose either Document References or Project References.**

2. **Click the Add button to the right of the header.**

   As shown in Figure 5-8, a menu pops up with options for adding a reference.

3. **Point to Add Internal Reference on the menu.**

4. **In the submenu that appears, follow the hierarchy and click the desired item.**

   The link appears in the References pane (see Figure 5-9).

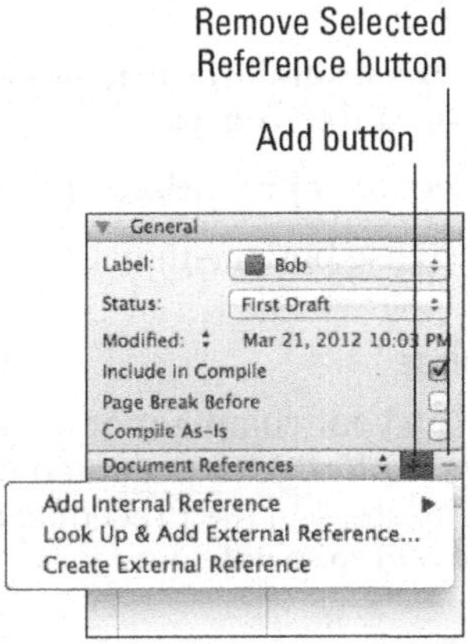

Remove Selected
Reference button

Add button

▼	General		
Label:	🔲 Bob	⬍
Status:	First Draft	⬍
Modified: ⬍	Mar 21, 2012 10:03 PM	
Include in Compile		☑
Page Break Before		☐
Compile As-Is		☐
Document References	⬍	⊞

Add Internal Reference ▶
Look Up & Add External Reference...
Create External Reference

Figure 5-8:
Click the
Add button
to create
an internal
reference.

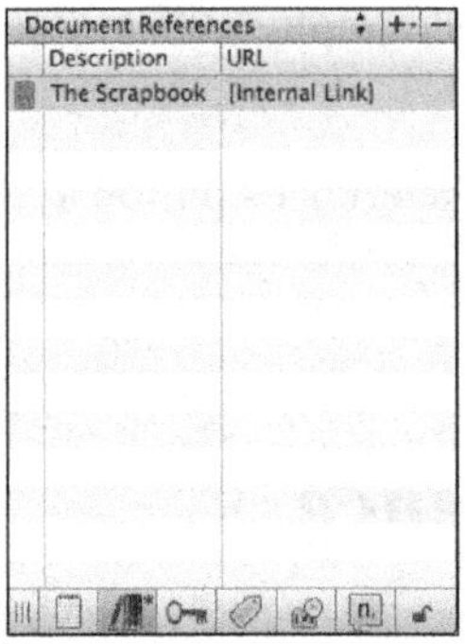

Figure 5-9:
A new
internal ref-
erence in the
References
pane.

You can also drag an item from the Binder and drop it on the References pane to create an internal reference.

Adding an external reference

External references are links to files outside of your project. They're handy for oversized files or when you want to always have access to the most up-to-date version of a file or website. You can link to most common file types with an external reference.

To add an external reference, you can look it up, type it in, or drag and drop. You start the first two methods by following these steps:

1. **Click the References header to open a drop-down list, and then select either Document References or Project References.**

2. **Click the Add button, and then select the appropriate option.**

   The following sections outline how to use both methods.

Looking up to add an external reference

You can use this method for files stored on your computer or on a drive that you can access from Finder (or Windows Explorer), such as an online storage site or external drive. After completing the steps in the preceding section, follow these steps to look up a reference and then link up:

1. **Select Look Up & Add External Reference from the Add drop-down list.**

   The Add References window appears.

2. **Select the file that you want to link, and then click Open.**

   The link appears in the References pane.

When you create a document reference, an asterisk appears in the References pane to denote that the current item has a reference.

Manually creating an external reference

This method is best for web pages, but also works for files stored on your computer if you know the file path. You need to know the *URL* (web address) of the page that you want, so if you don't know it by heart, pull up the page in your browser and copy the URL before following these steps:

1. **Select Create External Reference from the Add drop-down list.**

   A line appears in the References pane with New Reference selected in the Description field.

2. **Type the name of the reference in the Description field.**

   For example, you might enter **Bob's Vacation.**

3. **Press the Tab key to move to the URL field.**

4. **Type, or paste in, the resource URL, and then press Return.**

   The external reference you created now appears in the References pane. See the example in Figure 5-10.

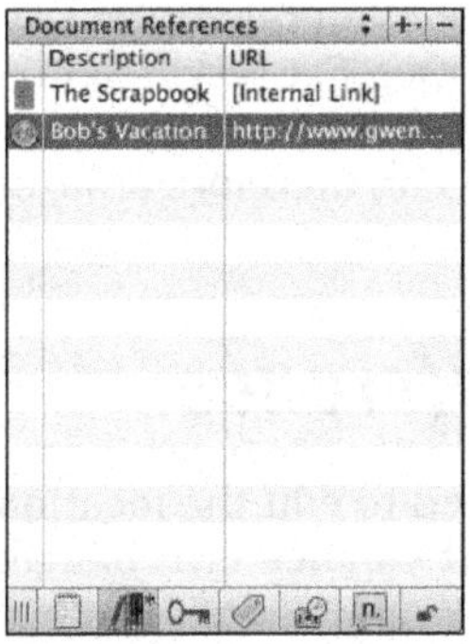

Figure 5-10:
A new external reference created manually.

Document References	
Description	URL
The Scrapbook	[Internal Link]
Bob's Vacation	http://www.gwen...

Dragging and dropping to create a reference

To add any kind of external reference, you can drag the file from Finder (or Windows Explorer) or your Internet browser's address bar (drag the icon just to the left of the URL, or the URL itself if there's no icon) directly to the References pane.

Just make sure you've selected either Document or Project References in the References header first.

Determining when to use external references

If you read about importing files in Chapter 2, you might be wondering how to decide whether to import your research or use an external reference.

Here's a list of things to consider when choosing between importing and referencing a file or website (for ease of reading, I use the term *file,* but the questions also apply to websites, images, and media):

- ✔ **How large is the file?** Every file you import to Scrivener adds to the project size. Although you shouldn't notice a slowdown while working in the project, file size impacts how quickly the project is backed up (more on backups in Chapter 21) and how much space it takes up on your hard drive.

  If the file is more than 1MB or you have a lot of files to add, consider using external references.

- ✔ **How often will you need to access the file?** If you plan to refer to a file frequently, it might be better to import it for quicker viewing.

- ✔ **Will the file's contents or location change?** If you don't need access to a file's updates or you're worried that it might change or move, you should import it. On the other hand, if you want to have access to the latest version at all times, use an external reference.

- ✔ **Will you work on your project on more than one computer?** If you open the same Scrivener project on multiple computers, external references to files on one computer don't work on another. For research files that you need to access from all computers, importing makes more sense because imported files are saved with the project and therefore always available.

Editing and deleting a reference

If you give a reference the wrong name or need to edit the location, you can do so anytime by double-clicking the part you need to change in the References pane and entering the new info.

On the other hand, you might add the wrong link or find one that no longer works. Or maybe you changed your topic from raccoons to giraffes, and you need to clean out the old research.

Follow these steps to delete an unwanted reference:

1. **Click the References header, and then select either Document References or Project References from the drop-down list that appears.**

2. **Select the reference that you want to delete from the References pane.**

   You can use multiple selection (covered in Chapter 2) to select more than one reference for deletion.

3. **Click the Remove Selected Reference button (refer to Figure 5-8).**

The selected reference (or references) disappears.

Viewing a reference

References don't do you any good if you can't view them, but how Scrivener displays a reference depends on where it's located and the type of file it is.

Viewing an internal reference

To view an internal reference, follow these steps:

1. **Click the References header to view the drop-down list, and then choose either Document References or Project References.**

2. **Double-click the icon next to the reference you want to view.**

By default, the Editor pane opens to a split screen with the reference in the upper pane. This setup lets you refer to your research while you write.

3. **If you don't want to work in Split Screen view, click the Split toggle button (shown in Figure 5-11) to exit that view.**

I talk about Split Screen view in Chapter 6.

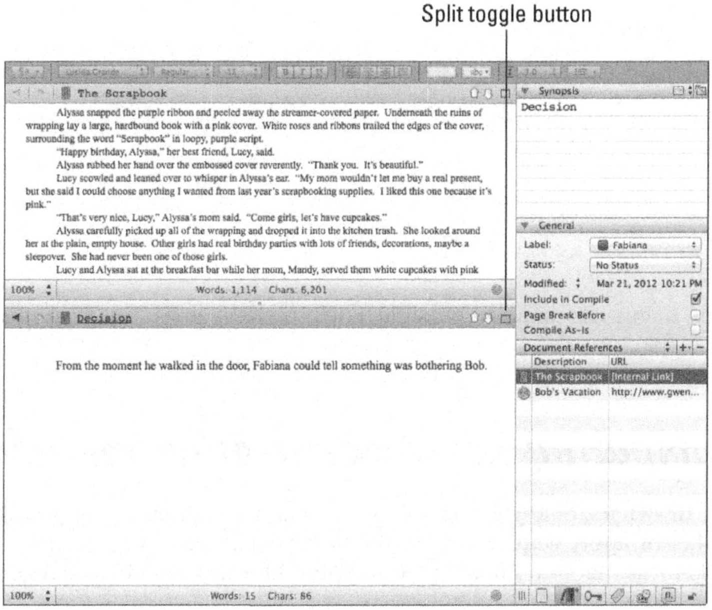

Split toggle button

Figure 5-11:
An internal
reference
open in
Split Screen
view.

Viewing an external reference

External references open in their native program (for example, Word, TextEdit, or your Internet browser). Open an external reference by following these steps:

1. **Click the references header, and then select either Document References or Project References from the drop-down list that appears.**

2. **Double-click the icon next to the reference that you want to view.**

   Scrivener launches the native program and opens the reference within it.

For more ways to open an external reference, right-click the reference. The Reveal in Finder option shows you where the file is located on your computer.

Assigning Keywords

Keywords allow you to add attributes to an item in your project. Keywords that have been applied to an item are visible from the Keywords pane, shown in Figure 5-12.

Remove Keyword
button

Add Keyword button

Figure 5-12:
The
Keywords
pane in the
Inspector.

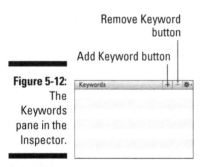

If the Keywords pane isn't visible, click the Keywords button at the bottom of the Inspector.

Comparing keywords to other metadata

The drawback of keywords is that you can't use them to color code the Binder or apply watermarks to the index cards like you can with the Label and Status metadata fields (see Chapter 4 for more on metadata).

However, keywords have their own strengths:

- ✔ You can view keywords as color tabs on index cards in the Corkboard or as words underlined by color in the Outliner.

- ✔ You can apply more than one keyword to an item.

- ✔ Just like with metadata, you can track point of view (POV), setting, part, characters present in a scene, the purpose of the scene, which subplot it belongs to, and more. Again, you're only limited by your own imagination and needs. And best of all, you can have keywords for all those categories, if you want.

Adding a keyword to an item

When you add a keyword to a document, it automatically becomes available for use within the whole project.

The keywords you create apply to your whole project but aren't available to other projects unless you save them into a custom project template (which you can read all about in Chapter 15).

To add a new keyword to both the selected item and the project, follow these steps:

1. **In the Binder, Corkboard, or Outliner, select the document for which you want to create a keyword.**

3. **Click the Add Keyword button in the Keywords header (refer to Figure 5-12).**

   A blank text box appears in the Keywords pane.

4. **Type the desired name of the keyword, and then press Return.**

   The new keyword appears with a Color box next to it, as shown in Figure 5-13. The color is now associated with that keyword and shows up on index cards when you view them in the Corkboard, if keyword colors are turned on (see Chapter 8 for more on the Corkboard).

   The asterisk in the Keywords button denotes that a keyword is applied to the current item.

After you have at least one keyword in the Keywords pane, you can select any keyword and press Return to add a new one. This shortcut gives you a quick way to add several keywords quickly.

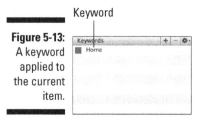

Keyword

Figure 5-13:
A keyword
applied to
the current
item.

Applying an existing keyword to a file

When you add a keyword to an item, you also add it to the project as a whole for use with other items. After the keyword you want to use already exists, you only need to apply it to the desired item. Just follow these steps:

1. **Select the item to which you want to add a keyword in the Binder, Corkboard, or Outliner.**

2. **In the Keywords header, click the gear button.**

   When you click the button, a pop-up menu appears.

3. **Choose Add Keyword, and then select the desired keyword from the list that appears.**

   The selected keyword appears in the Keywords pane.

Removing a keyword from an item

What happens when you're in revisions and you decide to kill off the hero's girlfriend a couple of scenes early? To avoid confusion, you want to remove her keyword from scenes in which she no longer appears.

You can easily remove a keyword from an item without deleting it from the project by following these steps:

1. **Select the desired item in the Binder, Corkboard, or Outliner.**

2. **In the Keywords pane, select the keyword(s) that you want to remove.**

3. **Click the Remove Keyword button in the Keywords header (refer to Figure 5-12).**

   Or you can just press the Delete key.

Removing a keyword this way affects only the selected document, not the whole project.

Working with the Project Keywords Window

The Project Keywords window floats over the Scrivener project window and lets you easily change keyword colors or delete keywords from the entire project.

Open the Keywords window by clicking the Keywords button in the Scrivener toolbar or choosing Project⊅Show Project Keywords. You can also click the gear button in the Keywords header of the Inspector pane, and then choose Show Project Keywords from the drop-down list that appears. The Project Keywords window shows all keywords available in the project. (To close the window, click the X in the upper-left corner.)

Figure 5-14 provides an overview of the Project Keywords window.

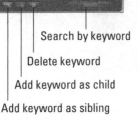

Figure 5-14:
The Project
Keywords
window.

Search by keyword

Delete keyword

Add keyword as child

Add keyword as sibling

Applying keywords

You can apply existing keywords to an item from the Project Keywords window easily. Just drag and drop the desired keyword from the window onto the item name in the Binder or into the Keywords pane in the Inspector.

TIP

If you want to add the same keyword to more than one file, select all the desired items in the Binder, and then drag the keyword from the window onto any one of the selected filenames.

Finding items by keyword

Want to know which documents have a keyword applied? Follow these steps to find out:

1. **In the Project Keywords window, select the keyword for which you want to search.**

2. **Click the Search button at the bottom of the window (refer to Figure 5-14).**

   A list of documents that contain the selected keyword appears in the Binder pane. You can choose any item from the list to view it in the Editor.

3. **Click the X at the bottom of the Search Results list (see Figure 5-15) to close the list and return to the Binder.**

Figure 5-15:
Searching by keyword returns all items with the selected keyword applied.

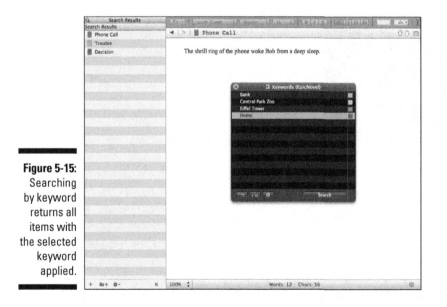

Adding a keyword to the project

If you're really organized, you can add a keyword to the project before you ever apply it to an item. You can even organize keywords into hierarchical groups, much like your documents are organized in the Binder.

To add a keyword to the project, follow these steps:

1. **In the Project Keywords window, click the Add New Keyword as Sibling button (refer to Figure 5-14) to add a keyword to the top level (or at the same level as a selected keyword).**

   A text box appears in the Project Keywords window.

2. **Type the desired keyword name, and then press Return.**

   The keyword is added to the list in alphabetical order.

To add a child keyword (one at a lower level than the selected keyword), click the Add New Keyword as Child button. (See Figure 5-14.)

Changing the keyword color

If the keyword colors chosen by Scrivener aren't to your taste, you can change them in the Project Keywords window by following these steps:

1. **Double-click the color square to the right of the keyword whose color you want to change.**

   The Colors window appears.

2. **(Mac only) Click the button for your favorite palette at the top of the window.**

3. **Select the desired color from the palette.**

   The color square in the window changes to the new color.

4. **Repeat Steps 1 through 3 until all the colors are to your liking.**

5. **Click the red X button to close the Colors window.**

   On a Windows PC, you click OK.

Modifying a keyword

Did you rename a character? Wrongly classify an item in your dissertation? Conjure up a new name for your species of alien? No problem. Just follow these steps to modify a keyword:

1. Double-click the text of the keyword that you want to edit.

The keyword text is selected and ready to change.

2. Type the new text, and then press Return.

Deleting a keyword

What if you kill off a character, remove a breed from your paper on the grooming habits of feral cattle, or eliminate a setting? Just follow these steps to delete a keyword:

1. Select the keyword that you want to delete.

2. Click the Delete button in the Keywords panel (refer to Figure 5-14).

If the keyword is in use, a pop-up window warns you of the consequences and asks you to confirm deletion.

3. If the pop-up window appears, read it, and then click OK.

Deleting a keyword applies to the whole project. After you delete a keyword, that keyword is no longer available in the Keywords panel, and it's removed from all documents to which you've already applied it.

Creating Custom Metadata

Custom metadata provides a way to tag items with a piece of information. But how is it different from the Label and Status fields (Chapter 4), or keywords (see the section "Assigning Keywords," earlier in this chapter)? Custom metadata works best when the field value might be different for every document but corresponds to a theme.

Here are some example uses of metadata:

✔ Say you want to keep track of the setting for each scene in your manuscript, but you want to be more specific than London, France, or Ladies' Underpants, and every scene takes place somewhere new. With custom metadata, you can create a Setting field and populate it with values such as John's Living Room Floor or Front Seat of Kerry's Car.

✔ An anthology editor might find value in tracking the author for each section via custom metadata, thus freeing up Label and Status for other things.

✔ Depending on how specific you want to be, a timeline can also fit nicely into custom metadata. For every scene or section, you mark it with something as high-level as the year or as detailed as the minute of the day.

✔ If you're writing book reviews, you can attach custom metadata for the ISBN, price, or even the Dewey Decimal number of the book to each document.

Here are a few of the pros of custom metadata:

✔ After you create them, you can add custom metadata values to any item in the project.

✔ You can sort documents by a custom metadata field in the Outliner.

✔ Like with other types of metadata, you can use custom metadata fields to create a collection (see Chapter 18), with which you can filter items during the compile (export) process outlined in Part IV of this book.

And now for the cons:

✔ Custom metadata fields are the least visible of all metadata. You can see them only in the Inspector pane and the Outliner.

✔ You can't create a drop-down list of values, so you have to enter the values manually, which can lead to data entry errors.

Click the Custom Meta-Data button in the Inspector (refer to Figure 5-1) to open the Custom Meta-Data pane. If you haven't added any fields before, the pane displays No Meta-Data Fields Defined and includes the Define Meta-Data Fields button.

Adding a custom metadata field

When you create a custom metadata field, it is available to every item in the project. Follow these steps to add a metadata field:

1. **Click the gear button (shown in Figure 5-16) in the Custom Meta-Data header to open a submenu.**

2. **Select Edit Custom Meta-Data Settings.**

The Meta-Data Settings window appears, with the Custom Meta-Data button already selected.

You can also access the Meta-Data Settings window by choosing Project⇨Meta-Data Settings or by clicking the Define Meta-Data Fields button in the Custom Meta-Data pane (only available when you haven't yet defined any custom fields).

3. **Click the Add New Meta-Data Field button.**

   A blank text box appears in the Custom Meta-Data Fields list.

4. **Type the name of the field, and then press Enter.**

   The new field name appears in the list.

   Don't type the values in this text box. Think of this as the heading under which values are added.

5. **(Optional) Select Wrap Text to force the value to wrap, instead of showing just the first line.**

6. **(Optional) Select Colored Text to apply the selected color to the values when you view them in the Outliner and the field name when you view it in the Custom Meta-Data pane in the Inspector.**

   To choose a color, select the metadata field in the list, click the color picker box at the bottom of the Meta-Data Settings window, and select a color from the Colors window that appears.

7. **Click OK to close the Meta-Data Settings window.**

   The new field appears in the Custom Meta-Data pane in the Inspector.

Adding a value

You can add values to a custom metadata field, either in the Inspector pane or directly within the Outliner row. I detail working with values in the Outliner in Chapter 9. To add a value in the Inspector, follow these steps:

1. **Select the desired item in the Binder, Corkboard, or Outliner.**

2. **In the Custom Meta-Data pane in the Inspector, click in the text box below the field to which you want to add a value.**

   The text box outline turns blue, and your cursor blinks within the text box.

3. **Type the desired value, and then press Return.**

   The new value appears in the field text box, as shown in Figure 5-16.

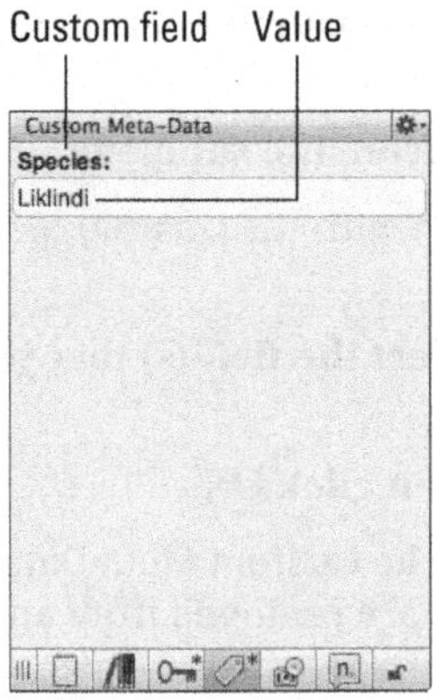

Custom field   Value

Figure 5-16:
A value
added to
a custom
metadata
field.

Although the field is added to the whole project, the value you just
entered is applied only to the current document. If you select a different
item, the value may be either empty or different, depending on whether
you already added a value to it.

Modifying a value

You can edit the value of a custom metadata field in either the Inspector pane
or Outliner row. (Modifying values in the Outliner is detailed in Chapter 9.)
To change a value in the Inspector, follow these steps:

1. **Select the desired item in the Binder, Corkboard, or Outliner.**

2. **Select the existing value in the text box below the appropriate field in
   the Custom Meta-Data pane in the Inspector.**

3. **Type the desired value.**

   Alternatively, you can delete the text to remove that value.

4. **Press Return.**

   The new value appears in the Inspector pane. If you deleted the value,
   the custom field's text box is blank.

Deleting a custom metadata field

Did you create a custom metadata field only to find you don't use it? Or
maybe it's served its purpose and you no longer want to retain the data.
Follow these steps to delete your custom field:

1. **Click the gear button in the Custom Meta-Data header to display a submenu.**

2. **Select Edit Custom Meta-Data Settings from the submenu.**

   The Meta-Data Settings window appears, with the Custom Meta-Data button already selected.

3. **In the Custom Meta-Data Fields list, select the field(s) that you want to delete.**

4. **Click the minus sign (–) button, and then click OK.**

   The selected fields no longer appear in the Custom Meta-Data Fields list or in the Inspector pane. The values are removed from any items to which they were applied.

Looking at the Remaining Document Support Options

The document support panes section of the Inspector offers several more functions: snapshots, comments and footnotes, and the Lock Inspector To Current Editor button. The following sections give you a brief overview, but each option is covered in its own chapter.

Snapshots

Like taking a picture before editing, snapshots allow you to keep multiple versions of your documents, compare them, and even revert back to an older version. With snapshots, you really don't have to kill your darlings. You can keep them all around for years to come.

Can't wait to zoom in? Chapter 19 focuses on snapshots.

Comments & Footnotes

Ever wish you could add notes in the margin while you write, edit, or read your manuscript? Need to add footnotes for your works cited or comic asides? The Comments & Footnotes pane lets you create, modify, and view all linked notes associated with an item.

For more information, beat feet over to Chapters 10 and 11.

Locking the Inspector

Did you notice the little Lock button at the bottom of the Inspector? No? Go on; look now. That Lock button binds the Inspector view to a specific Editor pane. This feature specifically applies to split-screen functionality, which you can read more about in Chapter 6.

Part III
Starting to Write

The 5th Wave   By Rich Tennant

"Do you use these 3x5 cards for anything other than charting your screenplay, or does the creature actually make a pineapple bundt cake at this point in the movie?"

In this part . . .

This part of the book is what it's all about, folks: Writing!

In this part, you can take a stroll with the Editor, create a distraction-free desktop, play with your scenes in the Corkboard, and take a high view in the Outliner. And when you've put some words down, you can go back and mark them up with annotations and comments, and create footnotes to keep track of your sources.

Chapter 6

Introducing the Editor: Where the Magic Happens

....

In This Chapter

▶ Diving into the parts of the Editor

▶ Viewing multiple items in Split Screen mode

▶ Working with QuickReference panels

▶ Viewing documents in Scrivenings mode

▶ Checking spelling and grammar

....

You can play with Scrivener's crazy-cool features all day, but in the end, you have to plant your rear in the chair and write something, or all your fooling around is for naught.

Enter the Editor. The Editor is where you actually write your novel, screenplay, blog post, magazine article, dissertation, class lesson, or memoir. It's where you make literary magic.

Available in Document view (for an individual file) or Scrivenings mode (when you're working with multiple documents), the Editor is the default display for Scrivener. Basically, if you're not in the Corkboard or the Outliner, you're in the Editor.

This chapter is a lesson on Editor anatomy, working in Split Screen mode, editing multiple documents at one time, and checking your spelling and grammar.

Dissecting the Editor

The Editor is composed of these major parts:

▶ **Format bar:** At the top, the Format bar provides options for changing the font, text color, alignment, and line spacing of your document.

> ✔ **Header and Footer bars:** Give you information about the document you're viewing and provide shortcuts to several document options.
>
> ✔ **Ruler:** Lets you set tabs and indents.

The following sections explain each element of the Editor. Figure 6-1 starts you off with a quick breakdown of the Editor pane. Dig in!

Header bar   Format bar

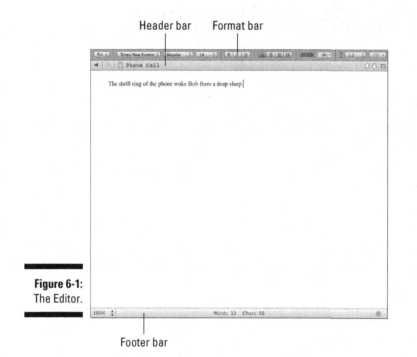

Figure 6-1:
The Editor.

Footer bar

The Format bar

The Format bar isn't strictly part of the Editor, but its options are available only while in Document view or Scrivenings mode (as opposed to the Corkboard or Outliner) or while working in the Notes pane of the Inspector. If you've ever used a word processor, most of the options should look familiar.

The Format bar is where you go to change the font, justification, font color, highlighting, and spacing, and to create bulleted or numbered lists. All the options available on the Format bar are also accessible from the Format menu.

If you're not sure what an option does, hover your mouse pointer over the button or drop-down list to get a *tooltip,* which provides a brief description of the button.

With the exception of bold, italic, and underline, whatever font settings you use within the Editor may not be the same as those used when you compile (export) your manuscript, depending on the Compile settings (see Part IV for more on exporting).

Scrivener provides formatting options that allow you to customize your writing experience and to offer bold, italic, and underline.

The good news is that if you like to type in 16-point blue Helvetica, you can do that and still have Scrivener export to Times New Roman or Courier without reformatting the entire manuscript within the Editor.

Figure 6-2 shows the Format bar for Mac and Windows, respectively.

Figure 6-2:
The Format bar on the Mac (top) and in Windows (bottom).

Choosing font options

The Format bar contains the common controls you need to format your text. Three buttons apply to font formatting:

✔ **Font Family:** Clicking this button lets you choose which style of font you want, from Arial to Zapfino.

Have you ever heard the terms *serif* and *sans serif* and wondered what the heck people were talking about? Here's an explanation:

• A *serif* font is one that has the extra little projections on the tips of the letters. For example, Times New Roman is a serif font.

• *Sans* comes from the French word for *without. Sans serif* means the font doesn't have the little projections. Arial is a good example.

✔ **Typeface:** When you click this button, you can choose from available variations of the font, such as italic, bold, oblique, light oblique, or condensed. Fonts all have their own set of variations based on what the font designer chose to include.

✔ **Font Size:** Click this button to choose the size of your text. The numbers are in points, which are roughly equal to $\frac{1}{72}$ of an inch, which means that if you want 1-inch letters, choose 72-point font. The standard for business and publishing is generally 12-point.

Font options apply to whatever text is selected when you make your choices. If no text is selected, font choices apply to whatever you type from the current cursor position forward.

Choosing text options

The Bold, Italic, and Underline buttons, located to the right of the font options on the Format bar, provide text formatting options. **Bold,** *italic,* and <u>underline</u> are generally used on small sections of text for emphasis.

If your cursor is within text that has one of the formats applied, the appropriate button appears depressed in the Format bar to show that format application.

Want to use italics while writing, but need to submit your manuscript with underlined words instead? You can! Use italics now, and when you're ready to compile (export) your file, you can convert the italicized words to underlined words. Check out Chapter 12 for more on Compile settings.

The Text Color and Highlighter Color buttons on the Format bar allow you to change text color and apply highlighting. Click either button once to use the displayed color, or press and hold the button (Windows users click the triangle to the right of the button) to reveal more color options in a drop-down list, where you can select the color you want to use.

With all the text formatting options, you can select a block of text and then apply one of the options, or you can choose the desired text option to make that option apply to text you add from your cursor point forward.

Applying paragraph formatting options

Paragraph formatting options are distinct from the others because they apply to the entire paragraph your cursor is located in, regardless of whether any text is selected:

✔ **Text Alignment:** The Text Alignment buttons let you choose left, center, or right alignment, or full justification, respectively. Each button shows a visual representation of the alignment it provides.

✔ **Line Spacing:** Choose the amount of space between lines of text from this drop-down list. For even more line spacing options, select Other from the list (select More in Windows).

✔ **Table:** Shown by default in Windows only, this button opens a window that allows you to modify properties of an existing table. For other Table options, click the arrow next to the button to view a drop-down list.

Mac users who want the Table option in the Scrivener toolbar can add it by going to View⇨Customize Toolbar and then dragging the Table icon from the window directly onto the toolbar above. Clicking the button when not in a table inserts a table and opens the Options window. If your cursor is within a table when the button is clicked, the Options window opens without inserting another table.

Table options are also accessible via Format⇨Table.

✔ **List Style:** The List Style button lets you apply a bulleted or numbered list format. With your cursor at the beginning of the line, press the Tab key to indent and demote the bullet or number line (make it lower on the hierarchy). Pressing Shift+Tab promotes a bullet or number line.

When you use list styles, the styles stay active with each subsequent paragraph you create until you press the Return key twice in a row, at which point, the text reverts to the previous paragraph style (either a higher level bullet/number, or normal paragraph text). Alternately, you can apply the list styles after the fact by selecting text and choosing a style.

Creating a preset

The very first button in the Format bar is for applying presets. A *preset* is a saved combination of formatting choices that you can apply to the selected text with a single button click — sort of like the button on a fancy car that memorizes each driver's seat options, temperature preferences, and wheel tilt.

Presets are useful when you have sections of your manuscript that you need to distinguish from the rest of the text in some way. For example, maybe your project has e-mails from one character to another, and you want to set them off with a different font, spacing, and alignment. Or maybe you use a block quote at the beginning of each chapter and don't want to recreate the settings each time you add a new one.

Presets are saved within Scrivener and become available to all projects.

Scrivener comes loaded with several presets, but you can also create your own by following these steps:

1. **Select a block of text and format it as desired, choosing from any of the options in the Format bar.**

   Alternatively, you can select from a section of text that is already in the format you desire.

2. **Choose Format⇨Formatting⇨New Preset from Selection.**

3. **Type a name for the preset in the New Style window that appears.**

   Use a name that will remind you of the preset's attributes.

4. **Select Save All Formatting from the drop-down list at the bottom-left of the window.**

Selecting this option ensures that character attributes (such as font color, bold, italics, and underline) are retained, along with paragraph styling (such as first line indents and line spacing).

5. **To save the font family and size with the preset, select the Include Font and Include Font Size checkboxes at the bottom-right.**

6. **Click OK.**

   The New Style window closes.

7. **Click the Presets button in the Format bar to see your new preset in the drop-down list that opens.**

Figure 6-3 shows the new preset I created called BlueScript14, based on the text in the document that I formatted as blue, Lucida Calligraphy, size 14.

Figure 6-3:
A new
formatting
preset.

| ¶a ▾ | Times New Roman ‡ | Regular ‡ | 14 ‡ | B I U | ☰ ☰ ☰ ☰ | ▮▮ | abc ▾ | I |

Presets
¶ Block Quote
    BlueScript14
¶ Body
a Char only
¶ Essay Block Quote (Preserved)
¶a Heading
¶a Sub-heading
¶a Title

...cinating. As a writer who wants plot ideas on demand, it can also

...ticle that said our brains don't work as well

...?) We can't force the ideas, they're more likely to

come when our conscious mind is occupied with other things. Like

driving, showering, jogging, walking the dog.

   My own--admittedly non-scientific--observation has borne this out. I can stare at the screen for hours and get zip, but tie on my running shoes and within minutes something's likely to bubble up. Good for my story and my hips!

Applying a preset

Creating a preset doesn't do you any good if you don't know how to apply it. Follow these steps to make it happen:

1. **Click in the desired paragraph.**

   If you want to apply the preset to more than one paragraph, select all the paragraphs to which you want to apply the preset.

   If a preset has only character attributes (meaning font family, typeface, size, bold, italic, underline, or color) saved, then you must select the desired text before you select the preset to apply.

   Presets that have only character attributes are designated with an underlined lowercase A (so it looks like a). The presets that have only paragraph formatting have a paragraph icon (backwards *P*). Presets that have both character and paragraph formatting show both icons.

2. **Click the Presets button in the Format bar, and then select the desired preset from the drop-down list that appears.**

   The selected text changes to display the attributes defined in the preset.

Deleting a preset

If you make a mistake or realize you don't want a preset anymore, you can delete it. Just choose Format➪Formatting➪Delete Preset, and then select the preset that you want to delete from the list of presets that appears.

If you delete a built-in preset, you can't get it back without re-creating it yourself or doing some fancy footwork.

If you want to remove your custom presets and restore the defaults, choose Scrivener➪Reveal Support Folder in Finder. Delete the `Styles.plist` file located in `~/Library/Application Support/Scrivener`. No need to restart Scrivener, the Presets list reverts to the original defaults.

Preserving formatting

Sometimes when you give a block of text within a document special formatting, you want it to stay that way, even when you compile (export) the rest of your manuscript in Times New Roman 12-point font that's double-spaced.

For example, a portion of your document might represent a handwritten note or contain a block quote, epigraph, or figure caption that has a style distinct from the rest of the text. To ensure that the formatting is preserved regardless of your compile settings, first select the portion of text that you want to preserve. Then, choose Format➪Select Formatting➪Preserve Formatting. The text is highlighted in pale blue with a dashed outline (see Figure 6-4) to indicate that its formatting will be preserved.

To remove Preserved Formatting, highlight the text and choose Format➪Select Formatting➪Preserve Formatting.

Figure 6-4:
The blue-highlighted text has its formatting preserved when you compile.

> ◄ | ► | 📄 Bubble Brain   🔒 ⊟
>
> I think the human brain is fascinating. As a writer who wants plot ideas on demand, it can also be frustrating.
>
> *Recently I read an article that said our brains don't work as well under stress. (Duh, right?) We can't force the ideas, they're more likely to come when our conscious mind is occupied with other things. Like driving, showering, jogging, walking the dog.*
>
> My own--admittedly non-scientific--observation has borne this out. I can stare at the screen for hours and get zip, but tie on my running shoes and within minutes something's likely to bubble up. Good for my story and my hips!

Changing the default document format

If you have specific text and paragraph settings that you want to use for all the documents you create in Scrivener, you don't have to apply them after the fact.

Instead, you can change the default setting by following these steps:

1. **On the Mac, choose Scrivener⇨Preferences to open the Preferences window, and then click Formatting to view the Formatting options.**

   Windows users, choose Tools⇨Options to open the Options window, and then select the Editor tab to view the Formatting options.

2. **Click in the Main Text Style box at the top of the window to activate it.**

   In Windows, click the Default Main Text Attributes box.

3. **Use the Format bar in the window to set your preferences for all new documents in Scrivener.**

   These settings don't apply to documents already created.

   In this Format bar, font settings are accessible from the A button, as shown in Figure 6-5.

4. **When you finish settings preferences, click the red X button to close the Preferences window.**

   Windows users, click OK to apply settings and close the window.

   The settings are saved automatically.

Click to access font settings

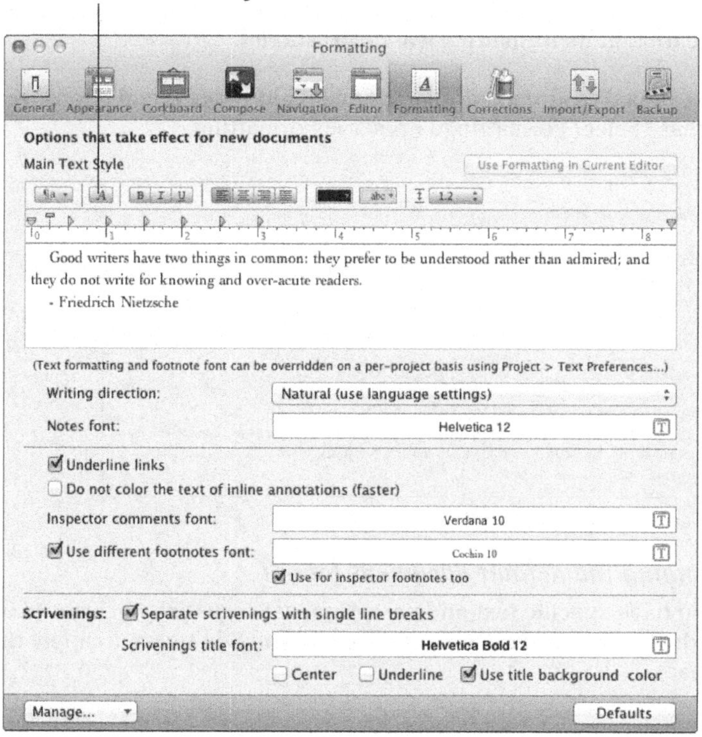

Figure 6-5:
The Formatting Preferences window.

Changing the default formatting applies to all projects, not just the one you're working in. To change it only for the current project, choose Project⇨Text Preferences to open the Project Formatting Preferences window, and then click the Override Text Formatting for This Project check box. When you set up your desired format, all new documents in the current project (and only in that project) use the specified settings.

The Header bar

Just below the Format bar in the Editor pane is the Header bar. In addition to providing information such as the title of the document being viewed in the Editor, it also offers a few handy functions. Figure 6-6 points out the key parts of the header, which I describe in this list:

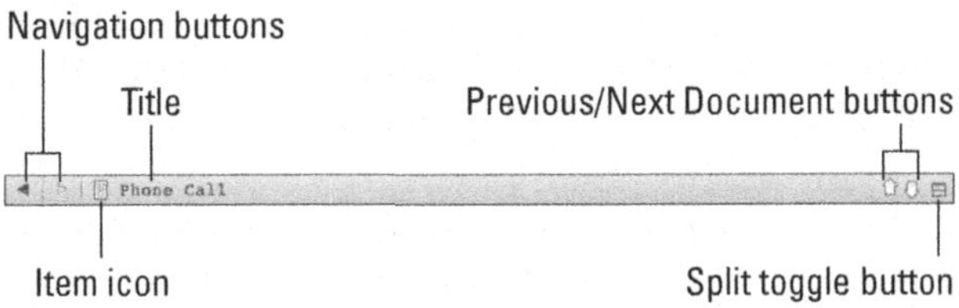

Navigation buttons

Title   Previous/Next Document buttons

Figure 6-6:
The Editor's
Header bar.

Item icon   Split toggle button

✔ **Navigation buttons:** The arrow buttons at the far-left of the header work much like the navigation buttons in a web browser, letting you step backward and forward through your document history.

Think of your document history as a linear timeline that you can skip through. For example, if you're working in Scene 1, and then you choose Scene 3 in the Binder, you can navigate back to Scene 1 by clicking the Back button. (Handy if you want to go back to a previous item but don't remember the name of it or where it's located in your vast hierarchy of files.) From Scene 1, you can click the Forward button to reopen Scene 3.

If you click and hold either button, a history menu appears; make a selection to jump directly to a file.

When you skip around with the Back and Forward buttons, the selected item in the Binder doesn't change to represent the document that has the Editor focus. (The Item icon menu has an option to deal with that.)

✔ **Item icon:** The icon in the Header bar is actually a button that you can click to display a shortcut menu, shown in Figure 6-7:

Figure 6-7:
The Item
icon menu.

- *Reveal in Binder:* If the selection in the Binder doesn't match the document that has the focus in the Editor, click Reveal in Binder to synchronize them.

- *Path:* Shows the hierarchical location of the current document in reverse order and lets you jump to a location on the path by clicking that location in the hierarchy.

- *Go To:* Choose any file in the project by following the hierarchy, pointing to each folder or subfolder to open it, until you reach the desired item. This feature is especially helpful when the Binder is hidden.

  When in Scrivenings mode (viewing multiple documents together in the Editor), Go To displays only a list of the items in the group being viewed. When you choose a document from the menu, Scrivener moves to that document's position among the files being viewed in the Editor, instead of loading the document by itself in the Editor.

- *Bookmarks:* Jump to a bookmark (covered in Chapter 17).

- *Take Snapshot:* Takes a snapshot of the current file. Read more on snapshots in Chapter 19.

- *Match Split Documents:* This option works only in Split Screen mode (see the section "Seeing Double with Split Screen Mode," later in this chapter, for the scoop on this mode). When you select this option, the document in the Editor pane of the Header bar you're using to access the menu opens in the other pane, as well, thus allowing you to work with the same document in both splits.

- *Lock in Place:* Locks the Editor so that clicking in the Binder doesn't change the document being viewed in the Editor. In Split Screen mode, this option locks whichever Editor's Header bar menu you're using. When locked, the Header bar turns a muted shade of red. Select the option again to unlock the Editor.

✔ **Title:** When a single item is viewed in the Editor, the Title section displays the document name. In this view, you can edit the document title by clicking in the title area, typing your change, and pressing Return.

In Scrivenings mode where a container is selected in the Binder, the Title section displays the container name followed by (Composite) and then the title of the item within the container that has the focus (where the cursor is).

In Scrivenings mode where multiple items are selected in the Binder, the Title section displays Multiple Selection followed by the title of the item that has the focus.

When in Scrivenings mode, you can't edit the title.

✔ **Previous/Next Document buttons:** Click the up- and down-arrow buttons in the Header bar to move up to the previous document or down to the next document in the Binder. These buttons ignore the hierarchy of the items when moving within the Binder, moving through every item in the list in order, even if containers are collapsed to hide their contents.

So, if you're in the Chapter 3 container and click the Previous button, you end up in the last scene of Chapter 2. Unlike with the History buttons, the item displayed in the Editor and the selection in the Binder always match.

✔ **Split toggle button:** Turn Split Screen mode on and off. The section "Seeing Double with Split Screen Mode," later in this chapter, has more on that subject.

The Windows Header bar has two Split toggle buttons, one for vertical split and one for horizontal split.

The Footer bar

The available options and information in the Footer bar change depending on what type of document you're viewing, but Figure 6-8 points out the elements of the Footer bar in the most common view, the Document view:

Figure 6-8:
The Editor's
Footer bar in
Document
view.

Text zoom   Target button

✔ **Text Zoom:** This drop-down list lets you change how large or small text appears in the Editor without changing the font size.

✔ **Word/Character Count:** The center of the Footer bar displays the word and character count for the current document. If you have a document target set (see Chapter 14), this part of the Footer bar shows the count divided by the goal.

If you don't see the Word and Character count, you may be in Scriptwriting mode. Choose Format⇨Scriptwriting. If Script Mode —

Screenplay has a checkmark next to it in the submenu that appears, select Script Mode — Screenplay to turn it off and return to standard Editing mode.

If you select a portion of the text in the document, the Footer bar changes to display the word and character count for the selection, adding the word Selection and turning the counts blue.

You can also select the desired text and right-click to view the selection word and character count at the bottom of the contextual menu that appears.

✔ **Target button:** Lets you set a word or character target for the current item. Chapter 14 covers document targets in more detail.

The Ruler

The Ruler lets you set indents and tab stops for the Editor. If it's not visible, click inside the Editor to give it the focus, and then choose Format⇨ Show Ruler. To hide the Ruler, choose Format⇨Hide Ruler.

Unlike most word processors, Scrivener doesn't revert to ½-inch tab stops when no tab stops are marked on the Ruler. If no tabs are marked on the ruler, pressing Tab moves the cursor to the next line without a paragraph break.

By default, however, most templates provide tab stops every ½ inch for the first 3 inches of typing space. Beyond that, you must add your own.

When you add, move, or remove tabs or change the indents, the settings apply to the paragraph in which the cursor appears or to all selected paragraphs. When the cursor is in a paragraph and you press Return, the first paragraph's settings carry to the new paragraph, but not to existing text elsewhere in the document.

Figure 6-9 shows the icons used in the Ruler.

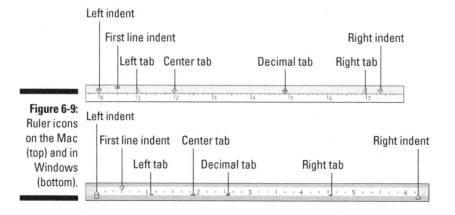

Figure 6-9: Ruler icons on the Mac (top) and in Windows (bottom).

Tabs

Scrivener offers four types of tab stops, each represented by a different icon:

- **Left:** A left tab is the standard tab used most often. Text is left-aligned, starting at the tab stop.

- **Center:** The center tab center-aligns the text on the tab stop.

- **Right:** With a right tab, text is right-aligned, with the right edge of the text at the tab stop.

- **Decimal:** Generally used to create columns of numbers, the decimal tab aligns the text with the decimal point at the tab stop. Text prior to the decimal is right aligned; text after the decimal is left aligned.

You can add a tab stop one of the following ways:

- For a left tab, click the desired location in the ruler and drag up into the gray space above that location.

- For all types of tabs, Control-click on a Mac (right-click on a Windows PC) in the Ruler and select the tab type from the contextual menu that appears. The chosen tab appears in the gray space above the Ruler (on the Mac) or within the Ruler (in Windows).

To remove a tab stop, drag it up or down out of the Ruler until the icon disappears.

If you want to move an existing tab, drag and drop the icon to the desired location.

Indents

Three indent controls are available in Scrivener:

- **Left:** The left indent specifies how far away from the left margin text is offset. Generally, you want this indent to be at the left margin — that is, zero — but if you need to make a paragraph stand out from the rest of the text, such as for block quotes, you might want to indent its left margin.

- **Right:** The right indent specifies the offset from the right margin. You generally want this indent all the way to the right so that the text wraps automatically unless you're attempting to create a special format for a section of text.

- **First line:** The first line indent is where the first line of a paragraph starts. If you don't want the first line indented at all, place the first line indent marker at the left margin. (A ½-inch first line indent is the default in Scrivener. To change the default, refer to the section "Changing the default document format," earlier in this chapter.)

To create a *hanging indent* — where the first line is further left than the rest of the paragraph — simply move the first line indent marker to zero and the left indent marker to the desired location (by dragging and dropping the icon in the Ruler). You might use hanging indents for bibliographies and pages of definitions, which generally indent each entry line after the first line.

Seeing Double with Split Screen Mode

In addition to the basic Editor layout (discussed in the preceding sections), Scrivener offers an *über*-fabulous option called a split screen. Just like it sounds, Split Screen mode lets you divide the Editor screen into two separate panes. After you divide the screen, each Editor pane works just like a full-size Editor, with all the same features and functions, including Header and Footer bars.

The two Editors function independently, so if you change settings in one pane, they aren't reflected in the other. For example, if you change the text scale or container view mode in the top pane, that setting doesn't change in the bottom pane.

In addition, Scrivener remembers your preferences for each pane and uses them next time you split the screen, regardless of the contents. However, if you have the same file open in both panes, changes to the text *are* applied in both panes because you're simply viewing the same file from two places at the same time.

Why on Earth might you want to split screens? I'm glad you asked. Here's a short list of possible reasons:

- ✔ To refer to another section, piece of research, or image in one Editor pane while working in the other. Also, you can copy and paste from one to the other.

- ✔ To view another part of the same document you're working on (viewing the same document in both panes). You can refer to something you wrote earlier in the document or copy part of the document without losing your current place.

   When the same document is open in both split panes, changes made to the text in one are immediately reflected in the other.

- ✔ To compare snapshot versions (see Chapter 19 for more on snapshots).

- ✔ To view the ending of the previous scene or chapter while writing the opening of the next one. Using the split screen in this way helps you maintain the tone of the piece and ensure that your transition makes sense.

- ✔ To view the Corkboard or Outliner while working on a document.

Which of the two split screens is active determines which file's attributes appear in the Inspector and which text is affected if you invoke any menu commands.

You can tell which pane is active by its underlined title, and by the color of its Header bar:

- ✔ **Gray:** The pane is inactive.
- ✔ **Blue:** The pane is active.
- ✔ **Red:** If the Header bar is light red, almost pink, it indicates that the Editor is locked (see the section "Locking the Editor," later in this chapter).

Drag the sizing handle between the two panes to adjust the amount of real estate allocated to each one.

Figure 6-10 shows an example of a split screen. The Header bars have different colors — the top pane is inactive (gray), and the bottom pane is active (blue). Because the preferences can be different between panes, the Ruler is visible in the lower pane but not the upper one.

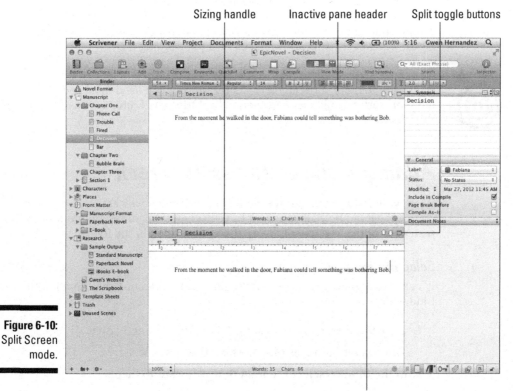

Figure 6-10: Split Screen mode.

Sizing handle   Inactive pane header   Split toggle buttons

Active pane header

Splitting the screen

Ready to split? You can cleave your Editor in two by following these steps (no axe required):

1. **(Optional) In the Binder, select one of the files that you want to work with.**

   The file appears in the Editor.

   Although you don't have to start with either file selected, it's helpful to have one already open in the Editor before you split the screen so that you don't have to add both of them to the Editor.

2. **On a Mac, click the Split toggle button in the Editor's Header bar (refer to Figure 6-10).**

   Windows users, choose either the vertical or horizontal split button to split the Editor.

   The screen splits into two Editor panes, both containing the document that had the focus in the Editor before the split. The following section explains how to open a different file in the second Editor.

To return to Single Screen view, click the Split toggle button in the Header bar of whichever pane you want to continue working with.

By default Scrivener (for Mac) splits the Editor horizontally (from left to right), but it splits vertically if that's the setting you used most recently. For more on vertical split, see the section "Splitting the Editor vertically," later in this chapter.

Adding a file to the split screen

When you first split the Editor, whatever document was active in the single pane appears in both. If you want to view something different in either of the panes (or both), use one of the methods described in the following sections.

Selecting an item

It's easy to add an item to one of the Editors by selecting that item in the Binder. Just follow these steps:

1. **Click anywhere in the desired Editor pane to activate it.**

   The Header bar turns blue to show that it's now active.

2. **In the Binder, select the item that you want to display.**

   The active pane now displays the selected file.

If you selected a container, the pane displays the last mode you used for a container. To change the view mode, choose View, and then select the desired view from the submenu that appears.

Dragging and dropping an item

Probably the quickest way to add an item to a split pane is to drag it from the Binder and drop it on the desired Header bar.

Be sure you drop the item on the Header bar of the pane — otherwise, Scrivener inserts the contents of the file into whatever you were viewing in the Editor pane. If you do insert the contents of the file by mistake, click in the affected Editor pane, and then choose Edit⟹Undo.

Locking the Editor

The ability to change the focus of a split pane by selecting an item in the Binder is great until you accidentally click something else and switch files. Locking the Editor pane — which you can do in Single Pane view, as well — prevents Binder selections from affecting the locked pane.

Locking the Editor doesn't affect the Inspector. The Inspector continues to display the information for whichever pane is active.

Follow these steps to lock down an Editor pane:

1. **Click the Item icon in the Header bar of the pane that you want to lock.**

   A menu appears.

2. **Choose Lock in Place.**

   The Header bar turns dusty red (think 1980s wedding-napkin pink) to indicate that it's locked.

Unlocking the Editor is as simple as following the preceding steps, choosing Lock in Place again to deselect it.

If you lock both panes, the Header bars don't change color to indicate which one is active. However, you can still tell the active pane by the underlined title in the Header bar.

As an alternative to locking the Editor, you can choose which Editor pane is affected by Binder selections. Just choose View⟹Binder Affects, and then select one of the following from the submenu that appears:

- ✔ **Current Editor:** The default. Selecting this option means that any item selected in the Binder appears in the active Editor pane.

- ✔ **Other Editor:** Choose this option to have Binder selections appear in the inactive Editor pane.

- ✔ **Top Editor:** Available in horizontal split only, selecting this option forces the item selected in the Binder to appear in the upper Editor pane.

- ✔ **Bottom Editor:** Available in horizontal split only, selecting this option forces the item selected in the Binder to appear in the lower Editor pane.

- ✔ **Left Editor:** Available in vertical split only, choosing this option forces the item selected in the Binder to appear in the left Editor pane.

- ✔ **Right Editor:** Available in vertical split only, choosing this option forces the item selected in the Binder to appear in the right Editor pane.

To cycle between the Editor panes and the Binder without using the mouse, press Control+Tab (Ctrl+Tab in Windows).

Selecting the active document in the Binder

If you lock one or both of the Editor panes and then start selecting items in the Binder, the Binder selection no longer matches the active pane. It might not match either one of the panes.

To match the Binder selection to the active document, click the Item icon button in the Header bar of the active Editor pane and choose Reveal in Binder from the menu that appears.

Locking the Inspector pane

In addition to locking the Editor, you can lock the Inspector, which forces the Inspector to continue displaying the data for the Editor pane that's selected at the time you lock the Inspector, even if you move the focus to the other pane. Think of it like handcuffing the Inspector to one Editor pane so that it can't run off with the other pane.

Locking the Inspector doesn't tie it to a specific file; rather, it's tied to the specific pane (upper or lower, left or right).

Lock the Inspector by following these steps:

1. **Activate the desired Editor pane by clicking in it.**

   The Inspector reflects the data for the active file.

2. **Click the Lock Inspector button at the bottom-right of the Inspector (see Figure 6-11).**

   Before you click the Lock Inspector button, it displays an image of an open padlock. After you click it, it displays a closed padlock.

To unlock the Inspector, click the Lock Inspector button again so that it appears unlocked.

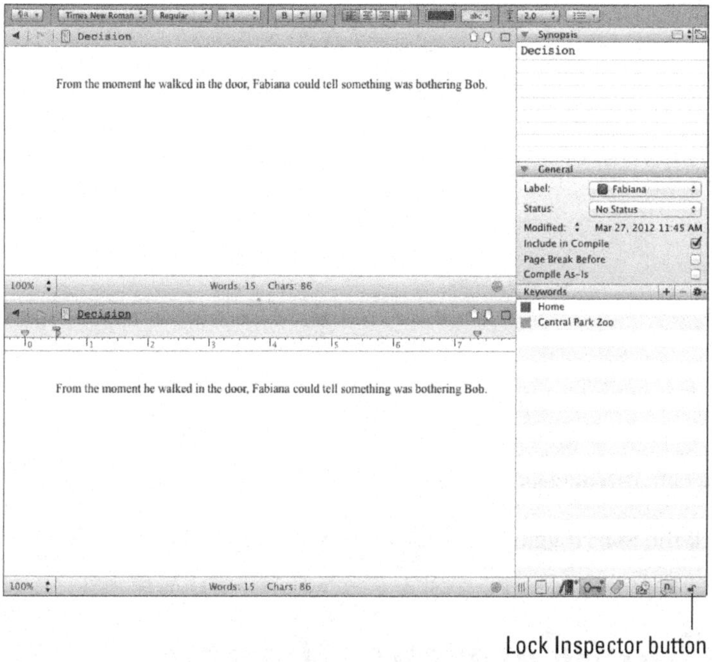

Figure 6-11:
The Lock
Inspector
button.

Lock Inspector button

Splitting the Editor vertically

You're not just stuck with a horizontal split option: You can also split the Editor vertically into left and right panes (see Figure 6-12).

To activate a vertical split on a Mac, press and hold the Option key while clicking the Split toggle button in the Header bar. If you're in Split Screen view already, it doesn't matter which Header bar's button you click. (Windows users have a separate Vertical Split button that appears just to the left of the Horizontal Split button in the Header bar.)

Use the same method to switch back to a horizontal split when in a vertical split or to choose a split type other than what's displayed on the button when in single pane view.

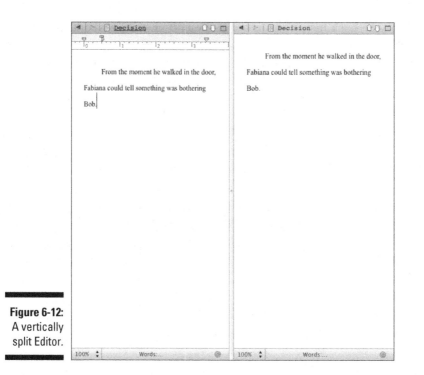

Figure 6-12:
A vertically
split Editor.

You can also access the split options by choosing View➪Layout.

Click the Split toggle button again to return to single pane view.

Using QuickReference Panels

Want to refer to something, but don't want to split the Editor to do it (or can't because you're in Composition mode)? Or maybe you need to work with more than two documents at the same time.

In either situation, try a QuickReference panel. Just like in split screen, you can edit the content, but the QuickReference panel has some advantages over the split Editor: You can move the QuickReference panel around and resize it, and you can have more than one open at a time.

Here are some easy ways to open a QuickReference panel:

✔ Select one or more documents in the Binder, and then press the space-bar. A QuickReference panel opens for each file selected.

✔ Select the desired document(s) in the Binder, Corkboard, or Outliner, and then click the QuickReference button in the toolbar.

✔ Drag the desired document(s) from the Binder, Corkboard, or Outliner, and then drop it onto the QuickReference button in the toolbar.

This method allows you to open a QuickReference panel without changing the Binder selection because you don't need to select the file before dragging it onto the toolbar button. Also, you can still use this option with a multiple selection, if desired.

✔ Choose View➪QuickReference and navigate to the desired document in the submenu that appears.

You can access QuickReference panels via this method in Composition (Full Screen) mode, but you must open each QuickReference panel one at a time if you want to use more than one.

If you already have QuickReference panels open, they stay open and are accessible when you enter Composition (Full Screen) mode.

When you open a QuickReference panel, it stays visible only as long as it's the active window. After you click in the Editor — or somewhere else within the Scrivener interface — the QuickReference panel hides behind the active window.

To view a QuickReference panel again, choose Window➪QuickReference Panels, and then choose the desired panel to view from the submenu that appears. Choose Window➪Float QuickReference Panels to allow the windows to remain visible while you work in the Editor or when you enter Composition (Full Screen) mode.

Within the QuickReference panel, you have access to the Label and Status metadata fields. You also can access other Inspector metadata by using the Display drop-down list at the bottom of the panel. Figure 6-13 shows you the QuickReference panel.

Label drop-down list   Status drop-down list

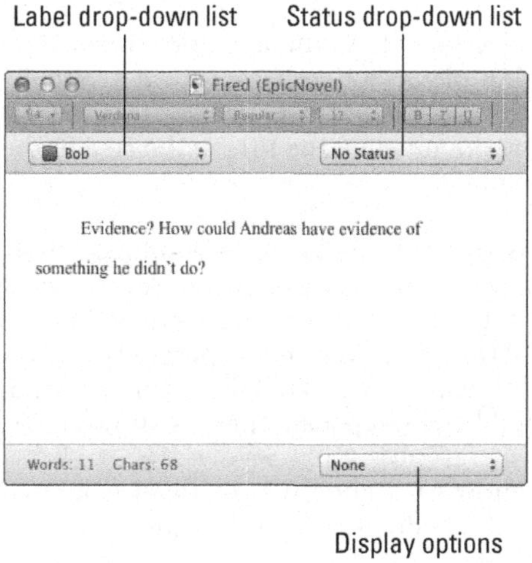

Figure 6-13:
A Quick-
Reference
panel.

Display options

If you close a QuickReference panel during the current session, you can quickly access it again by choosing Window⇨Closed QuickReference Panels and choosing the document from the submenu that appears. After you close the Scrivener project, however, the Closed Panels submenu is cleared.

Using Scrivenings Mode to View Documents Together

Scrivenings mode just sounds fun, doesn't it? But it's not a fancy phrase for sitting down to write. *Scrivenings mode* means viewing multiple documents in the Editor.

When you select a container (a folder or file group) in the Binder, Scrivener displays the files within that container in whatever view you used last (Corkboard by default when you first use Scrivener).

To view the text of files together in one long document, follow these steps:

1. **Select a container in the Binder.**

   Alternatively, you can select multiple items in the Binder.

   Scrivener can't display non-text files in Scrivenings mode.

2. **Choose View⇨Scrivenings.**

   The files appear in one continuous document in the Editor, as demonstrated in Figure 6-14. Note how the Header bar displays the container name followed by (Composite) in front of the title of the active document to indicate Scrivenings mode.

   If multiple items are selected in the Binder, rather than a container, the Header bar displays Multiple Selection before the active file's name.

While you move through the documents, the title in the Header bar changes to display the active file's name.

Did you notice the divider bars (or dashed lines in Windows) shown in Figure 6-14? If you don't like them, turn them off by choosing Scrivener⇨Preferences and clicking the Formatting button at the top of the window that appears. Below Scrivenings at the bottom of the window, select Separate Scrivenings with Single Line Breaks. The Editor displays small brackets rather than bars to mark the end of one document and beginning of another, as shown in Figure 6-15.

To exit Scrivenings mode, choose Corkboard or Outliner from the View menu (or the toolbar), or select a single document in the Binder.

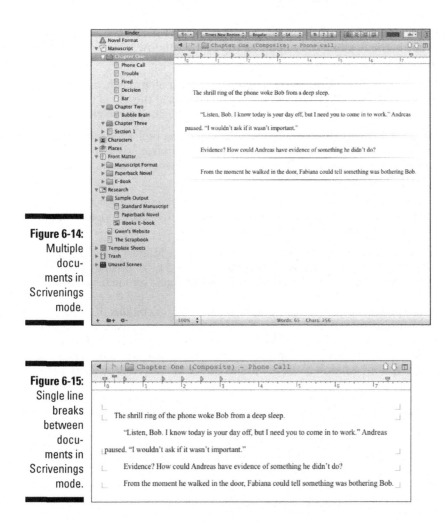

Figure 6-14:
Multiple docu-ments in Scrivenings mode.

Figure 6-15:
Single line breaks between docu-ments in Scrivenings mode.

Checking Your Spelling and Grammar

I know you're a word whiz and probably aced all your spelling exams in sev-enth grade, but just in case you can't remember whether accommodation has two M's or two C's (yes to both), your favorite teacher will never know because Scrivener has a built-in spelling guru.

You can either have Scrivener check your spelling and grammar while you type or only when you ask it to:

✔ **Automatic:** To turn instant spell checking on or off for the current proj-ect, choose Edit➪Spelling and Grammar➪Check Spelling While Typing. (Windows users, choose Tools➪Options to open the Options window.

Select the Auto-Correction tab, and then select Check Spelling as You Type in the Spelling section at the top of the window. This setting affects all projects.)

To change the spelling and grammar settings for all projects on the Mac, go to Scrivener⇨Preferences, select Corrections at the top of the window that opens, and select the desired options in the Spelling section.

✔ **Manual:** If you have instant spell checking turned off, then when you're ready to have Scrivener check your spelling, choose Edit⇨Spelling and Grammar⇨Show Spelling and Grammar (Windows users go to Tools⇨Spelling).

A window pops up — similar to the one in most word processors — that lets you step through the document error by error and add unique words to the personal dictionary.

To spell check the entire manuscript, select the Manuscript (Draft) folder in the Binder and go to Scrivenings mode by choosing View⇨Scrivenings. Then activate the Spelling and Grammar window.

For more Spelling and Grammar options, such as auto-capitalization, auto-completion, and substitutions, choose Scrivener⇨Preferences, and then select Corrections at the top of the Preferences window that appears. (Windows users, choose Tools⇨Options, and then select the Auto-Correction tab at the top of the Options window.) These options affect all Scrivener projects.

Chapter 7

Getting Rid of Distractions with Composition Mode

. . . .

. . . .

Composition mode (called Full Screen mode in Windows) can't take away the kids, the neighbor's boring dog, or the guy mowing his lawn. It also can't force you to turn off your e-mail, Twitter, or Facebook.

What Composition mode *can* provide is a distraction-free virtual workspace. (You're on the hook for the babysitter and the noise-canceling headphones.)

This chapter shows you how to create a little spot of visual serenity in your hectic writing world — kind of like your own personal rock garden.

Comparing Composition Mode to the Full Screen Function

In Mac OS X Lion, Apple introduced a full screen function that not only maximizes the window, but hides the menu bar and dock (similar to what happens when you press F11 in Windows). To avoid confusion, the good people at Scrivener renamed the former Full Screen mode to Composition mode in the Mac version. On Windows, it's still known as Full Screen mode, so when you see Composition mode in this chapter, I'm also referring to Scrivener for Windows Full Screen mode.

Whichever operating system you're using may have its own version of full screen, but Composition mode is more than merely an expanded window. Here's what you get from Composition mode:

- ✔ A simple view of the Editor with no visible menus, status bars, Binder, Inspector, docks, or taskbars (except when you want them).
- ✔ A customizable background that can be transparent or solid (solid black, by default) to block out the windows behind the screen.
- ✔ *Typewriter scrolling* (whatever line you're editing is always at the center of the screen).
- ✔ Quick access to Composition mode settings, Inspector metadata, and keywords.

Entering Composition Mode

Follow these steps to turn on Composition mode:

1. Select the item(s) in the Binder that you want to work with.

If you choose a container item, ensure that you're in Scrivenings mode (choose View⇨Scrivenings) before entering Composition mode. Otherwise, you see only any text in the container item, not the text from all its subdocuments.

2. Choose View⇨Enter Composition Mode.

Windows users, choose View⇨Enter Full Screen.

Alternatively, you can click the Composition Mode button on the toolbar.

As shown in Figure 7-1, the screen opens to a plain Editor that has a black background (unless you've changed it at some point). Don't you feel calmer already?

The control strip pops up at the bottom for a second before disappearing, just to remind you that it's there. The following section discusses the control strip in more detail.

To exit Composition mode, click the Exit Full Screen Mode button in the control strip or press the Esc key on your keyboard.

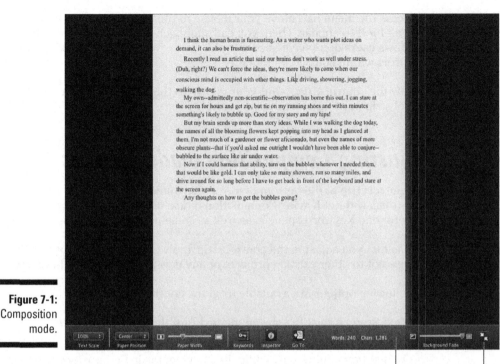

Figure 7-1:
Composition
mode.

The control strip

Exit Composition mode

Personalizing the Composition Mode Experience

Black not your color? Maybe you read about how a blue background is best for creativity and red is best for tasks such as editing. Or maybe you want a tranquil mountain scene to set the mood.

In Composition mode, you can change more than the background color; you can modify the paper color, paper width, and more. The following sections lay it all out for you.

Using the menu bar and control strip

While in Composition mode, you still have access to the menu bar (in the Mac version only), as well as another menu called the control strip, which provides options to adjust the view.

To access the menu bar, move your mouse to the top edge of the screen and wait for it to appear. Then, you can simply click the desired menu item. (Windows users don't have access to the menu, but keyboard shortcuts still work from within Full Screen mode.)

To view the control strip, point your mouse to the bottom of the screen. The control strip pops up, as shown in Figure 7-1.

Adjusting Composition mode settings

The control strip at the bottom of the screen allows you to modify some of the settings without leaving Composition mode. It also provides access to the Inspector and Keywords panels, as well as some navigation options.

Options that you adjust in the control strip apply only to the current project settings, not to other existing projects or any new projects you might create.

The following options are available from the control strip:

- ✔ **Text Scale:** Adjust the size of the text (not the font size, just its appearance).

    This option applies only while the document is in Composition mode; it doesn't change your settings in the standard Editor.
- ✔ **Paper Position:** Place the paper on the left, center, or right side of the screen.

- ✔ **Paper Width:** Use the slider to make the paper wider or narrower.

    To adjust the paper height, hold the Option key (the Alt key in Windows) to change the Paper Width slider to a Paper Height slider.
- ✔ **Keywords:** Displays the Keywords panel (I cover keywords in detail in Chapter 5).
- ✔ **Inspector:** Displays the Inspector panel, which I talk about in the "Viewing the Inspector Panel" section, later in this chapter.
- ✔ **Go To:** From this menu, you can choose a different item to view without leaving Composition mode.
- ✔ **Words/Chars:** Displays the word and character count for the document or for a selection of text.
- ✔ **Background Fade:** Use the slider to adjust the level of background color transparency.
- ✔ **Exit Full Screen Mode:** This button exits Composition mode and returns to the standard Scrivener interface.

Changing Composition mode settings for all projects

In addition to project-specific changes (which I discuss in the preceding section), you can modify the Composition mode settings for all projects from within the Preferences window's Compose tab (or the Options window's Appearance tab in Windows).

Below are some of the key Composition mode settings that you can modify:

- ✔ **Hide Main Window in Composition Mode:** The Scrivener program window doesn't show through the background when your background is translucent. Instead, you see the other open windows on your desktop.

- ✔ **Highlight Current Line:** Highlights the line where your cursor is. This setting can be especially handy when you're editing because the typewriter-scrolling default always moves the line you're editing to the center of the window. The highlighting helps your eye follow the cursor's jump from wherever you started typing back to the center of the screen.

- ✔ **Scroller Type:** Adjust the characteristics of the scroll bar on the right side of the Composition mode Editor so that it's either visible, auto-hidden unless pointed to, or never shown.

- ✔ **Customizable Colors:** Wanna recreate the old DOS terminal look with black screen and green text? Hey, it's your computer. Here's where you can change the colors of every element in Composition mode. You can find out more about customizing colors in the following sections. (This option appears as Colors in Windows.)

    Changing colors in the Compose tab (or the Appearance tab, Full Screen section in Windows) applies only to Composition mode.

- ✔ **Default Settings for New Projects:** Choose to use current Composition mode settings (those that can be adjusted via the control strip) for all projects that you create in the future.

Changing the background color

The background color can be anything you choose. Got a thing for orange? Go for it. Just follow these steps:

1. **Choose Scrivener⇨Preferences to open the Preferences window.**

   Windows users, choose Tools⇨Options to open the Options window.

2. **Choose Compose at the top of the window to view the Composition Mode options.**

   Windows users, click the Appearance tab to view the Appearance options.

3. **In the Customizable Colors section of the window, select Background, as shown in Figure 7-2.**

    In Windows, click Full Screen in the Colors section, as shown in Figure 7-2, and then select Background from the list.

4. **Click the Background color box and select your desired color from the Colors window that opens.**

5. **Click the red X to close the Colors window.**

    Windows users, click OK to close the window and apply the selected color.

6. **Close the Preferences window by clicking the red X.**

    Windows users, click OK to close the Options window.

    When you enter Composition mode, the background color reflects your choice.

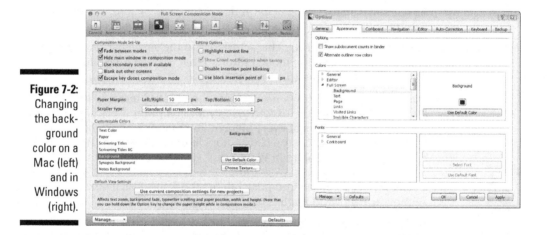

Figure 7-2: Changing the background color on a Mac (left) and in Windows (right).

Changing the paper color

In addition to the background color, which I talk about in the preceding section, you can also change the color of the paper in Composition mode. If bright white isn't to your liking, try a hint of gray, blue, yellow, or pink for a more soothing writing experience.

Get your paper color on by following these steps:

1. **Choose Scrivener⇨Preferences to open the Preferences window.**

    Windows users, choose Tools⇨Options to open the Options window.

2. **Choose Compose at the top of the window to view the Composition Mode options.**

   Windows users, click the Appearance tab to view the Appearance options.

3. **In the Customizable Colors section, select Paper.**

   Windows users, click Full Screen in the Colors section, and then select Page.

4. **Click the Paper color box, and then choose your desired color from the Colors window that appears.**

   Ever wish you could return to the glory days of green text on a black screen or some other color combination? You can change the text color in Composition mode by choosing Text, rather than Paper, and selecting Override Text Color With Color. The text color is changed only for Composition mode. The color appears normal when you return to the standard Editor.

5. **Close the Colors window by clicking the red X.**

   Windows users, click OK.

6. **Close the Preferences window by clicking the red X.**

   Windows users, click OK to close the Options window.

   Now, when you enter Composition mode, the paper matches your chosen color.

Adding a background image

In addition to colors, you can now add a background image to Composition mode. From an energizing display of colorful hot air balloons to a restful beach scene, as long as the picture is accessible within your project or on one of your computer's drives, you can use it for your Composition mode background.

The following steps change only the background image for the current project, so you can use a different image for each project you're working on.

Follow these steps to add or change the background image:

1. **Choose View⇨Composition Backdrop⇨Choose.**

2. **In the window that opens, navigate to and select an image from your files, and then click Open.**

   The File Selection window closes.

   Alternatively, you can choose from the list of images already in your project that appears in the Choose submenu.

When you enter Composition mode after making the changes in the preceding step list, the background displays your selected photo, as shown in Figure 7-3. The image is stretched to fill the screen either vertically or horizontally.

When you use a background image, the Background Fade option in the control strip changes to Paper Fade, allowing you to adjust the transparency of the paper.

Working in Composition Mode

Writing in Composition mode works just like in Editor mode, except that wherever you're typing is always at or above the center of the page by default. Called *typewriter scrolling,* this feature keeps you from always having to work at the bottom of the screen when typing.

When you're editing, typewriter scrolling can be disorienting because you can click a spot at the bottom of the screen to insert or edit text, and suddenly you're working in the middle of the screen.

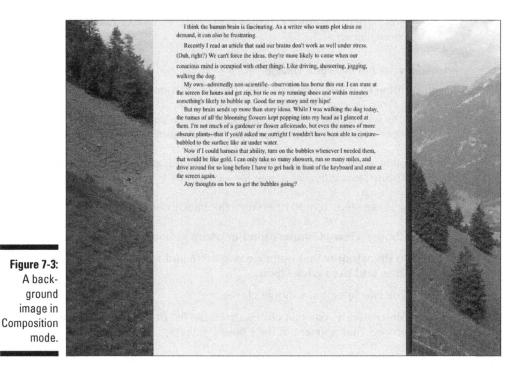

Figure 7-3:
A back-
ground
image in
Composition
mode.

Personally, I think after you get used to it, you'll wish your word processor had typewriter scrolling.

However, if you don't like it, here are two options for turning it off (or back on) that you can use while in Composition mode:

 ✔ Choose Format➪Options➪Typewriter Scrolling.

 ✔ Use the shortcut Ctrl+⌘+T (Windows+Ctrl+T for Windows).

Typewriter scrolling is on by default in Composition mode and off by default in the regular Editor. You can turn typewriter scrolling on or off while in the regular Editor, as well.

What if you're typing along in Composition mode, but you need to access another program? No need to exit Composition mode, you can view a menu of all open programs on your computer by pressing ⌘+Tab (Alt+Tab in Windows). Hold down the ⌘ (or Alt) key and advance through the menu by one program every time you press Tab.

Viewing the Inspector Panel

Do you love working in Composition mode, but want access to the Inspector's metadata without leaving your virtual den of Zen? No worries. The control strip has Inspector access built right in, allowing you to view the Synopsis; change Label and Status values; and work with the project and document notes, references, keywords, custom metadata, snapshots, and comments and footnotes.

To view the Inspector panel, follow these steps:

1. **If you're not already in Composition mode, choose View➪Enter Composition Mode.**

   Windows users, choose View➪Enter Full Screen.

2. **Point to the bottom of the screen until the control strip appears.**

3. **Click the Inspector button.**

   The Inspector panel appears, as shown in Figure 7-4. The drop-down list at the top of the panel provides access to the various elements of the Inspector. At the bottom of the panel, the Label and Status fields are available, as well. (In Windows, the Inspector panel displays a floating version of the Inspector pane instead, much like the one in the standard Scrivener interface.)

4. **View and modify any of the document's metadata from the Inspector panel, just like you can from the normal Editor view.**

   See Part II to read all about the Inspector.

5. **(Optional) Adjust the Inspector panel, as necessary.**

   You have a couple of options for modifying your Inspector panel experience while in Composition mode:

   - *Move it.* Drag the title bar of the panel to change its location.

   - *Resize it.* Drag the edge or corner of the panel window to change its size.

6. **Close the panel by clicking the X in the upper-left corner.**

Chapter 8

Planning Your Project with the Corkboard

. . . .

In This Chapter

▶ Accessing the Corkboard

▶ Setting up your index cards

▶ Using the Corkboard

▶ Tailoring the Corkboard to your tastes

▶ Getting your virtual index cards onto paper

. . . .

Do you like to storyboard? Need to follow a subplot or character from start to finish? Want to get a high-level view of your latest chapter? Then the Corkboard is for you.

The basis of the Corkboard is the index card. Each index card represents an item in the Binder and displays the Synopsis, if one exists (see Chapter 3 for more on the Synopsis). Index cards can also display Label and keyword colors, as well as Status values.

Even if you prefer to play with your story on paper index cards first, you can transfer your scenes to the Scrivener Corkboard when you're ready to start writing. After you enter them, you always have them with you when working on your story, you can quickly edit them, and you don't have to worry about the cards getting out of order.

With virtual index cards, you can easily erase, edit, and modify the Synopsis, as well as move the index cards to try new story flows — no sharp pins or wall space required.

This chapter will have you storyboarding like a pro in no time.

Viewing the Corkboard

The Corkboard isn't very interesting unless you have something to look at. You must choose a container or selection of files if you want to see anything but cork. Follow these steps:

1. **Select the desired container or files in the Binder.**

   Selecting a single file doesn't show anything in the Corkboard.

   Depending on the last multiple-selection view you used, Scrivener may or may not display the Corkboard.

2. **If the Corkboard isn't visible, choose View⇨Corkboard.**

   The center pane displays the Corkboard, with index cards representing each file at the top level of the container (or all files within the multiple selection) you chose in Step 1.

3. **To select an item in the Corkboard, click it.**

   A blue border appears to designate that card as the one with the focus.

   As shown in Figure 8-1, the Synopsis for each file appears on an index card. Depending on your settings, and whether you've added metadata values (see Chapters 4 and 5), your index cards might also have colored tabs, a colored background, an image, pushpins, or a watermark.

Selected container

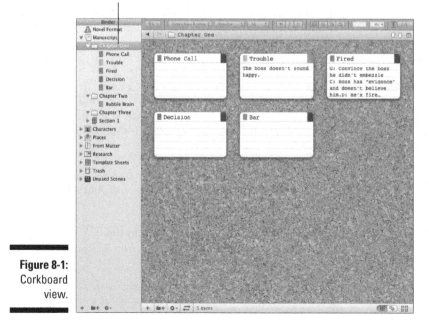

Figure 8-1:
Corkboard
view.

Understanding Index Card Elements

By default, index cards display the item icon, title, Synopsis, and color label or pushpin. In addition to these standard elements, you can choose to view card numbers, the Status stamp, and keyword indicators.

The following sections take you through the default and optional elements of the index card.

Default elements

The following items are displayed on index cards (as shown in Figure 8-2) unless you make changes to your settings:

- ✔ **Icon:** The icon matches the item's Binder icon. If you chose to use the Label color in the icon (see Chapter 4), the icon is tinted.

- ✔ **Title:** The title in the Synopsis is the document title seen in the Binder. Change the item title in the index card by double-clicking to select the title text.

- ✔ **Synopsis:** The index card Synopsis is the same as the Synopsis in the Inspector panel. You can edit it in either place.

- ✔ **Color Label/Pushpin:** If a Label value is applied to the document, the color shows in the upper-right corner as a corner swatch or in the center as a pushpin (see the section "Modifying the Corkboard Preferences," later in this chapter, for more on pushpins).

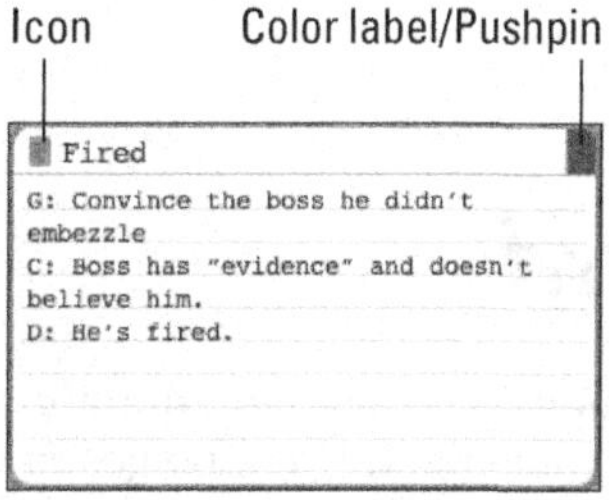

Icon   Color label/Pushpin

Figure 8-2:
The default index card elements.

Fired

G: Convince the boss he didn't
embezzle
C: Boss has "evidence" and doesn't
believe him.
D: He's fired.

Optional elements

You can turn on the following elements, if desired. A check mark next to an option in the menu indicates that it's already on. Here are the optional elements you can add (see Figure 8-3):

- ✔ **Card numbers:** This option numbers the cards by their place in the container. If you move the cards, the number changes to reflect the new order.

    To turn on card numbers, choose View➪Corkboard Options➪Show Card Numbers.

- ✔ **Status stamp:** To display a watermark-like stamp of the Status value across your index cards, choose View➪Corkboard Options➪Show Stamps.

- ✔ **Keyword indicators:** If you have keywords applied to a document (you can read about keywords in Chapter 5), they appear as color bars down the right side of the index card when you turn on this option.

    To view keyword colors, go to View➪Corkboard Options➪Show Keyword Colors.

Status stamp

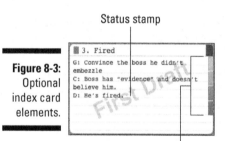

Figure 8-3:
Optional
index card
elements.

Keyword indicators

Working in the Corkboard

From within the Corkboard, you can rename a document, modify or add Synopsis text, and add keywords. You can make these changes in the Corkboard:

- ✔ **Renaming a document:** To rename a document in Corkboard view, simply double-click the title and type the new name.

- ✔ **Modifying the Synopsis text:** To add, edit, or delete the Synopsis text, double-click in the Synopsis area of the card to activate it. ***Note:*** Formatting options (such as font style and size) aren't available in the Synopsis section.

After you're in Title or Text Edit mode (by double-clicking in the title or text area, respectively), you can move through the index cards — alternating between the title and text portion of each card, in turn — by pressing the Tab key to move forward, or Shift+Tab to move backwards.

✔ **Adding keywords to a card:** You can add keywords to documents while in Corkboard view (for more on keywords and how to use them in your project, visit Chapter 5). Follow these steps:

1. *Click the Keywords Panel button in the toolbar.*

   The Keywords panel appears.

2. *Drag the desired keyword from the panel and drop it onto the desired card.*

   If keyword colors are turned on, the new color chip appears along the right side of the index card. (The "Understanding Index Card Elements" section, earlier in this chapter, discusses how to make keywords visible.)

   If you select multiple cards before you drag the keyword onto one of the selected cards, the keyword is added to all selected cards.

✔ **Opening an item from the Corkboard:** Struck with inspiration for one of your documents while looking at the big picture in Corkboard view? No need to hunt down the desired document in the Binder. When you're ready to add text to a document, simply double-click the index card's item icon to open the item in Document view (the Editor).

   If the item is a container, the container opens in the Corkboard, instead.

Modifying the Corkboard Layout

When you first open the Corkboard, it displays three columns of cards, ordered from left to right. Depending on your screen size and resolution, the cards might by tiny or huge. No worries. You can adjust the size and spacing of the cards in the Corkboard by clicking the Corkboard Options button. A small menu pops up, shown in Figure 8-4.

Changes made with the Corkboard Options menu apply only to the current project.

Here's a description of each option:

✔ **Card Size:** This slider resizes the index cards, but it works only if the Size to Fit Editor check box is deselected.

   If you make the cards large, some of them may "disappear" off the edge of the screen. You can fix this problem by adjusting the Cards Across setting.

➤ **Ratio:** The Ratio slider changes the shape of the cards (not the size). The 3x5 setting provides the standard index-card look, but if you prefer another rectangular shape, this setting is for you.

➤ **Spacing:** The Spacing slider adjusts the amount of space around each card.

➤ **Cards Across:** This option determines how many cards appear in each row.

If you choose Auto, Scrivener selects the number needed to display all cards in the Corkboard at their current size.

➤ **Keyword Chips:** Choose how many keyword colors to display on each card. If you set it to three but a document has five keywords attached, only the first three keyword colors appear.

Show Keyword Colors must be turned on, as outlined in the "Understanding Index Card Elements" section, earlier in this chapter.

➤ **Size to Fit:** Selecting this check box overrides the Card Size setting to ensure that all cards appear on the Corkboard. This option isn't available if the Cards Across option is set to Auto.

➤ **Use Small Font:** Applies the small font designated in the Corkboard Preferences (which are covered in the "Modifying the Corkboard Preferences" section, later in this chapter).

To close the Corkboard Options menu, click anywhere outside of it. (Windows users, click the X button at the top-right of the menu.)

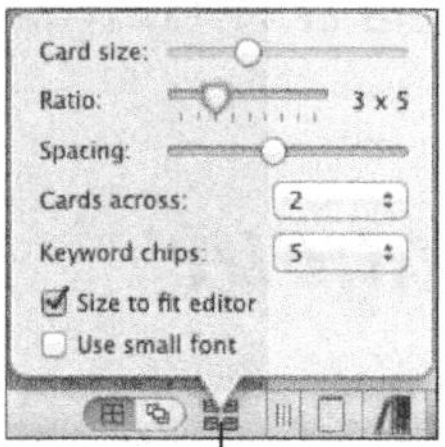

Figure 8-4:
The
Corkboard
Options
menu.

Card size:
Ratio: 3 x 5
Spacing:
Cards across: 2
Keyword chips: 5
☑ Size to fit editor
☐ Use small font

Corkboard Options
button

Understanding the Types of Corkboards

Scrivener has three types of Corkboards: linear, freeform, and stacked. The Linear Corkboard is the standard one that appears when you choose Corkboard view. The Freeform Corkboard lets you play with the order of your cards without affecting their order in the Binder until you're ready. Stacked Corkboards allow you to view multiple containers in Corkboard view side by side.

Linear Corkboard

The Linear Corkboard is aptly named because it allows you to display cards only in neat rows or lines. Index cards appear in hierarchical order in the way they appear in the Binder. If you move cards around in this mode, you affect their order in the Binder hierarchy.

If you select a group of items individually (for example, through contiguous or noncontiguous selection, which I discuss in Chapter 2), instead of by choosing a container, Scrivener doesn't let you move them because it can't be certain of the hierarchy with respect to the rest of the Binder. You can't move a group of items in this way, even if you individually select all items within a single container.

The default background for the Linear Corkboard is the cork texture. Find out how to change the background in the "Modifying the Corkboard Preferences" section, later in this chapter.

Moving a card in the Linear Corkboard is as simple as dragging it from one location to another. The vertical blue bar designates where the index card will land. After you move an item, that item's new location is reflected in the Binder, as well.

To change the location, you can also drag and drop one or more cards from the Corkboard to the desired location in the Binder.

If you chose a multiple selection in the Binder, rather than a container, you can't move the cards.

Freeform Corkboard

The Freeform Corkboard is like the hippie cousin of the Linear Corkboard because it lets you rearrange index cards freely. Not only can you place cards anywhere that you want on the board — no more rigid rows and columns — but moves don't affect the Binder hierarchy unless you choose to apply the new card order.

To enter Freeform Corkboard mode, click the Freeform Corkboard button in the Corkboard footer, as shown in Figure 8-5. The background changes to a gray grid to indicate that you're in Freeform mode.

Moving cards

In Freeform mode, you can move the cards anywhere on the field you want. Like circles? Go for it. Just drag each card to the desired location.

Selected container

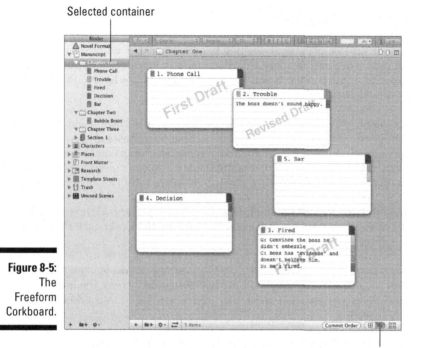

Figure 8-5:
The
Freeform
Corkboard.

Freeform Corkboard button

I find it helpful to turn on card numbers in the Freeform Corkboard so that I can quickly see the original order of the documents. (I demonstrate how to use card numbers in the "Understanding Index Card Elements" section, earlier in this chapter.) Card numbers are especially useful if you like to collapse or hide your Binder for a clutter-free workspace.

Committing the card order

After you have your index cards in an order you like, it's time to commit. Don't worry — you don't need an expensive ring, and you can always change your mind again later without hurting anyone's feelings.

To make the new arrangement permanent, follow these steps:

1. **Click the Commit Order button in the footer.**

   A window appears, providing options for how Scrivener should interpret your disordered mess, er, new story flow.

2. **In the Start At column, select where you want Scrivener to look for the first card.**

   You have the options of Top, Bottom, Left, or Right.

3. **In the Order From section, choose which direction Scrivener should read from your starting position to determine the card order.**

   Your options are Left to Right or Right to Left.

4. **Click OK.**

   Your items are reordered — and renumbered, if you were using card numbers — in the Binder.

You don't actually have to commit the order at all. If desired, you can leave your Freeform Corkboard uncommitted as an alternate way to view the cards in a container.

Stacked Corkboards

Stacked Corkboards are less of a type, and more of a way of viewing more than one Corkboard at a time. They're handy when you divide your manuscript into chapters or parts, but want to see the contents of more than one container at a time, while still retaining the ability to move cards.

In a Stacked Corkboard, you can even move index cards between containers. The only limitation is that Stacked Corkboards are available only in Linear mode. If you're in Freeform mode and you add an additional container to the selection, Scrivener switches to a Linear Corkboard.

To activate the Stacked Corkboard, select more than one container (for example, a folder or file group) by using noncontiguous selection in the Binder (using ⌘-click on the Mac or Ctrl-click in Windows, covered in Chapter 2). If you're already in Corkboard view, simply add additional containers to the current Binder selection.

The contents of the containers are displayed with a dividing line between them and shading differences, as shown in Figure 8-6. Notice the image card. Chapter 3 discusses how to display a pictorial Synopsis instead of a text Synopsis. Image files saved in your project also appear as image cards in the Corkboard, even if they don't have a pictorial Synopsis.

If you use contiguous selection to choose items in the Binder, you're selecting all the individual documents between the two containers, which triggers a Linear Corkboard based on multiple selection, not a stacked Corkboard.

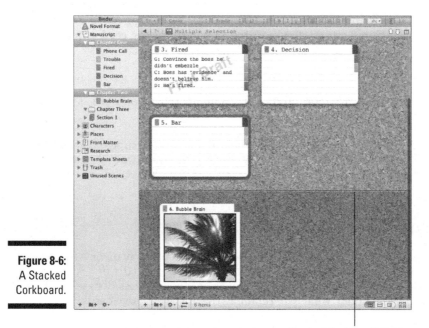

Figure 8-6:
A Stacked
Corkboard.

Stacked Corkboard divider

Modifying the card arrangement

By default, Stacked Corkboards wrap the cards for each container as designated in the Corkboard Options menu. However, you can also view them in rows or columns by clicking the Arrange Cards in Rows button or the Arrange Cards in Columns button in the footer.

Figure 8-7 shows you where the buttons are and how Stacked Corkboards appear when laid out in columns.

To return to the standard view, click the Wrap Cards button.

Numbering cards by section

To force the card numbers to start over with each container, choose View➪Corkboard Options➪Number Per Section. This option works only if Show Card Numbers is already turned on, as outlined in the "Understanding Index Card Elements" section, earlier in this chapter.

You can use the same procedure to change back to continuous numbering.

Stacked Corkboard divider

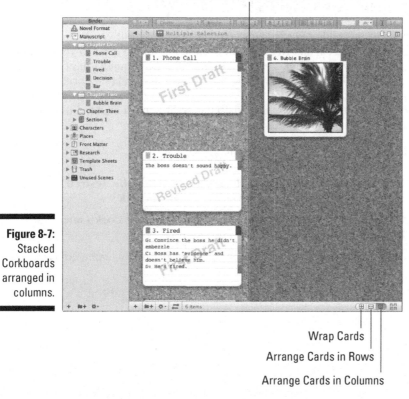

Figure 8-7:
Stacked
Corkboards
arranged in
columns.

Wrap Cards

Arrange Cards in Rows

Arrange Cards in Columns

Adding a New Document in the Corkboard

Want to start your story or article from scratch by creating a card and Synopsis for each scene before you write? You can add a new document to your project without leaving the Corkboard, whether you're in Linear, Freeform, or Stacked view. Just click the Add button in the toolbar. A new card appears, ready to be named.

To insert a card after an existing card, select the existing card before clicking Add in the toolbar.

That's it. Really. Now, go forth and multiply.

Viewing the Corkboard in Split Screen

Say you've created index cards for your next chapter, but you haven't actually written the scenes. While writing, you want to be able to refer to your index cards. The answer is Split Screen. It works just as I outline in Chapter 6, but rather than two Editor panes, you can view one Editor and one Corkboard pane.

Or you can have two Corkboards visible in Split Screen, instead of using a Stacked Corkboard.

You know you want to try it. Just follow these steps:

1. **If you're not already in Corkboard view, select the desired container in the Binder, and then choose View⊃Corkboard.**

2. **Click the Split toggle button in the header of the Corkboard (see Figure 8-8).**

   The Corkboard splits into two panes, displaying the same container in both.

3. **Click in the pane in which you want to view the Editor.**

Split toggle buttons

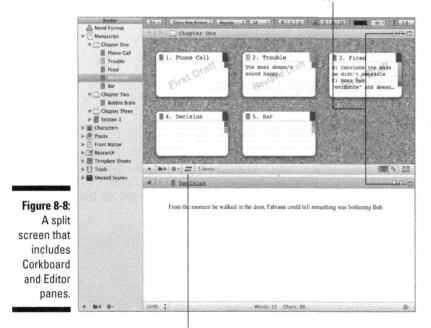

Figure 8-8:
A split screen that includes Corkboard and Editor panes.

Automatically Open Selection in Other Editor button

4. **Select the file that you want to edit in the Binder.**

   The file appears in the pane you activated in Step 3. Figure 8-8 shows an example of a split screen that has Corkboard and Editor panes.

5. **To exit Split Screen view, click the Split toggle button in whichever pane you want to continue working with.**

TIP

If you're working in Editor mode and want a split view with a Corkboard, split the panes, then add a container to the active pane and choose Corkboard view.

TIP

Want to use the Corkboard as a navigation tool while in Split Screen mode? Click the Automatically Open Selection in Other Editor button (see Figure 8-8). Every time you select an index card in the Corkboard, the document opens in Document view in the other pane. With this option, you can hide the Binder (by choosing View➪Layout➪Hide Binder) but still quickly open documents for editing.

Modifying the Corkboard Preferences

You can modify the Corkboard settings for all projects, including the look of the cards, whether images appear, the background, font, and so on. Follow these steps to modify the preferences to meet your needs:

1. **Choose Scrivener➪Preferences.**

   Windows users, choose Tools➪Options.

   The Preferences window appears.

2. **Choose Corkboard.**

   The Corkboard options appear in the window.

3. **Select the check boxes for items that you want to enable.**

   Alternatively, you can choose the desired setting from a drop-down list or slider bar.

   Most of the options are self-explanatory, but I'll highlight a few:

   - *Index Card Theme:* Called Corners in Windows. Change the shape and colors of the cards. The Rounded theme is the default, but the other two themes display the pin (Label) colors as pushpins, rather than squares.

   - *Allow Drop Ons:* In Windows, this option is Allow Dropping Dragged Items onto Cards. If this option is selected, you can drop one card onto another to create a file group. By keeping this option deselected, you prevent accidental drop ons.

- *Double-Clicking on Corkboard Background:* In Windows, this appears as the Empty Space Double Click Will option. You can designate the behavior triggered by double-clicking the Corkboard background.

  If you plan to add a lot of new index cards from the Corkboard view, consider selecting Creates a New Card from this drop-down list.

Printing Index Cards

Did you just get a little giddy when you saw that you could print your index cards? Yes, you can print index cards, and you can even do it without leaving the Corkboard. Index cards are set up to work with Avery Perforated Index Card stock, but you can print them on plain paper or card stock, and then cut them out, if desired.

Follow these steps to move your virtual index cards into the physical world:

1. **Go to File⇨Page Setup.**

   The Page Setup window appears.

2. **In the Settings drop-down list, select Scrivener.**

   The window changes to a list of margin settings.

3. **Click Options.**

   The Print Options window appears.

4. **Click Index Cards in the center row of buttons.**

   The window displays Index Card print options, as shown in Figure 8-9. The sample index card in the top half of the window reflects the options chosen in the bottom half. Here are the options:

   - *Include Titles:* Prints the document title at the top of each card.

   - *Include Card Numbers:* Numbers the cards by their order in the hierarchy.

   - *Ignore Cards with Titles Only:* If this option is selected, Scrivener prints only cards that contain Synopsis text.

   - *Highlight Titles with Label Color:* Adds the Label value color to the title of the card.

   - *Include Keywords:* Adds underlined keywords below the title.

   - *Print Cutting Guides:* Adds dotted lines and corner marks around each card for easier cutting.

   - *Force Landscape Orientation:* When this option is selected, the cards print on the paper in landscape — rather than portrait — orientation, which allows you to fit more cards per sheet.

Don't select this option if you're using Avery stock, which is always printed in portrait orientation.

- *Embolden Titles:* Makes the titles bold.

- *Print Using Font:* Lets you choose the desired font and font size.

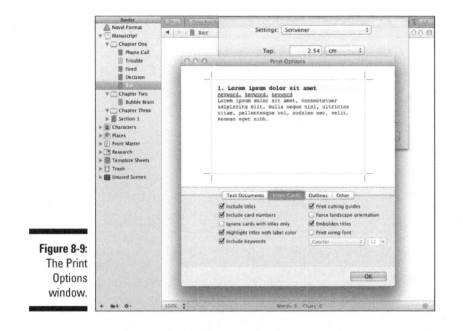

Figure 8-9:
The Print
Options
window.

5. **After making your option selections, click OK to close the Print Options window, and then click OK to close the Page Setup window.**

    Now you're ready to move on to the second part of the process: printing.

6. **Make sure the container (or files) for which you want to print index cards is selected in the Binder.**

7. **Choose File⇨Print Current Document.**

    The Print window appears.

8. **Make sure the settings are as desired (the appropriate printer and number of copies), and then click Print.**

    Image files and cards that are set up to display a pictorial Synopsis (such as the one shown in Figure 8-6) print as image cards.

If you want to preview the index cards before you commit to printing them, click the PDF button at the bottom-left of the Print window, and then choose Open PDF in Preview from the drop-down list that appears before you click Print. If you like what you see, print directly from Preview, or close the Preview window by clicking the red X button and then repeat Steps 7 and 8.

Chapter 9

Getting a High-Level View of Your Project with the Outliner

In This Chapter

▶ Viewing the Outliner

▶ Customizing how the Outliner appears

▶ Working in the Outliner

▶ Printing your outline

*I*f you're like me, an outline makes you think of boring book reports from grade school. But in Scrivener, outlining can be fun and helpful. Want to see a hierarchical representation of your manuscript that includes metadata? The Outliner is what you're looking for.

View your items and whatever combination of attributes (custom metadata, keywords, Label, Status) that you want. And unlike the Corkboard (covered in Chapter 8), you can easily view, edit, and move all levels of your documents in one screen.

This chapter outlines everything you need to know to get started with the Outliner.

Accessing the Outliner

You use the Outliner to view multiple selections of files, especially containers, so selecting a single document shows nothing in the Outliner. The beauty is that you can select a high-level container, such as your Manuscript folder, and still be able to view all the lower-level folder contents, too.

Follow these steps to get into the outlining groove:

1. Select a container in the Binder.

Alternatively, you can select a noncontiguous group of files, if you want.

Depending on the last view mode you used, Scrivener may or may not show the Outliner view. Most likely, you see the Corkboard.

2. If the Outliner isn't visible, choose View⇨Outline.

The Outliner appears, displaying the files as a list. Figure 9-1 shows an example of a lower-level container view. Yours might look slightly different, depending on the level of container you choose, additional columns you may have added in the past, and your Label color preferences (see Chapter 4 for more on Label colors).

Selected container

Figure 9-1:
The Outline
view.

Arranging the Outliner

The first time you use the Outliner, it displays the title and Synopsis for each item in the Binder selection. From there, you can organize and adjust the Outliner to suit your purpose: expand or collapse subfolders, add and move columns, adjust the column width, move items within the Outliner, and sort your list. The following sections explain how to customize your outline.

Expanding and collapsing items

When you choose a high-level container, such as your Manuscript folder, the Outliner displays all top-level items within that container. You can expand subfolders and file groups to show their contents or collapse them to hide those contents.

Figure 9-2 shows the Outliner with the Manuscript folder selected. If the triangle next to each folder points to the right, the folder is collapsed, so its contents are hidden. If the triangle points down, the folder is expanded, meaning its contents are visible.

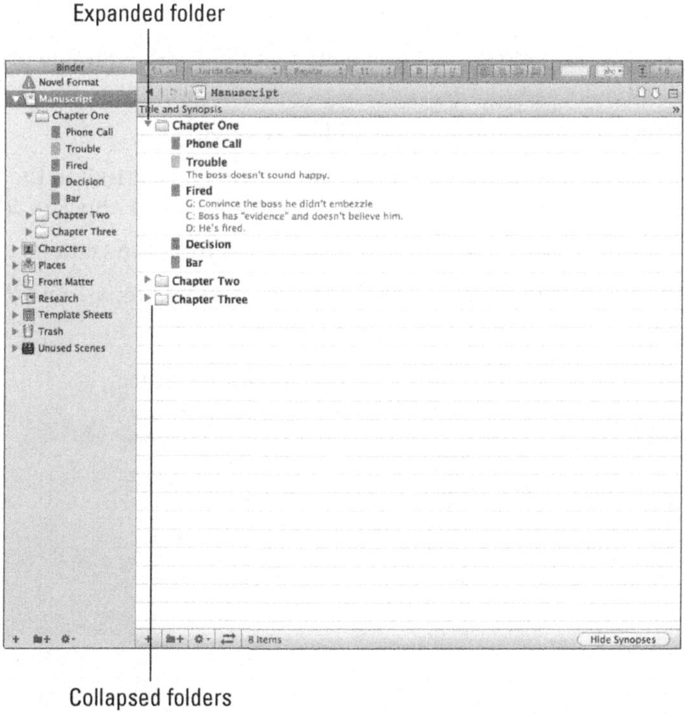

Expanded folder

Figure 9-2:
An outline
with folder
items.

Collapsed folders

To collapse or expand a folder or subfolder, simply click the triangle.

Note: On Windows XP and older, a plus sign (+) is used for collapsed folders, and a minus sign (–) is used to designate expanded folders.

Pressing the Option key (Alt on Windows) while expanding an item expands all its subfolders and file groups, too.

Adding and removing columns

All the metadata items you can add in the Inspector — Label, Status, keywords, custom metadata, as well as document and aggregate targets for each container (called Totals) — can be displayed in the Outliner.

Follow these steps to add or remove a column:

1. **Click the Column List button at the right of the field headers, as shown in Figure 9-3.**

   Alternatively, you can go to View➪Outliner Columns.

   A list of available metadata appears. Items that have a check next to them are currently visible in the Outliner.

   The Species field is a custom metadata field I added to my project (as covered in Chapter 5).

2. **Select the field you want to add or remove.**

   If you select a field that doesn't have a check next to it in the Column list, the new column appears in the Outliner and a check is added.

   If you select a checked field, it disappears from the Outliner.

3. **To add or remove additional columns, repeat Steps 1 and 2.**

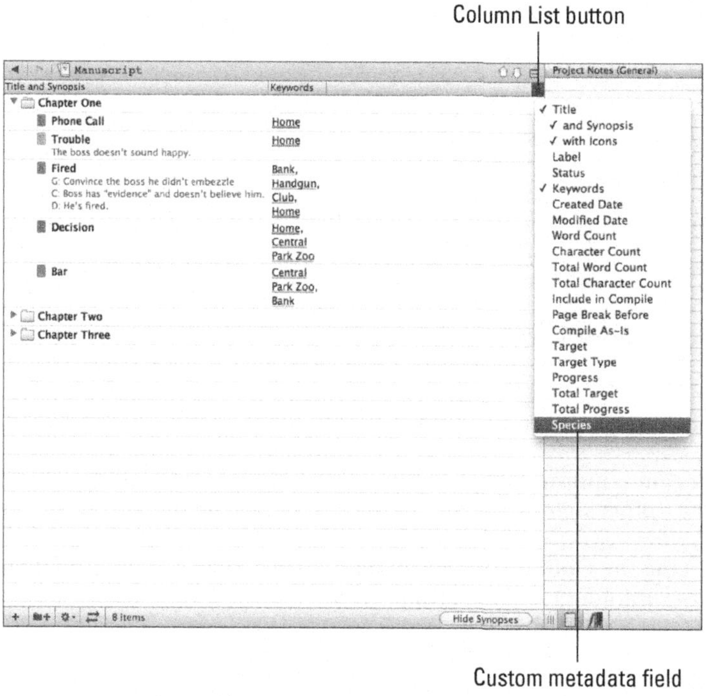

Column List button

Figure 9-3:
Adding columns to the Outliner.

Custom metadata field

Scrivener adds the columns from left to right in the order you choose them, but you can put them in any order you want by dragging and dropping the title bar of the column to the desired location.

Adjusting column width

Is your outline getting a bit crowded? Did your columns run right off the page? No problem. Adjusting the width of the columns is a piece of cake. You have two options:

- ✔ **Manually adjust the column width.** Place your cursor on the divider bar to the right of the column title. A two-sided arrow cursor appears. Click and drag to resize.
- ✔ **Let Scrivener auto-fit the column width.** Double-click the bar to the right of the column title. The column width resizes to fit the values in that column.

Moving items within the Outliner

If you want to change the order of your documents or folders while in the Outliner, you can. Just drag the desired item to its new location and drop it like a hot potato.

The blue target lines and boxes show you where your file will land, just like when moving items in the Binder (see Chapter 2 for more on using the Binder).

The item order is changed in the Binder, as well.

Figure 9-4 shows the New Job file being moved from Chapter Three to Chapter Two. Notice the blue target bar below Bubble Brain, which shows where in Chapter Two the file will be placed. There's also a blue box around Chapter Two to designate it as the new container for New Job.

Sorting by column

One of the Outliner's many useful features is the ability to sort by column. Why might you do that? Here are a few reasons off the top of my head:

- ✔ **Sort by Progress, Word Count, or Status:** See which documents need the most attention. (I talk more about document targets in Chapter 14.)
- ✔ **Sort by POV:** Group each character's scenes together.

✔ **Sort by Day or Date:** You can use this option if you've created a timeline-type field to make sure that your scenes are in the appropriate order.

For example, you can create a custom metadata field and enter a date value in a sortable format, such as **2012-06-01**. If you have documents that have the same date, add a time to the value by using the 24-hour clock, such as **2012-06-01-1830**.

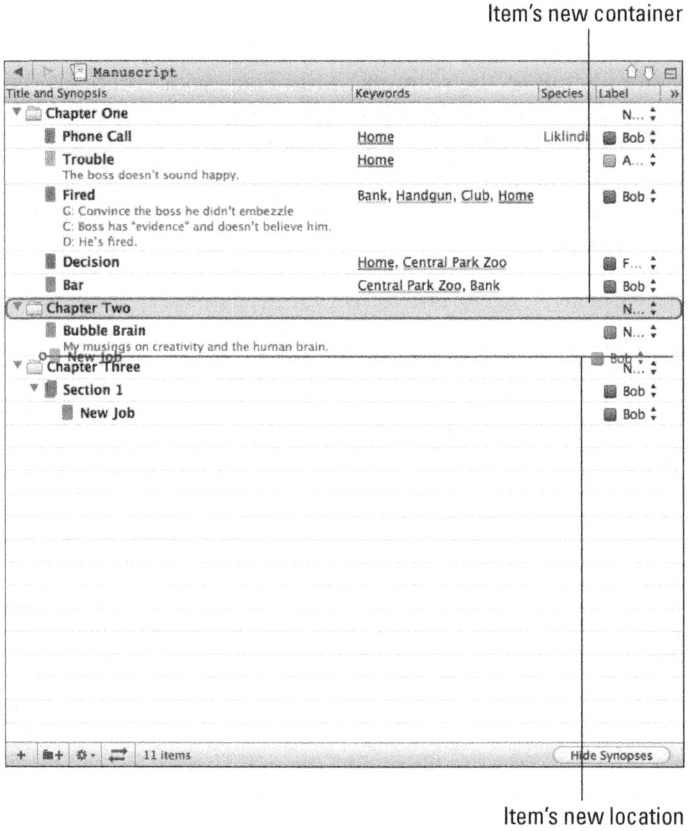

Item's new container

Figure 9-4:
Moving a
file in the
Outliner.

Item's new location

The sort starts over in each container. To sort by all files, use a noncontiguous selection (⌘+click on the Mac, Ctrl+click in Windows) of items when you're viewing more than one container. Just beware that you can't move files within an outline that's based on multiple selection, except to drop one file on another, which turns the dropped-on item into a file group that contains the dropped file.

REMEMBER

Sorting by a column doesn't change the item order in the Binder.

So, now do you want to know how to sort? Just click the column header box — for example, to sort by word count, click the Words column header, as shown in Figure 9-5: a small triangle appears in the Words header to designate the sort, and the header box turns blue. Each chapter is now sorted in ascending order by word count, but the order in the Binder is unchanged. Here's what the triangles signify:

- ✔ A triangle pointing up denotes an ascending sort (for example, A to Z).
- ✔ A triangle pointing down denotes a descending sort (Z to A).
- ✔ No triangle means the items are in hierarchical order (Binder order).

To toggle through ascending sort, descending sort, and no sort, keep clicking the header.

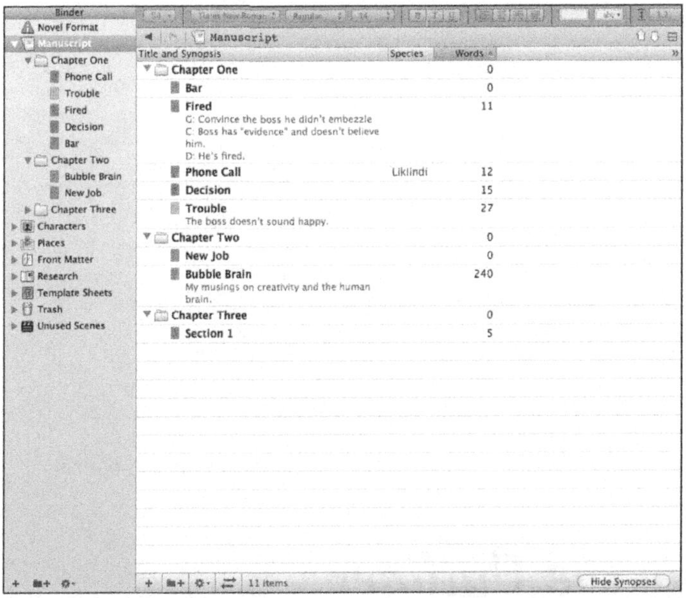

Figure 9-5:
Items sorted
by the
Words
column.

Hiding and showing the Synopsis

If your outline is looking a bit cluttered, you can hide the synopses for a cleaner view. You could remove the Synopsis field through the column list (which I talk about in the "Adding and removing columns" section, earlier in this chapter), but you have a quicker option.

To remove the Synopsis with one click, click the Hide Synopses button in the Outliner footer. As shown in Figure 9-6, the Synopses disappear from the Outliner, and the button changes to Show Synopses.

To reinstate the Synopses, click the Show Synopses button.

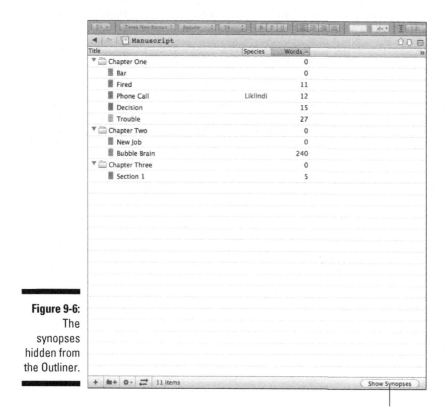

Figure 9-6: The synopses hidden from the Outliner.

Hide/Show Synopses button

Editing in the Outliner

Need to add a Label value, edit the title, or modify the Synopsis for an item? No need to change views, you can do it right from the Outliner:

- ✓ **Text fields:** Double-click to select the text, and then type the new value.
- ✓ **Fields with values:** Provide a drop-down list that offers value choices (for example, the Label or Status field). Figure 9-7 shows the Status field's drop-down list.

The values in the drop-down list match those in the Inspector. You can even edit the values that appear right from the drop-down list. (For more on modifying the Label and Status fields, see Chapter 4.)

To apply the same Label (or Status) value to multiple items, select the desired items and right-click. Choose Label (or Status) from the contextual menu that appears, and then choose the desired value from the submenu.

✔ **Add a Keyword:** To add one or more keywords from the Keywords panel (covered in Chapter 5), open the Keywords panel by clicking the Keywords button in the toolbar, and then drag the keyword(s) from the panel onto the desired file.

To apply the same keyword to more than one item, select the desired items in the Outliner, and then drag the keyword onto one of the selected items. The keyword is added to all selected items.

Want to open an item to work on it in the Editor? You don't need to find it in the Binder — simply double-click the item icon.

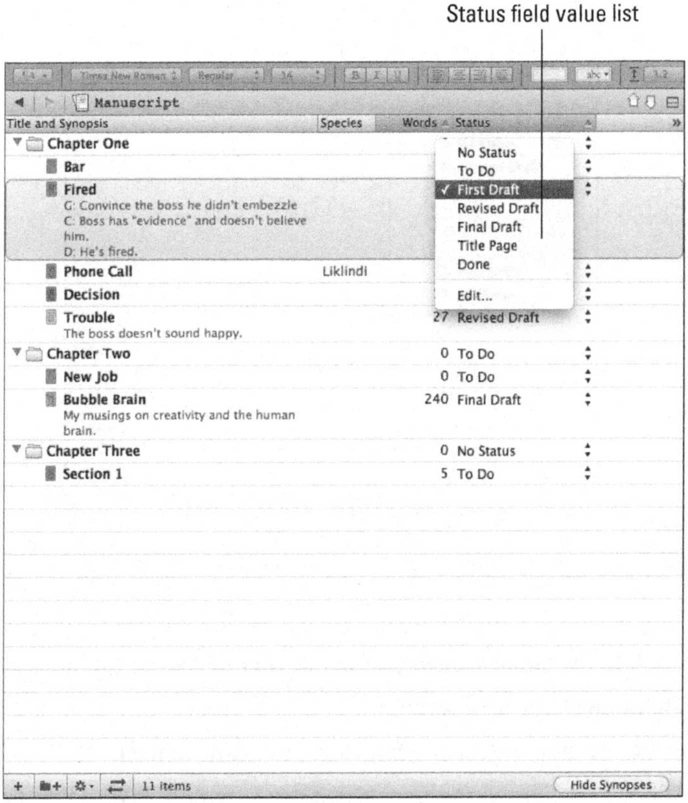

Status field value list

Title and Synopsis	Species	Words ▲	Status
▼ 📁 Chapter One			
▋ Bar			No Status
▋ Fired			To Do
G: Convince the boss he didn't embezzle			✓ First Draft
C: Boss has "evidence" and doesn't believe			Revised Draft
him.			Final Draft
D: He's fired.			Title Page
▋ Phone Call	Liklindi		Done
▋ Decision			Edit...
▋ Trouble		27	Revised Draft
The boss doesn't sound happy.			
▼ 📁 Chapter Two		0	To Do
▋ New Job		0	To Do
▋ Bubble Brain		240	Final Draft
My musings on creativity and the human			
brain.			
▼ 📁 Chapter Three		0	No Status
▋ Section 1		5	To Do

+ ▤+ ✿ ▾ ⇄   11 Items   (Hide Synopses)

Figure 9-7:
Changing
the Status
value in the
Outliner.

Viewing Your Outline in Split Screen

Just like with the Editor (covered in Chapter 6) and Corkboard (see Chapter 8), you can view the Outliner in Split Screen mode. Follow these steps to split the screen and then view a single document in one of the panes:

1. **Click the Split toggle button in the header of the Outliner (as shown in Figure 9-8).**

   The Outliner splits into two panes, displaying the same container in both.

   The Outliner layout — which columns are visible, their order, and the column widths — is specific to each split when you work in Split Screen mode (covered in more detail in Chapter 6).

Automatically Open Selection in Other Editor button

Editor pane   Outliner pane   Split toggle button

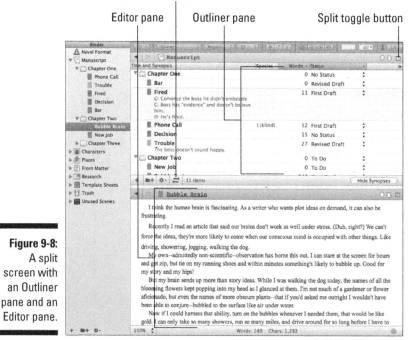

Figure 9-8:
A split
screen with
an Outliner
pane and an
Editor pane.

2. **Click in the pane where you want to view the single document.**

   That pane becomes active.

3. **In the Binder, select the file that you want to edit.**

   The file appears in the pane that you activated. Figure 9-8 shows an example of a split screen with Outliner and Editor panes.

4. **Click the Split toggle button again to exit Split Screen mode.**

TIP

If you're working in Editor mode and want a split view with an Outliner pane, split the Editor and then add a container to the active pane. If the Outliner doesn't appear, choose Outline from the View menu or the toolbar.

TIP

If you want to use the Outliner as a navigation tool while in Split Screen mode, click the Automatically Open Selection in Other Editor button (refer to Figure 9-8). Every time you select an item in the Outliner, the document opens in Document view in the other pane. With this option, you can hide the Binder (by choosing View⇨Layout⇨Hide Binder) but still quickly open documents for editing.

Printing Your Outline

Yep, just like with index cards (which you can read about in Chapter 8), you can print your outline. It doesn't come out looking like the nice spreadsheet you set up on your screen (see the following section for how to export your outline for use in a spreadsheet), but you still get a hierarchical list of the items in your selected container.

Follow these steps to print your outline:

1. **Choose File⇨Page Setup.**

   The Page Setup window appears.

2. **In the Settings drop-down list, select Scrivener.**

   The window changes to a list of margin settings.

3. **Click Options.**

   The Print Options window appears.

4. **Click Outlines in the center row of buttons.**

   Figure 9-9 shows the Print Options window that appears. The sample outline at the top of the window reflects the options you can choose in the bottom.

   Here are your options:

   - *Include Titles:* Prints the document title for each item.

   - *Include Synopses:* Prints the Synopsis text for each item.

   - *Include Label and Status:* Adds the Label in parentheses next to the title and highlights the title in the corresponding Label color. Includes the Status value in parentheses at the bottom of the entry.

   - *Include Keywords:* Displays keywords below the title of each item.

   - *Include Custom Meta-Data:* Lists custom metadata items below the title and any keywords.

- *Indent By Level:* Indents items by hierarchy. If left unchecked, the list of items appears in order, but all are aligned to the left.

- *Print File Name:* Adds the name of the selected container to the header of the printout.

- *Include Word Count:* Includes the document word count on the last line of the item entry.

- *Include Character Count:* Includes the document character count on the last line of the item entry.

- *Include Targets with Counts:* If the target value is greater than zero, this option displays the target value with the word count as a fraction (for example, Words: 200/1000). For more on document targets, see Chapter 14.

- *Prefix Titles with Number:* Adds a number to each document title in order.

- *Font:* Click the drop-down lists to select the font and font size for printing.

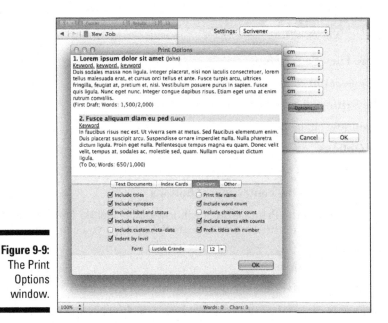

Figure 9-9:
The Print
Options
window.

5. **After making your option selections, click OK in the Print Options window to close it, and then again in the Page Setup window to close it.**

   Now you're ready to actually print the outline.

6. **Make sure the container (or files) for which you want to print the outline is selected in the Binder.**

7. **Choose File⇨Print Current Document.**

   The Print window appears.

8. **Make sure the settings are as desired (the appropriate printer and number of copies appear), and then click Print.**

   Figure 9-10 shows a preview of the Chapter One outline with all print options selected. The documents within each chapter are indented to indicate their lower level in the hierarchy.

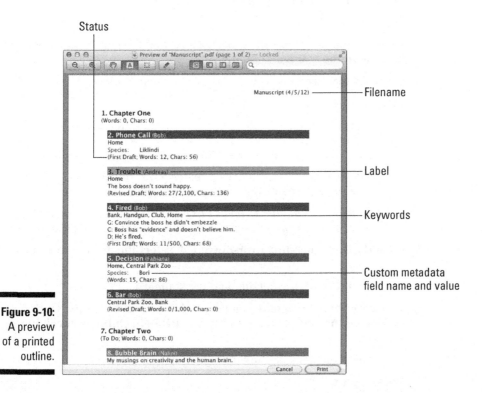

Status

Filename

Label

Keywords

Custom metadata field name and value

Figure 9-10: A preview of a printed outline.

If you want to preview the outline before you commit to printing it, click the PDF button at the bottom-left of the Print window and choose Open PDF in Preview before you click Print. If you like what you see, click the Print button at the bottom of the Preview window.

For other ways to print an outline of select items within your Manuscript, check out Chapter 13.

Exporting Your Outline to a Spreadsheet

If you want the nice columns like the ones you see in the Outliner, you can export your outline for use in a spreadsheet program (for example, Apple Numbers or Microsoft Excel). Just follow these steps:

1. **Display the desired container or selection of files in the Outliner.**

   I describe how to do this step in the section "Accessing the Outliner," earlier in this chapter.

2. **Choose File⇨Export⇨Outliner Contents as CSV.**

   The Export window opens.

3. **Enter a filename in the Save As text box, and navigate to the desired location in the column at the left.**

4. **In the Format drop-down list, choose the desired format.**

   You have these options:

   - *Comma Separated Values (CSV):* The standard option recognized by most spreadsheet programs. It creates a text document with each value separated by a comma and each item on a new line.

   - *Tab Separated Values (TSV):* Creates a text document with tabs between each value and each item on a new line.

   - *Semi-Colon Separated Values (TXT):* Creates a text document with semicolons between each value and each item on a new line.

5. **From the Text Encoding drop-down list, select the desired encoding type.**

   Unicode (UTF-8) is the default, and the standard.

6. **To view only the columns you currently have visible in the Outliner, make sure the Only Include Columns Visible in Outliner check box is selected.**

   If the box is unchecked, the output includes all columns.

7. **Click Export.**

   The file is saved to the location you specified in Step 3.

   To view the output in a spreadsheet, open the file from within the spreadsheet program. The values should be automatically placed in separate columns, with each item in its own row.

Chapter 10

Marking Up Your Text with Inline Annotations and Comments

. . . .

In This Chapter

▶ Working with annotations in the text

▶ Using comments in their own pane

▶ Exporting annotations and comments to their own file

. . . .

*O*ne of the biggest drawbacks to writing on the computer is that you can't easily mark up your manuscript. Struggling with that paragraph but need to move on? Need more research here? Have to remember to insert a hook or transition there?

Scrivener has a function for that — two, actually: Annotations and Comments.

Annotations are embedded within the text, whereas comments are stored outside the text, accessible by a hyperlink or the Comments & Footnotes pane in the Inspector. When you're ready to compile your manuscript, you can either hide annotations and comments (the default), leave them visible, or convert them to footnotes or endnotes (see Chapter 11 for more on footnotes).

This chapter introduces you to the next best thing since the red pen.

Using Inline Annotations to Insert Notes into Your Text

Inline annotations are notes inserted directly into the text of your document. You can put them anywhere, even in the middle of a sentence, if desired. You can use inline annotations when you want the notes to be highly visible, right there on the page.

Add annotations for plot notes, to mark passages for more research or consideration, to critique another person's work, or to provide reminders.

You can even insert images and hyperlinks directly into annotations, which you can use while working on the file, and then remove them when you compile the project.

Creating an annotation

When you're ready to unleash your inner editor, follow these steps to add an inline annotation to your work:

1. **Click in the document to position your cursor where you want the inline annotation to start.**

2. **Choose Format➪Inline Annotation.**

   Here's a handy keyboard shortcut: Shift+⌘+A for Mac users, Ctrl+Shift+A for Windows users.

3. **Type your annotation.**

   Your text appears in a red bubble (unless you changed the color, which I describe how to do in the following section), as shown in Figure 10-1.

   Notice the lack of spacing around the annotation. Extra spaces before or after annotations show up in your compiled manuscript after you strip out those annotations, so treat the spacing as if the annotation wasn't there.

   To add buffer spaces, make sure they're inside the annotation bubble.

4. **Click outside the color bubble.**

   Alternatively, you can choose Format➪Inline Annotation.

   Annotations are turned off, and you return to normal typing mode.

To create an annotation from an existing line of text, select the text that you want to convert into an annotation, and then choose Format➪Inline Annotation. The text is encased in a colored bubble.

Figure 10-1: An inline annotation.

◄ | ▸ | 🖺 Phone Call

The shrill ring of the phone woke Bob from a deep sleep. Is there a better option than a ringing phone? What if I skip this part and go straight to the next scene? He groped for the handset, knocking his alarm clock off the nightstand.

Changing annotation color

Not so red-hot for red? You can choose any color you want for your annotations, and even use different colors for different types of notes. Just follow these steps:

1. **Click inside an existing annotation.**

   You don't need to select all the text.

2. **Choose Format⇨Font⇨Show Colors.**

3. **Choose a color that works for you from the Colors window that appears.**

   The annotation text and bubble change to your selected color. Until you change colors again, all future annotations use the new color.

4. **Close the Colors window by clicking the red X button.**

Windows users can change the default annotation color by following these steps:

1. **Choose Tools⇨Options.**

2. **In the Options window that appears, select the Appearances tab.**

3. **Choose Editor in the Colors list, and then click Annotation Text.**

4. **Click the Color box to choose a new color from the Select Color window that appears.**

5. **Click OK to close the Select Color window, and then click OK again to close the Options window.**

   All annotations — existing and new — appear in the new color.

Splitting an annotation

If you want to convert one note into two or more separate annotations right next to each other, you can split the original note by changing the color of the part that you want to differentiate. Split the annotation by following these steps:

1. **Within an existing annotation, select the portion of text that you want to split off.**

2. **Choose Format⇨Font⇨Show Colors.**

3. **From the Colors window that appears, pick a color that's different from the original annotation.**

   The selected text changes to the new color and gets its own bubble, as shown in Figure 10-2, where the text What if I skip this part and go straight to the next scene? was split from the original annotation.

4. **Click the red X button to close the Colors window.**

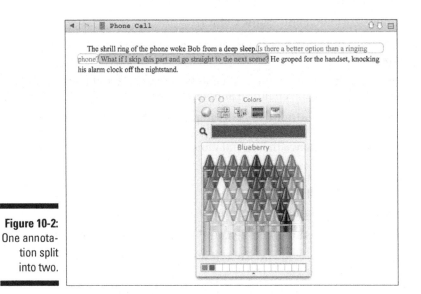

Searching for an annotation

Having all these notes embedded in your text isn't much good if you can't find them again when you need them. Luckily, Scrivener includes a robust search feature.

Follow these steps to find an annotation in your manuscript:

1. **Choose Edit⇨Find⇨Find by Formatting.**

   The Formatting Finder window appears, as shown in Figure 10-3. You can search not only by type of formatting, but also by text and color.

2. **In the Find drop-down list, select Inline Annotations.**

3. **If you're looking for a specific string of text, enter it into the Containing text box.**

TIP

For easy searching, consider adding unique strings to your annotations to help classify them, such as **RRR** for research, **EEE** for editing notes, and **ZZZ** for all others. Pick something that doesn't appear in a common word.

4. **In the Search drop-down list, select All Documents to search the entire manuscript.**

   Alternatively, you can choose Selected Documents if you want to limit your search only to documents selected in the Binder.

5. **Make a selection from the Color drop-down list.**

   This list gives you three choices:

   • *Any Color:* Searches for all annotations, regardless of color.

   • *Limit Search to Color:* Searches only for annotations matching the specified color. Specify the color by clicking the Color Chooser box and then selecting a color from the Colors window that appears.

   • *Exclude Color from Search:* Searches for all annotations except annotations of the specified color.

6. **When you have all the settings to your liking, click Next.**

   Scrivener highlights the first annotation after the position of your cursor and goes to the next instance in the manuscript or document every time you click Next.

7. **Click the red X button to close the Formatting Finder window when you're done.**

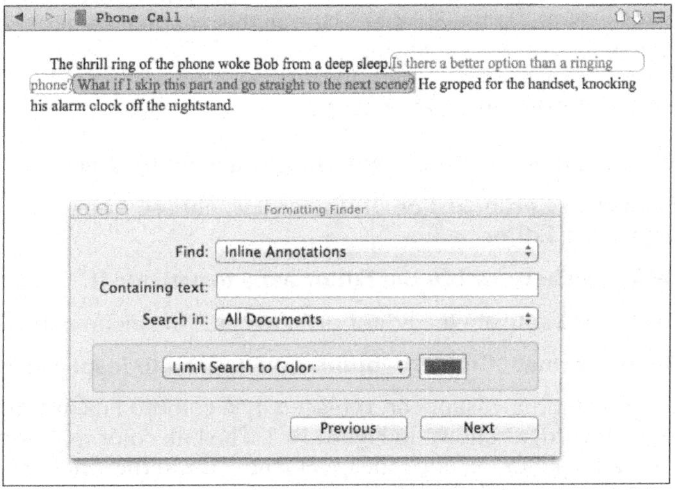

Figure 10-3:
Searching for annotations.

Editing and deleting an annotation

Need to change the wording of an annotation? Or maybe you've handled the issue and want to delete the note.

No problem, the process is simple for both:

- ✔ **Modifying:** Simply select the annotation text that you want to modify, and then type the new text.
- ✔ **Deleting:** Select the entire annotation text and delete it by pressing the Delete key.

 The colored box around an inline annotation is just a special type of formatting. If you paste regular text into the annotation, you split it. Likewise, if you copy text from an annotation and paste it into your regular text, you create another inline annotation. To avoid adding a new annotation, choose Edit⇨ Paste and Match Style to paste text into — or copied from — an inline annotation.

Converting annotations to comments

Annotations and comments are two sides of the same coin. Whereas annotations are inserted directly into the text, comments are stored off to the side, out of the way, designated by a colorful link in the text.

If you want to keep the annotations you made, but get them out of your way, you can convert them to comments (see the section "Using Comments to Create Linked Notes in the Sidebar," later in this chapter, for more on working with comments).

Follow these steps to make the change:

1. **Select the item(s) in the Binder that you want to affect.**

2. **If you're in Corkboard or Outliner view, choose View⇨Scrivenings to display the Editor pane.**

3. **Click anywhere within the Editor pane to activate it.**

   You have to activate the Editor pane to make the menu options available.

4. **Choose Format⇨Convert⇨Inline Annotations to Inspector Comments.**

   The annotations disappear, replaced by a colored link around the nearest word, as shown in Figure 10-4. The link color matches the annotation color, as does the comment color in the sidebar.

5. **Click a link to view the comments in the Comments & Footnotes pane.**

   Alternatively, you can click the Comments & Footnotes button at the bottom of the Inspector panel to open the Comments & Footnotes pane.

Figure 10-4:
Inline
annotations
converted to
comments.

The shrill ring of the phone woke Bob from a deep sleep. He groped for the handset, knocking his alarm clock off the nightstand.

Comments & Footnotes

▾ Comment:
Is there a better option than a ringing phone?

▾ Comment:
What if I skip this part and go straight to the next scene?

Stripping all notations from a document

Ready to delete all the annotations or comments from a document? You don't have to select and delete them one by one. You can strip them all at the same time — although still only one document at a time — by following these steps:

1. **Select the desired document in the Binder.**

2. **Choose Edit⇨Select All to select the document text.**

   Alternatively, you can click and drag over the text you want to select.

3. **Choose Edit⇨Copy Special⇨Copy Without Comments or Footnotes.**

4. **Choose Edit⇨Paste.**

   The copied text — without annotations or comments — replaces the annotated text.

This procedure strips out not only annotations and comments, but also footnotes. Be absolutely sure you're ready to ditch them all before following the preceding steps.

To keep a copy of the document with annotations, comments, and footnotes embedded, take a Snapshot (covered in Chapter 19) before removing the notes as outlined in the preceding steps.

Using Comments to Create Linked Notes in the Sidebar

Comments are similar to annotations, but instead of being inline with the text, they're tucked out of the way in the Comments & Footnotes pane, quickly accessible via a link within the text.

Just like annotations, comments are equally handy for making plot notes, marking passages for more research or revision, critiquing another's work, and adding reminders to yourself.

To view existing comments in a document, click the Comments & Footnotes button at the bottom of the Inspector, or click a comment link in the Editor to open the Comments & Footnotes pane.

Adding a comment

To add a comment, follow these steps:

1. **Click the spot within the text to which you want to link your comment.**

   Alternatively, select a portion of text if you want to associate the entire selection to a comment.

2. **Choose Format⇨Comment.**

   The nearest word is underlined and highlighted in yellow (or the most recently used comment color), and the Comments & Footnotes pane opens, displaying a new Comment text box. The author name, date, and time that appear automatically are selected, so any typing you do over-writes them.

3. **Type the desired comment, and then click outside the Comment text box to save it.**

   Alternatively, after you enter a comment, you can press the Esc key to save the comment and return to your place in the Editor.

Figure 10-5 shows a new comment and the corresponding link in the text. Both are the same color. The asterisk in the Comments & Footnotes button in the Inspector indicates the presence of a comment or footnote in the selected document.

Editing and deleting a comment

Need to change a comment? It's as easy as double-clicking the comment within the Comments & Footnotes pane, and then making your changes.

To delete a comment, click the X button in the upper-right corner of the Comment text box.

To delete one or more comments, select the desired comments, and then click the Delete Selected Comments & Footnotes button (refer to Figure 10-5), or press the Delete key.

However you delete it, the comment and its link disappear.

Comment link   Delete Selected Comments & Footnotes button

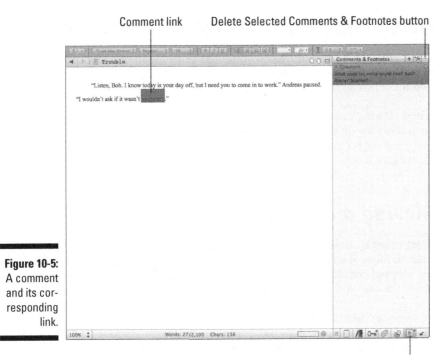

Figure 10-5:
A comment
and its cor-
responding
link.

Comments & Footnotes button

Changing the comment color

Were you dismayed to see that new comments showed up yellow, even if you changed the annotation color? Never fear, comment colors are changeable, too, if you follow these steps:

1. **In the Comments & Footnotes pane, select the comment(s) that you want to change.**

2. **Choose Format⇨Font⇨Show Colors.**

    The Colors window appears.

3. **Select the desired color.**

    The selected comments change to the new color, as do their corresponding links in the text.

    Any new comments appear in the new color until you change it.

4. **Close the Colors window by clicking the red X button.**

Using comments to navigate a document

When you're ready to address a comment in your project, you can quickly jump to the corresponding location within a document by clicking the Comment box in the Comments & Footnotes pane.

When viewing multiple documents in the Editor (Scrivenings mode), the comments for all the documents appear in the Comments & Footnotes pane. Just click each comment in turn to navigate to the parts of your project that need more work.

Moving a comment

Need to get a comment out of the way for easier text editing? Or maybe you want to move it to another place in the document. You don't have to delete the original comment and create a new one from scratch. You can simply move the one you already have to a different location.

To move a comment, follow these steps:

1. **Select the new text to which you want to attach the comment.**

2. **In the Comments & Footnotes pane, right-click the comment that you want to move.**

3. **Choose Move to Selection from the contextual menu that appears.**

For an even faster move, drag the desired comment from the Comments & Footnotes pane and drop it on the word in the Editor to which you want to apply it.

Converting a comment to an inline annotation

Are the comments too out of the way for your liking? Do you wish the comment was embedded in the text for quick, easy reading? Then convert your comments to inline annotations.

Follow these steps to make the change:

1. **Select the document(s) in the Binder that you want to affect.**

2. **If you're in Corkboard or Outline view, choose View⇨Scrivenings to display the Editor pane.**

3. **Click anywhere within the Editor pane to activate it.**

   This step makes the menu options available.

4. **Choose Format⇨Convert⇨Inspector Comments to Inline Annotations.**

   The comments disappear from the Comments & Footnotes pane, and the links are removed. The comment text appears to the right of the original link in a colored bubble that matches the comment color.

Exporting Comments and Annotations

Want to see all your comments and annotations in one list that's print-ready? Follow these steps:

1. **If you only want to export the comments and annotations from specific documents, selected those documents in the Binder.**

   If you want to export all comments and annotations, skip this step.

2. **Choose File⇨Export⇨Comments & Annotations.**

   A Save As window appears, as detailed in Figure 10-6.

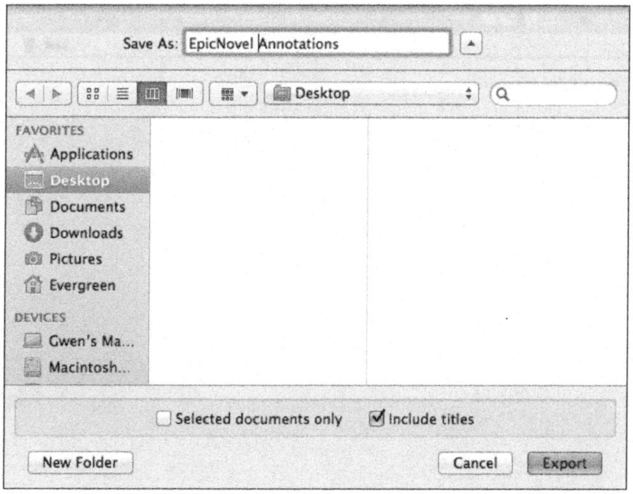

Figure 10-6:
The Save As window.

3. **In the Save As text box, type the name of the file.**

4. **Select a location in which to save the file.**

   If necessary, click the Expand button to the right of the Save As text box to see more location options (Windows users, click the Browse button).

5. **(Optional) To export comments and annotations for only the files selected in the Binder, click the Selected Documents Only check box.**

6. **(Optional) To organize comments and annotations by document titles, select Include Titles.**

7. **Click Export.**

   The comments and annotations are exported to an RTF (Rich Text Format) file that has the name and location you specified. RTF files are compatible with most word processors, including Microsoft Word.

Figure 10-7 shows an example of an exported comments-and-annotations file. The bold headings are the names of the documents in which the notations appear. The entries below Phone Call are inline annotations. The text below Trouble is from a comment.

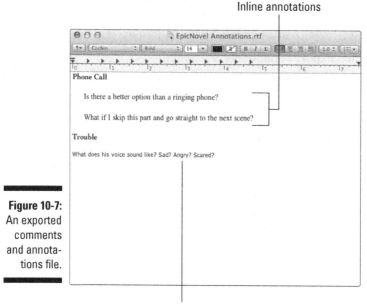

Inline annotations

Comment

Figure 10-7:
An exported comments and annotations file.

Chapter 11

Citing Your Sources with Footnotes

. . . .

In This Chapter

▶ Sorting out footnote types

▶ Including footnotes in your document

▶ Looking at footnotes in the sidebar

▶ Changing or removing a footnote

▶ Deleting all footnotes from a file

▶ Importing and exporting files with footnotes

. . . .

*I*f you need to add explanatory asides or copyright permissions to your work, or cite your sources at the bottom of each page, Scrivener offers a footnotes feature. Although it doesn't visually organize footnotes the way a word processor might, when you export (compile) your project, you can include the footnotes as either footnotes or endnotes. (You can find more on footnote options during compiling in Chapter 12.) Scrivener takes care of the numbering for you.

If you've already worked with inline annotations or comments, featured in Chapter 10, footnotes look mighty familiar because they actually work in a similar way. The main difference is that footnotes are generally intended to be included in the final manuscript, whereas comments and annotations usually aren't. You can, however, choose to compile a project without including footnotes.

This chapter shows you how to include footnotes in your work and outlines the available options for displaying them within your manuscript.

Understanding the Types of Footnotes

Scrivener offers two basic styles of footnotes: linked and inline. Both styles give you the same ultimate result when you compile the manuscript. The choice is merely a matter of personal preference.

Linked footnotes

Linked footnotes appear within the text as an underlined word in a gray box, while the actual footnote text is relegated to the Comments & Footnotes pane in the Inspector, thus minimizing distraction while still being visible.

Linked footnotes are especially suited for long notes that might visually disrupt the flow of your text while you're working, or for times when you want to view all footnotes in a document together in one place (the Inspector sidebar).

For even less intrusive footnoting, you can set up linked footnotes so that they use a special marker, instead of linking to a word. See the "Using footnote markers" section, later in this chapter, for more information.

Inline footnotes

Inline footnotes place the footnote text in its entirety within the manuscript, surrounded by a gray box. Inline footnotes are best if you want to be able to view them immediately with the text they reference or don't want to have to use the mouse to access their contents.

Inline footnotes also have the added advantage of not needing an anchor, which means they can be placed anywhere within the document — at the beginning or end, or in a document that doesn't yet contain text.

A special type of inline footnotes — called *referenced footnotes* — allows you to use inline notes but store the text of the footnote elsewhere in the document for easier reading. Referenced footnotes use a reference word that's later stripped out.

Adding a Footnote

The method for adding a footnote varies, depending on which type of footnote you choose. You can add a linked, linked with marker, inline, or referenced footnote.

Adding a linked footnote

If you're used to creating footnotes in a standard word processor or you're not sure where to start with footnotes, linked footnotes are probably the easiest to work with.

Linked footnotes are anchored to a word or words within the document. The anchor becomes a link that you can click to access the footnote. To add a linked footnote, follow these steps:

1. **Select the position where you want the footnote number to appear in your manuscript text.**

2. **Choose Format⇨Footnote.**

   A gray box appears around the selected word (which is now underlined to denote a link) or the word preceding the location you chose, and the Comments & Footnotes pane appears. When you compile your project, the footnote number appears just after the linked word.

3. **Type your footnote text in the Footnote text box that appears in the Comments & Footnotes pane.**

4. **To exit and save the footnote, press the Esc key to move the cursor back to your position in the Editor pane.**

   Alternatively, you can click outside the footnote.

Figure 11-1 shows a footnote added at the end of the first paragraph. In this example, when the manuscript is compiled, the footnote number will appear at the end of the first paragraph, after the period. If only the word *speech* were highlighted (and not the period), the footnote number would appear just before the period.

Note that you can also add a footnote by using the Add Footnote button in the Comments & Footnotes pane, and you can hide the footnote text by clicking the Collapse button (the small triangle at the left of each Footnote text box).

Viewing linked footnotes in the sidebar

When you add a new linked footnote, the Comments & Footnotes pane opens in the Inspector. However, if you want to view footnotes at a later time and the pane isn't visible or the Inspector is hidden, just click the footnote's link to open the sidebar and view all notes for the document you're working in.

If the Inspector is visible but open to a different pane, click the Comments & Footnotes button to open the Comments & Footnotes pane.

To navigate to a footnote anchor location within your document, click the desired footnote in the Comments & Footnotes pane.

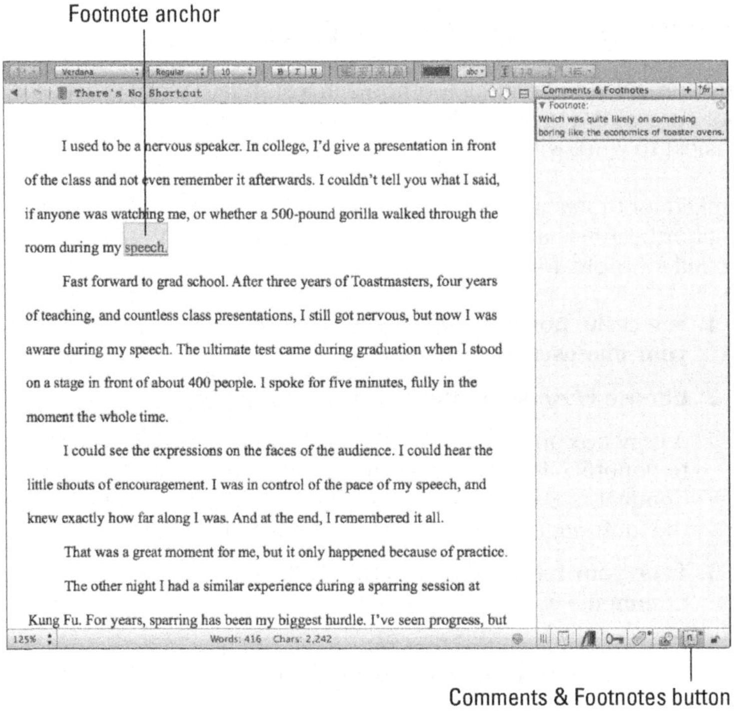

Footnote anchor

Figure 11-1:
A linked
footnote.

Comments & Footnotes button

Moving a linked footnote

Is your footnote in the wrong place? Want to temporarily move it out of the way while editing text so you don't lose it? No need to delete the original footnote and create a new one. Simply drag the desired footnote from the Comments & Footnotes pane and drop it in the location in the Editor where you want the anchor to be.

Using footnote markers

If you like linked footnotes but prefer they be even less visible, you can designate a *footnote marker* — a single character that appears where the footnote number will be inserted when you compile the project.

Be sure to stick with a character after you choose it for a project. If you change the marker character part way through the writing process, footnotes created with the old marker aren't automatically updated to use the new symbol.

Follow these steps to specify a footnote marker:

1. **Choose Project⇨Text Preferences.**

    The Project Formatting Preferences window appears.

2. **Select Use Footnote Marker.**

3. **(Optional) If you want to use a marker other than the default asterisk (*), enter it in the text box that's enabled when you click the check box in Step 2.**

    The footnote marker settings are specific to each project.

4. **(Optional) If you want to apply this marker to all new projects, click the Make Default button.**

    You can turn the footnote marker off in any project by deselecting Use Footnote Marker in the Project Formatting Preferences window.

4. **Click OK to close the Project Formatting Preferences window.**

If you turn off footnote markers — or change the marker symbol halfway through your project — but still have them embedded in your manuscript, the markers show up when the document is compiled. However, you can mix the different types of footnotes within a single project.

After you set your footnote marker, follow these steps to add a footnote:

1. **Place your cursor within the document exactly where you want the footnote number to appear.**

2. **Choose Format⇨Footnote.**

    The gray footnote bubble appears with your selected footnote marker in it, and the Comments & Footnotes pane appears in the Inspector. Figure 11-2 shows footnotes created that use a footnote marker. Note the placement of the marker and its reduced footprint on the page.

3. **Type the text of your footnote in the Footnote text box in the Comments & Footnotes pane.**

4. **Press Esc to move your cursor back to the Editor and save the footnote.**

    Alternatively, you can click outside the Footnote text box to save the footnote.

Footnote markers

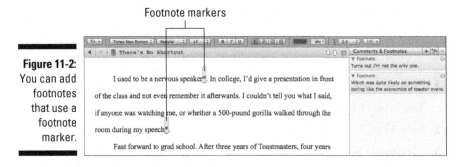

Figure 11-2:
You can add
footnotes
that use a
footnote
marker.

Adding an inline footnote

Inline footnotes are embedded right in the text of the manuscript for quick, easy viewing without clicking a link or using the Comments & Footnotes sidebar. Add an inline footnote by following these steps:

1. **Select the desired footnote location or the text that you want to convert to a footnote.**

   When you compile your project, the inline footnote bubble is replaced with the footnote number, so choose your location carefully.

2. **Choose Format⟹Inline Footnote.**

   If you selected a location but no text, nothing happens visually yet. If text was already selected, it's surrounded by a gray box.

3. **Type the desired footnote text.**

   The text appears in a gray box, as shown in Figure 11-3.

   No corresponding entry appears in the Comments & Footnotes sidebar for an inline footnote. Also, no extra spacing appears between the text and the inline footnote. Added spacing before or after an inline footnote shows up in the final manuscript, even though the footnote text is moved to the bottom of the document. However, extra spaces before and after the footnote text *within* the inline footnote box are stripped out during the compile process.

Adding a referenced footnote

A referenced footnote is a type of inline footnote that uses a reference word *(anchor)* that's stripped out of the manuscript when you compile. The anchor is placed where you want the footnote number to appear when the project is compiled, and also with the actual footnote text, to link the footnote location and text together.

Inline footnote

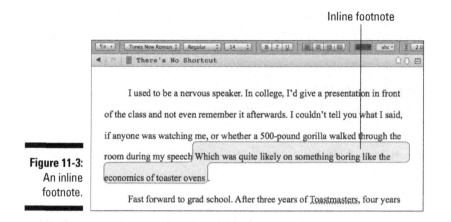

Figure 11-3:
An inline
footnote.

Keep a couple of important things in mind when you use a referenced footnote so that you can avoid random words ending up in your outputted manuscript:

- ✔ Each footnote within a document must use a unique anchor, although you can use the same word as a referenced footnote in a separate document.

- ✔ The anchor must match exactly in both locations.

- ✔ The anchor and the footnote text don't have to be located in the same document, but if they're not, have a unique anchor for every referenced footnote in the project to avoid confusion when Scrivener compiles the project.

- ✔ The reference anchor and footnote text must both be encased in the inline footnote formatting (surrounded by the gray bubble that denotes an inline footnote).

Ready to add a referenced footnote? Follow these steps:

1. **Decide on a reference word or characters for the footnote anchor.**

   The ideal anchor is something you aren't likely to use for another footnote. So, for a paragraph on golden retrievers, you might use **dog**, and **twain** might work for a reference to a quote by Mark Twain.

2. **Place your cursor in the desired footnote location in the document text.**

3. **Choose Format⇨Inline Footnote.**

   Nothing appears until you start typing.

4. **Type your anchor surrounded by square brackets, as shown in Figure 11-4.**

   The anchor appears in a gray bubble.

5. **Reposition your cursor wherever you want to put the footnote text.**

   You could add the text at the bottom of the document, the end of the paragraph, in a document set aside just for footnotes, or wherever you want to put it to be out of the way.

6. **Choose Format⇨Inline Footnote.**

7. **Type the anchor in brackets, followed by the footnote text.**

   The anchor and text appear in a gray bubble.

8. **Choose Format⇨Inline Footnote to turn off inline footnote formatting.**

   Alternatively, click anywhere outside the inline footnote to turn off the formatting.

Figure 11-4 shows an example of a referenced footnote setup. The order in which the footnotes appear doesn't matter, only that the reference words match and are unique for each footnote within the document. During the compile process, the footnotes are added in the order the anchors appear within the text.

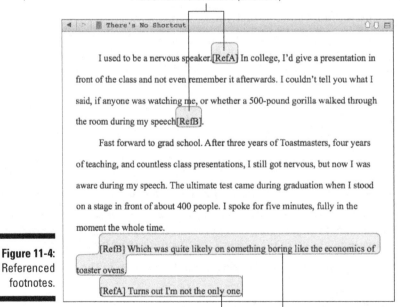

Placement references (anchors)

Figure 11-4:
Referenced
footnotes.

Footnote text with references

Figure 11-5 shows the compiled output with footnotes included. You can see that the footnote number is placed exactly where the anchor bubble used to be, so in Footnote 1, it appears after the period, but Footnote 2 occurs before the period. For more on footnote settings during the compile process, see Chapter 12.

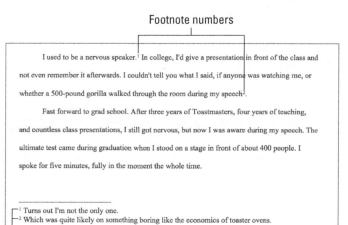

Footnote numbers

I used to be a nervous speaker.[1] In college, I'd give a presentation in front of the class and not even remember it afterwards. I couldn't tell you what I said, if anyone was watching me, or whether a 500-pound gorilla walked through the room during my speech[2].

Fast forward to grad school. After three years of Toastmasters, four years of teaching, and countless class presentations, I still got nervous, but now I was aware during my speech. The ultimate test came during graduation when I stood on a stage in front of about 400 people. I spoke for five minutes, fully in the moment the whole time.

[1] Turns out I'm not the only one.
[2] Which was quite likely on something boring like the economics of toaster ovens.

Figure 11-5: Footnotes in a compiled manuscript.

Footnotes

Editing or Deleting a Footnote

You edit a footnote differently, depending on the type of footnote:

- ✔ **Linked footnote:** Double-click the text in the Comments & Footnotes pane to enter Edit mode, and then make your changes.

- ✔ **Inline footnote:** Click in the gray bubble in the Editor and make changes, as needed.

TIP

The gray box around an inline footnote is simply a special type of formatting. If you paste regular text into the footnote, you split it. Likewise, if you copy text from a footnote and paste it into your regular text, you create another inline footnote. To avoid this split, choose Edit⇨Paste and Match Style to paste text into, or copied from, an inline footnote.

To delete footnotes, use these procedures:

- ✔ **A single linked footnote:** Click the X in the upper-right corner of the footnote box in the Comments & Footnotes pane (refer to Figure 11-1). Alternatively, you can delete the text anchor (the link) in the manuscript.

- ✔ **Multiple linked footnotes:** Select them in the Comments & Footnotes pane, and then click the Delete Selected Comments and Footnotes button (refer to Figure 11-1) or press the Delete key.

- ✔ **Inline footnotes:** Select all the characters and spaces within the inline footnote bubble, and then press the Delete key.

Stripping All Notations from a Document

You can choose to leave the footnotes out when you compile your project (Chapter 12 has more on compiling with footnotes), but if you want to remove all the footnotes from a document, you don't have to select and delete them one by one, or even have the Comments & Footnotes pane open.

Strip them all at the same time — although still only one document at a time — by following these steps:

1. **Select the desired document.**

2. **Choose Edit⇨Select All to select the document text.**

   Alternatively, you can click and drag to select a portion of text.

3. **Choose Edit⇨Copy Special⇨Copy without Comments or Footnotes.**

4. **Choose Edit⇨Paste.**

   The copied text — without footnotes, annotations, or comments — replaces the annotated text.

This procedure strips out not only footnotes, but also annotations and comments. Be absolutely sure that you want to remove everything before taking the steps in the preceding list.

To keep a copy of the document with footnotes, annotations, and comments embedded, take a Snapshot (covered in Chapter 19) before removing the footnotes, as outlined in the preceding steps.

Importing and Exporting with Footnotes

I cover importing and exporting (compiling) in Chapters 2 and 12, respectively, but here are several things to keep in mind when working with footnotes:

✔ **To import a file that has footnotes into Scrivener, convert it to RTF format first.** You can usually save a file in RTF format through a Save As command in your word processor.

✔ **When compiling your manuscript for use in a word processor, the RTF format is the best at handling footnotes.** Thus, you should compile to RTF format, even if you plan to open the manuscript in Word. After you open the file in Word, you can save it as a DOC file.

If you don't want to use RTF, most formats retain the footnotes but convert them to endnotes.

✔ **If you use a footnote marker for part of the manuscript, but then turn the marker setting off, the markers show up in the exported draft, alongside each footnote number.**

To avoid this problem, you can move the link from the marker to a word in the text by using one of the following methods:

- Select the text in the Editor that you want to use as the new link, and then right-click the footnote in the Comments & Footnotes pane and choose Move to Selection from the pop-up menu that appears.

- Drag and drop the footnote from the Comments & Footnotes pane to the spot within the text where you want the footnote to appear. Regular linked footnotes link to the nearest word, and footnote markers are placed exactly where you drop them.

If you're switching from footnote markers to text links, be sure to delete the markers manually; otherwise, they appear in the compiled manuscript.

✔ **You can use any combination of the different types of footnotes together in one manuscript.** Scrivener numbers them all sequentially without regard to footnote style. When compiling to RTF, you can even choose to have Scrivener export one type of footnote as end-of-page footnotes, and another footnote type as endnotes. You can also export comments (covered in Chapter 10) as footnotes or endnotes.

✔ **If you have footnote markers turned on but want to create a standard linked note, highlight the text to link before choosing Format⇨ Footnote.** Instead of adding a gray bubble with the marker inside it, Scrivener turns the selected text into a link and opens the Comments & Footnotes pane with a footnote text box ready for you to type in. Footnote markers aren't turned off by this action, only circumvented.

Part IV
Getting Your Manuscript Out There

The 5th Wave   By Rich Tennant

"The margins on your script are sooo even, Ms. Holly, and the type so black and crisp. I'm sure whatever the story's about is also good, but with centered headlines and flush left columns like this, we'd be fools not to put it into production."

In this part . . .

Part of the power of Scrivener is the ability to store your work in small chunks, whether scenes, chapters, sections, poems, or recipes. But what do you do when you want to turn those pieces and parts into one cohesive document?

You compile them.

This part of the book walks you through the compile settings, takes you through the compile process, and shows you how to save your settings for future use and lower stress.

Chapter 12

Setting Up the Compile Options

. . . .

In This Chapter

▶ Choosing the right format and output type

▶ Selecting the contents and structure of your compilation

▶ Formatting the elements for output

▶ Converting text for use in other programs

▶ Working with e-book and script formats

. . . .

Scrivener is designed so that you can write in small chunks, but that
means when you're ready to export your project, the software must
compile all those bits and pieces of writing into one complete document.
For this reason, the process of exporting your work from Scrivener is called
compiling.

Think of the Compile function as a team of specialists standing ready to
give your manuscript a makeover. You send in the project littered with
comments and annotations, and plagued by mismatched fonts, and out
comes a groomed and polished manuscript. Or e-book. Or web page.

One key thing to understand about the compile process is that it doesn't
change the look of the original documents in the Scrivener project. It
essentially makes a copy of the documents you select to include, applies the
changes you desire, and collates them into a new file type (or prints them out).

In an effort to avoid being your go-to cure for insomnia, this chapter doesn't
cover every possible setting available in Compile. But it does take you
step-by-step through the must-know and often-confused sections, explaining
what they're for, how to use 'em, and when you need 'em.

Deciding on a Format and Output Type

Open the Compile window by choosing File➪Compile. Scrivener provides two compile options:

- ✔ **Summary:** Shown in Figure 12-1. Provides a quick, easy way to compile your project without worrying about all the extra options.

- ✔ **All Options:** Presents a series of options tabs that changes based on which output type you choose. Options within the tabs allow you to customize exactly how Scrivener compiles your project. You can change the font, auto-number chapters, add a header or footer, modify the format, add a book cover, choose only a portion of your project to export, and so much more.

If you don't want to deal with all the nitty-gritty details of formatting within Scrivener — or you'd rather handle formatting in your word processor — then the Summary option is for you (and is covered in more detail in Chapter 13).

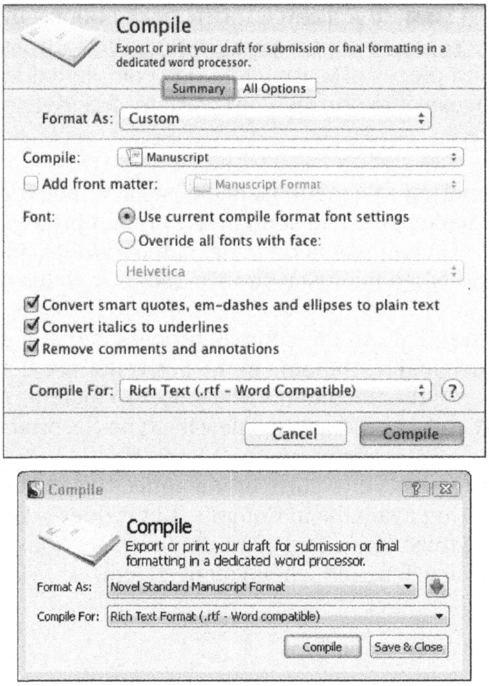

Compile

Export or print your draft for submission or final formatting in a dedicated word processor.

Summary | All Options

Format As: Custom

Compile: Manuscript

☐ Add front matter: Manuscript Format

Font: ⦿ Use current compile format font settings
       ◯ Override all fonts with face:
       Helvetica

☑ Convert smart quotes, em–dashes and ellipses to plain text
☑ Convert italics to underlines
☑ Remove comments and annotations

Compile For: Rich Text (.rtf - Word Compatible) (?)

Cancel | Compile

Compile

Export or print your draft for submission or final formatting in a dedicated word processor.

Format As: Novel Standard Manuscript Format

Compile For: Rich Text Format (.rtf - Word compatible)

Compile | Save & Close

Figure 12-1:
The Compile window in Summary mode on the Mac (top) and in Windows (bottom).

Predefined compile formats

Scrivener comes preloaded with an impressive number of formats representing some of the most common compile setups, which you can view by clicking the Format As list (refer to Figure 12-1). In this case, the format refers to the appearance of the outputted file. Formats contain settings for font style and size, line spacing, chapter numbering, margins, page numbers, headers, and so on.

You can use a format as-is or take it as a starting point for creating your own. How a document gets formatted during the compile process depends on how you structure that document in the Binder. Most formats assume that folders are chapters and documents are scenes or sections, but because everyone has their own preferred way to set up a project, a preexisting format may not work perfectly for you without some tweaks.

The project template you're using determines which format is selected by default, but you can choose any format you want.

Many of the formats are described in the following list, but for the most current and complete list of available formats, refer to the Scrivener User Manual. Chapter 13 discusses creating your own, and revealing hidden, format presets.

The list is a bit different in each version of Scrivener, but here are some commonly offered formats:

- **E-Book:** A simple format for use on electronic readers that treats containers as chapters and text documents as sections for scenes. If you have extra levels, such as Part folders, you might need to make some adjustments, or use the hidden format called E-Book (with Parts). Chapter 13 reveals how to view hidden formats.

- **Enumerated Outline:** This format provides a numbered list of document titles in a hierarchical fashion. When you use this format, the All Options page allows you to add synopses in the Formatting tab, if desired.

- **Non-Fiction Manuscript Format:** A common academic format that treats folders and top-level file groups as chapters, and gives titles to top-level files within those folders and file groups. This format is the non-fiction equivalent of Standard Manuscript Format.

- **Paperback Novel:** This format is set up to produce a good result for PDF output, suitable for submission to print-on-demand (POD) services such as CreateSpace.

- **Plain Text Screenplay (Celtx, Movie Magic):** Outputs the file into a plain-text format that's compatible with several screenplay software programs, including Celtx and Movie Magic.

✔ **Proof Copy:** Creates a double-spaced manuscript that allows for easy note taking, and includes a disclaimer in the header and after each chapter that says Not for Distribution. This format treats folders as chapters and all lower-level containers as sections.

✔ **Script or Screenplay:** This format uses settings for integration with Final Draft (version 8 or later), using the FDX format.

✔ **Standard Manuscript Format:** Outputs the manuscript in Courier, 12-point font, double-spaced. It adds scene separators, changes italics to underlines, inserts page numbers, and treats folders as chapters and all lower level containers as sections. This format is best used with RTF, PDF, or Print output.

✔ **Original:** This first option in the list when using a blank template moves to the bottom when you're working from any other project template. This option is basically a lack of format that carefully preserves your draft the way you formatted it within Scrivener.

This format doesn't add any page breaks, titles, or format adjustments. It just compiles the documents exactly as they appear in the Editor, with an empty line between each and a page break after each document that's followed by a folder.

All other format presets are a modified version of Original. To experiment with Compile settings, choose Original, and then try out the different options on the All Options page until you get the results you want. (The All Options page is covered in the section "Accessing the Compilation Options," later in this chapter.) Chapter 13 even shows you how to save your custom format for future use.

✔ **Custom:** This format represents the current settings if you've made any changes to the options on the All Options page. The bulk of this chapter is devoted to customizing the Compile options.

You may also find a preset at the very top of the list, separate from the others (for example, Novel). This preset represents the original compile formatting created for the specific project template you chose. (I talk about project templates in Chapter 15.)

Output types

After you decide on the format of your draft (as discussed in the preceding section), you need to choose the type of output. How you plan to use the compiled project determines your choice. Want to view your work on an e-reader? Choose one of the E-Book options. Want to print your manuscript for a read-through on paper? Pick Print.

Find the output options in the Compile For list (refer to Figure 12-1). Depending on which version of Scrivener you're using, your output options may be slightly different, but most of the options in this list should be available to you:

- **Print:** Use this option to send the project to your printer.

- **PDF:** Saves the file to PDF format.

- **Rich Text (.rtf – Word Compatible):** Usually the best choice when exporting for use in a word processor, even Microsoft Word, because it retains more of your format options than any other type. The RTF file supports images, bullets, comments, footnotes, and tables, and it's compatible with most word-processing programs.

- **Rich Text With Attachments (.rtfd):** This Mac-only option creates an RTFD file, mainly useful for exporting to Apple Cocoa applications such as TextEdit or Pages, especially when your file contains images. Not compatible with most word processors or non-Apple operating systems.

- **Microsoft Word 97-2004 (.doc):** Exports to DOC format, but isn't as quick as using the RTF exporter. And, depending on your computer setup, you may lose some formatting, such as indents, line spacing, footnotes, comments, and bullets. If you have issues with this format, try RTF, instead.

- **Microsoft Word (.docx):** Exports to DOCX format for newer versions of Word, but still has the same issues as the DOC version.

  This option is available on Windows if Word 2007 or higher is installed on your computer. Choose Tools⇨Options, and then select the General tab on the Options window that appears. In the Import/Export section, specify that you want to use Word for the conversion. You may need to close and reopen Scrivener for the setting to take effect.

- **Open Office (.odt):** Creates an ODT file but may lose formatting such as line spacing, indents, bullets, comments, and footnotes. For best results, use the RTF format.

- **Plain Text (.txt):** Creates a plain-text file with no formatting that's compatible with almost any software on any platform.

- **Final Draft 8 (.fdx):** Use this option when exporting for Final Draft version 8 or newer. This output format converts synopses to scene summaries and supports scene titles and custom script-element formatting.

- **Final Draft 5–7 Converter (.fcf):** This Mac-only option converts output to FCF format for use with older versions of Final Draft. Only maintains basic screenplay formatting.

- **ePub eBook (.epub):** Creates an EPUB file compatible with most e-readers. Supports formatting, table of contents, hyperlinks, and footnotes (converted to endnotes).

- **Kindle eBook (.mobi):** Outputs a MOBI file for use with Amazon Kindle devices. Supports formatting, table of contents, hyperlinks, and footnotes (converted to endnotes). Requires Amazon's KindleGen software.

For Mac, KindleGen works only on Intel machines (to check yours, choose ♦⇨About This Mac, and then look next to Processor in the window that appears).

✔ **Web Page (.html):** Outputs an HTML file for web publication.

✔ **Web Archive (.webarchive):** Exclusive to Mac, this option is generally compatible with only Safari and some Mac OS X applications. This option produces a .webarchive file that's like HTML with images bundled into a single file.

✔ **eXtensible Web Page (.xhtml):** This Windows-only option creates a single XHTML file. Good for newer web platforms.

✔ **PostScript (.ps):** Available for Windows only. Produces a file similar to a PDF that appears the same on any platform. Commonly used in design and publishing.

✔ **MultiMarkdown:** Exports a plain-text MultiMarkdown (.mmd) file that can be archived or modified after export.

✔ **MultiMarkdown->LaTeX:** Creates a LaTeX (.tex) file with full MultiMarkdown parsing. For LaTeX files without MultiMarkdown (MMD), use the plain-text MMD exporter.

✔ **MultiMarkdown->RTF:** For Mac only. Uses HTML to create an RTF file with partial MMD support. Features are limited, and the result isn't equal to the standard RTF file.

✔ **MultiMarkdown->HTML/MultiMarkdown to Web Page (.html):** MultiMarkdown->HTML applies to the Mac, and MultiMarkdown to Web Page (.html) appears in Windows. Creates a W3C-compliant HTML file (.html) for web publication or additional modification.

✔ **MultiMarkdown->Flat XML (.fodt):** Listed as MultiMarkdown to OpenDocument Flat XML (.fodt) in Windows, this option creates a single OpenDocument flat XML file for use in OpenOffice.

✔ **MultiMarkdown to Outline Processor Markup Language (.opml):** Windows only. Produces output suitable for OPML, an XML format for outlines.

Accessing the Compilation Options

Compilation options are the real meat of the Compile window. These options let you tell Scrivener how you want your selected content to look after it goes through the compile metamorphosis.

When you click All Options (on the Mac) or the Expansion button (in Windows) within the Compile window, a list of options tabs appears along the left side, as shown in Figure 12-2. This list changes depending on which output type you selected, so yours might look slightly different.

Each of the options tabs provides access to customizable settings for the output type that you chose. They're loaded with defaults based on your selection, but you can change the settings to suit your needs.

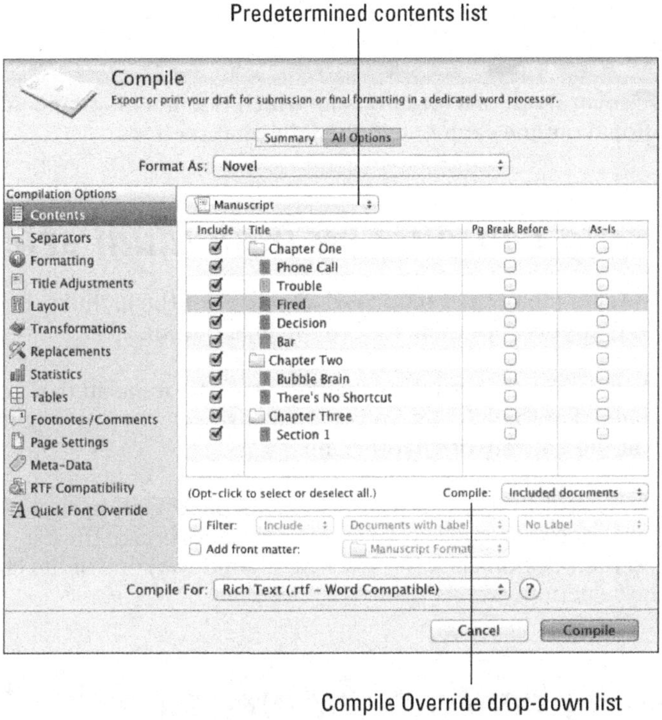

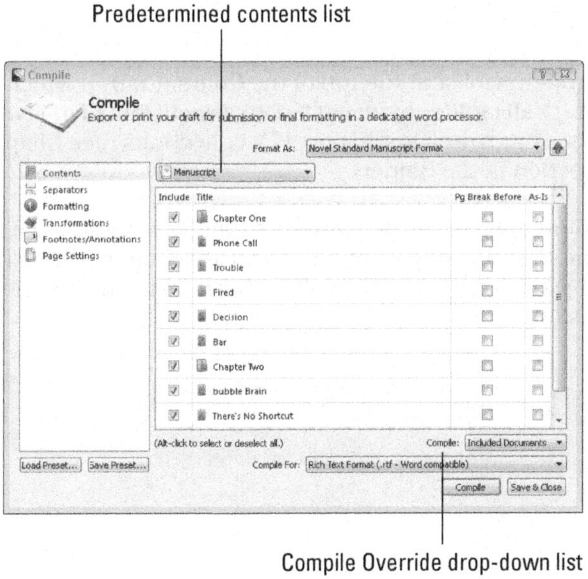

Predetermined contents list

Compile Override drop-down list

Predetermined contents list

Figure 12-2:
The Compile window in All Options mode on the Mac (top) and in Windows (bottom).

Compile Override drop-down list

Choosing which Documents to Export

Are you exporting your entire project or just the first three chapters? Or maybe only your essays from last March. Whatever you want in the final output, content selection is handled on the Contents tab of the Compile window.

You have several options for choosing which documents to include in the compilation. I outline each one in the following sections.

Choosing contents by individual selection

In the Contents tab of the Compile window, select the Include check box for each item that you want to include in the final output.

If you select a container, such as Chapter One, the items in that container aren't included automatically, so you must also select each document within if you want the entirety of Chapter One.

To select or deselect all items in the Contents pane, Option-click (Alt-click in Windows) one of the boxes. To toggle only a portion of the list, select the items, and then Option-click (or Alt-click in Windows) one of the check boxes within the selection.

Choosing contents by predetermined selection

Click the drop-down list at the top of the Content tab — which shows the Manuscript (Draft) folder by default — to select from high-level containers, saved searches (covered in Chapter 17), collections (see Chapter 18), and the current selection in the Binder.

Choosing something other than the root folder narrows down the items available for selection. For example, if you add a filter (which I talk about in the following section), it applies only to those items within the selection you make in this list.

Narrowing contents with a filter

A filter lets you narrow your list of files to those that match the criteria you select. For example, you might limit your output to only those scenes written from a specific point of view, essays written about the same topic, or scenes that take place in a particular setting.

The filter applies only to the list of items already selected.

To apply a filter, follow these steps:

1. **Select the Filter check box.**

2. **Select Include or Exclude from the first drop-down list to specify whether you want to filter by including files or excluding them.**

3. **Select which criteria you want to filter by from the middle drop-down list.**

   You can choose Documents with Label, Documents with Status, Documents in Collection, or Current Selection.

   When you filter by a collection, only those collection items located in the Manuscript (Draft) folder are available for compile. Files in the collection that are located outside the Manuscript (Draft) folder aren't included.

4. **If you picked one of the first three criteria in Step 3, select the desired value from the last drop-down list.**

   The list in the Contents pane changes based on your selections.

As an example, the filter settings shown in Figure 12-3 compile all documents with the Label value of Bob. The Contents list reflects the choices made in the filter section so that you can check your results before compiling.

Overriding the contents list selections

The Compile Override drop-down list (refer to Figure 12-2) changes how the Contents list is handled, depending on which option you choose:

✔ **Included Documents:** Outputs items with a check mark. This is the default setting.

✔ **Excluded Documents:** Outputs only those items *not* checked.

✔ **All:** Compiles all items on the list, regardless of their Include status.

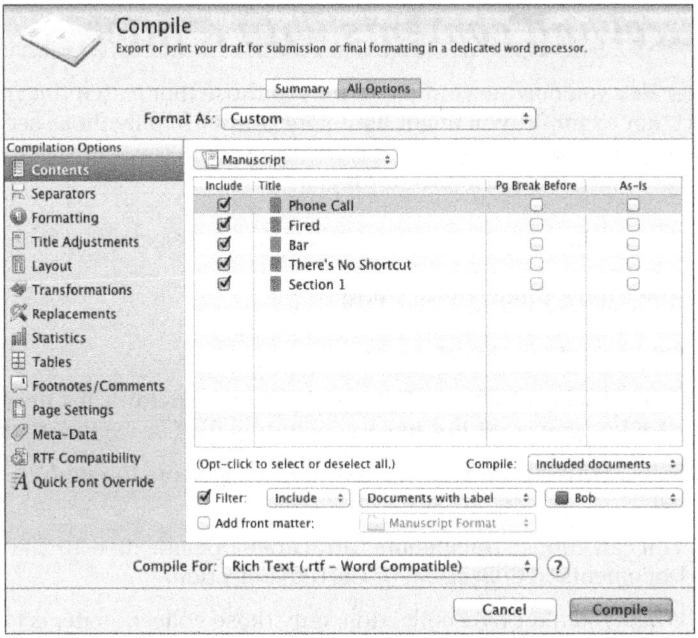

Figure 12-3:
Using a filter
to select
compile
items.

Adding front matter to the compilation

You can include front matter items (a title page, table of contents, dedication, acknowledgements, and so on) by selecting the Add Front Matter check box in the Contents pane.

The Add Front Matter drop-down list lets you choose from items outside the Draft folder, as shown in Figure 12-4. Some project templates (such as the Novel template used for this example) come with predesigned front matter items, but you can also create your own.

You can organize different types of front matter into folders, and then select the folder appropriate for the type of output you're creating. For example, a submission to an agent needs a title page complete with contact information, but you probably don't want to include the same in an e-book for public distribution. After you make a selection, the front matter items are added to the Contents list.

If you choose a subgroup of the draft from the Predetermined Contents drop-down list, you must select Treat Compile Group as Entire Draft from the Compile Group Options drop-down list that appears; otherwise, the Add Front Matter option is unavailable. The same is true if you choose Current Selection for your contents.

Selecting Treat Compile Group as Entire Draft forces Scrivener to renumber the chapters like they're the only ones in the manuscript. Leaving the option unchecked is useful if you want to print only a portion of the manuscript but use the correct chapter numbering.

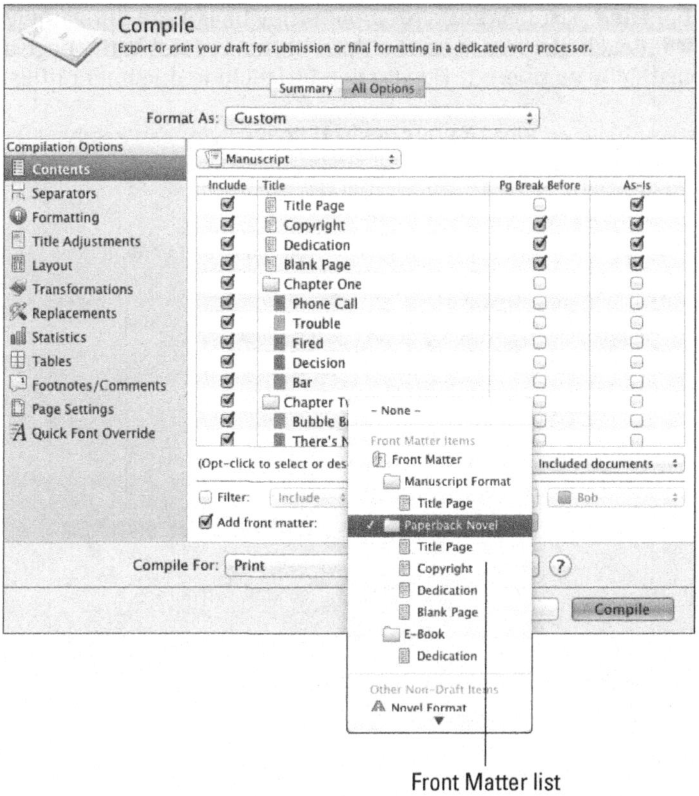

Figure 12-4:
Adding front
matter.

Front Matter list

Formatting the Compiled Output

Looking at the Formatting section often makes people cross-eyed, but it's not as bad as it appears. I promise! Plus, if you master this section, you can fix almost anything. In the Formatting pane, you can control the font, font size, line spacing, chapter numbering, title format, and more.

Figure 12-5 points out the two sections of the Formatting pane:

✔ Structure and Content table
✔ Formatting Editor

The two sections work together. In the Structure and Content table, you choose the level that you want to work on, and you make the desired changes in the Formatting Editor.

Before getting started, think about how your project is laid out and how you want to format each level of your project. For example, do you want part numbers and part headings, or should they be left out altogether? Do you want each chapter to start a third of the way down the page and be automatically numbered? Do you need to include document titles or not?

After you have an idea of your desired layout, you can easily make the necessary styling decisions.

Structure and Content table

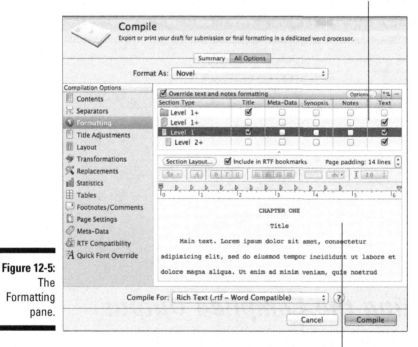

Formatting Editor

Figure 12-5:
The
Formatting
pane.

Understanding the Structure and Content table

In the Structure and Content table, you can choose the content elements that you want to include for each type of item in the Binder (for example, folder, subfolder, file group, document, and subdocument).

Level 1 items are those at the top of the hierarchy. Level 2 items are those contained within Level 1 items. Level 3 items are contained within Level 2 items, and so on.

The elements selected for inclusion — and the formatting set up in the Formatting Editor — can be different for each hierarchy level. So Level 1 folders might include only a title, whereas Level 2 folders could include a title and any text within the folder that serves to introduce the section.

You also use the Structure and Content table to select items whose formatting you want to customize in the Formatting Editor (in the lower half of the pane).

The following list explains the levels in the Structure and Content table that appears in Figure 12-6:

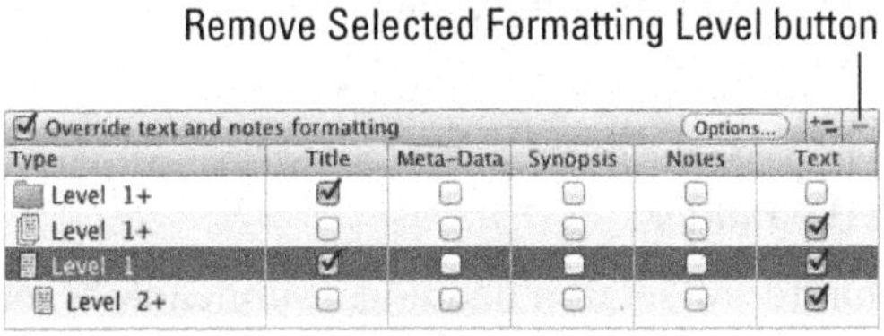

Remove Selected Formatting Level button

Figure 12-6:
Item type
levels in the
Structure
and Content
table.

✔ **Level 1+ folder:** Represents all folders at the top level or lower. So, if your book had Part folders and Chapter folders, this option applies to all of them unless you create a lower level (which I cover in the following section).

✔ **Level 1+ file group:** Represents all *file groups* (text files that have subdocuments) at or below the top level.

✔ **Level 1 text document:** Applies to all text documents at the top level of the hierarchy (just below the Manuscript or Draft folder).

✔ **Level 2+ text document:** Applies to all text documents at level 2 or lower.

Figure 12-7 shows how Binder items match up with the levels in the table. Level numbers are relative to the root (Manuscript) folder, which you can think of as level 0.

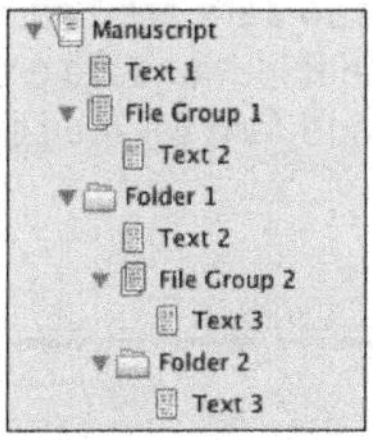

Figure 12-7:
Hierarchy
levels.

For each item type, you can choose to include one or more elements of content. In the final output, each element is included in the order listed. When you make changes, the Format Editor at the bottom of the Formatting pane shows an example of the final output for the level selected in the table. Here are the elements you can include:

- ✔ **Title:** Displays the title of the item. If only this option is selected, the compiled output is a list of titles. Note that certain templates are set up to automatically number the folders CHAPTER ONE and so on, which is added separately from the title. For more on auto-numbered chapters, see the section "Working with chapter titles and subtitles," later in this chapter.

- ✔ **Meta-Data:** Displays the Created date/time, Modified date/time, Status and Label values, keywords, and custom metadata.

- ✔ **Synopsis:** Adds the Synopsis. For a printable Synopsis list, select Title and Synopsis in the table for text file types.

- ✔ **Notes:** Adds notes from the Document Notes pane.

- ✔ **Text:** Includes the text of the item (what's in the Editor pane when the item is selected in the Binder).

Want to include chapter or section headings, subheadings, or introductions? No problem. Folders and file groups can contain text just like a text document. Simply add the desired text to the folder or file group in the Editor. Then, in the Structure and Content table on the Formatting tab of the Compile window, select the Text element for the appropriate level. Scrivener then includes the heading, subheading, or introduction in the final output.

Using levels

How you use levels depends completely on how your project is set up. For example, if you use folders for each chapter and have documents for each scene within a chapter, you need only a Level 1+ for each item type and can select the Title element for the folder item and the Text element for the text item.

If you have part folders with chapter subfolders that contain documents for each scene, you might want a Level 1 folder item to handle the part headings, a Level 2+ folder item to select and set up the chapter headings, and a Level 1+ text item for the documents. (See the section

"Adding and deleting levels," in this chapter, to find out about adding levels.) Deselect all elements in the Level 1 folder item to leave out part headings, select Title for the Level 2+ folder row to include chapter headings, and select Text in the Level 1+ text item row to include only the text from each document.

For a project in which each chapter is a text document and no folders are used, deselect all elements for the folder and file group levels, and include Title and Text for the Level 1+ text item.

Adding and deleting levels

If you have a project that has several layers for the same item type — for example, part, chapter, and section folders — creating additional levels in the Structure and Content table allows you to format each level differently. For example, your manuscript could have part headings centered in all caps and 16-point font, chapter headings centered in title case with 12-point bold font, and section headings left aligned and italicized in 12-point font.

Add a level by following these steps:

1. **Select the row of the desired item type (folder, file group, or text file) in the Structure and Content table.**

2. **Click the Add Another Formatting Level button.**

   A new row appears, as shown in Figure 12-8. The higher-level folder no longer has a plus sign (+) next to it, which means the settings for that row apply only to that level in the hierarchy. (Settings applied to the Level 2+ item affect all items at level 2 and below.)

   The new item has the same settings as the original item. If the levels will be fairly similar in format, save time by formatting the top-level item before adding lower levels.

Figure 12-8:
A new
folder level.

New folder level

If all levels of each item type have the same settings, you can delete extra levels from the table to simplify the view. Follow these steps:

1. **In the Structure and Content table, select the level(s) that you want to delete.**

2. **Click the Remove Selected Formatting Level button.**

   The selected level(s) disappears from the table.

Copying settings from one level to another

If the thought of tweaking the settings for every level individually has you contemplating a nap or worse, keep your eyes open for one more second. You can adjust the settings for one level and then copy the settings to the other levels. Then, all you have to do is make a few minor changes for any differences between levels, and you're done.

To copy all settings (from both the Structure and Content table and the Formatting Editor) from one level to another, follow these steps:

1. **In the Structure and Content table, select the formatted level that you want to copy.**

2. **Press ⌘+C (Ctrl+C for Windows) to copy the formatting.**

   Alternatively, you can choose Edit⇨Copy.

3. **Select the row to which you want to apply the formatting.**

4. **Press ⌘+V (Ctrl+V for Windows) to apply the formatting.**

   Choosing Edit⇨Paste works, too.

5. **Repeat Steps 3 and 4 until you've applied formatting to all desired levels.**

After you apply the formatting, you can tweak that formatting for each level, as needed (covered in the following section).

Changing the final format with the Formatting Editor

No matter what font and layout you've been using to write, you can change the appearance of the compiled output to something entirely different in the Formatting Editor. You can also set up the format for headings, titles, and subtitles.

The Formatting Editor is directly tied to the Structure and Content table. (See the section "Understanding the Structure and Content Table," earlier in this chapter.) When a row is selected in the table, a sample appears in the Formatting Editor that shows how the format and contents of items of the selected type and level will look. (Windows users, click the Modify button to access the Editor.)

The Notes and Text sections in the Formatting Editor may be grayed out and inaccessible, but the other elements selected in the Structure and Content table can still be modified in the Editor. (See the following section for how to make the grayed-out sections accessible.)

To adjust the appearance of each type of content, click in that area within the Editor and use the Format bar and ruler (covered in Chapter 6) to adjust font settings, alignment, color, line spacing, tab stops, and indents.

For example, to underline the title, as shown in Figure 12-9, you click the word Title and then click the Underline button in the Format bar.

REMEMBER

To exempt a specific Binder item from global formatting, select the As-Is check box in the Contents pane (see the "Preserving the format of a document" section, later in this chapter) or select Compile As-Is in the general Meta-Data section of the Inspector (covered in Chapter 4).

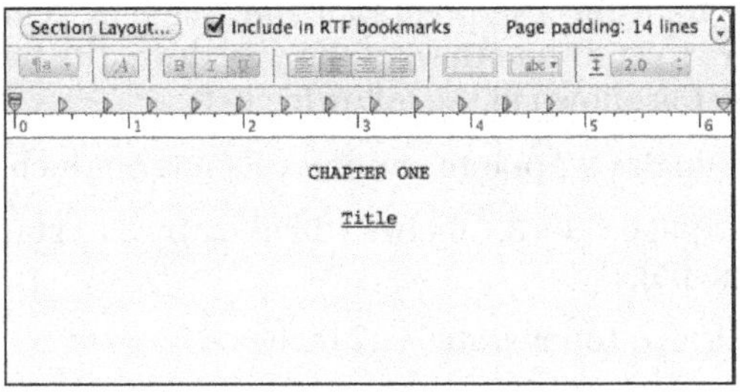

Figure 12-9:
Use the
Format bar
to modify
element
formats.

Several options may appear in the header of the Formatting Editor, depending on the chosen output type:

- **Include in RTF Bookmarks:** This option appears when you're exporting to RTF, and it's turned on for every level by default. If it's selected for a certain level, every item at that level in the Binder is given a bookmark (using the title for a name), which you can use in compatible word processors and to create a table of contents.

  If you add a table of contents to your project by choosing Edit⇨Copy Special⇨Copy Documents as ToC (covered in Chapter 22), be sure this option is selected for every item level included in the table of contents.

  If you prefer not to have every level bookmarked, uncheck the Include in RTF Bookmarks box for each level that you want to exclude.

- **HTML Elements:** When outputting to an HTML format (including e-books), a drop-down list appears next to the Section Layout button in the header of the Formatting Editor.

  For each level in the Structure and Content table, you can assign an HTML heading style from this drop-down list.

- **Page Padding:** This option, located at the right of the Formatting Editor header, lets you designate how many lines to insert at the top of a new page following a page break.

  In most books and manuscript submissions, it's standard for each chapter to start about a third of the way down the page. Page Padding is how you add that extra space automatically.

  Windows users, click the Modify button to access the Page Padding.

  This option doesn't preview in the Formatting Editor, and it's not available for MultiMarkdown output types.

Your output has approximately six lines per inch when you use a 12-point font size (72 points per inch divided by 12 points per line). To figure out how much page padding you need, determine how many inches down the page you want to start, subtract the top margin, and then multiply the remaining inches by the number of lines per inch.

For example, if you're using a 12-point font and 1-inch margins, and you want your chapters to start one-third of the way down the page, choose 16 lines of padding (as shown in the following list):

- 72 points per inch ÷ 12 points per line = 6 lines per inch
- 11 inches per page ÷ 3 = 3.7 inches (dividing by 3 to start ⅓ of the way down the page)
- 3.7 inches − 1 inch top margin = 2.7 inches
- 2.7 inches × 6 lines per inch = 16.2 lines, rounded to 16

Overriding text and notes formatting

If you've been writing in pink Comic Sans 16-point font but want the final manuscript in black Times New Roman 12-point, you can override the format you've been using.

To enable the Editor so that you can format the Text and Notes elements, select the Override Text and Notes Formatting check box in the Structure and Content table; otherwise, the text area of the Editor is inaccessible (although the other fields are always accessible in the Formatting Editor).

For Windows users, all elements are accessible in the Editor pane; however, changes to the Text and Notes formatting aren't applied unless the Override Text and Notes Formatting check box is selected.

After you select the override option, simply click in the Text or Notes area of the Formatting Editor and make your changes by using the Format bar.

If you're outputting to e-book format, the font you choose may not appear on an e-reader because each reader has its own preferred font settings.

Inserting subtitles between elements

If you select more than one element — other than the Title — for a level in the Structure and Content table, you can add predetermined subtitles before each text-type element selected (for example, Synopsis, Notes, or Text).

This option operates on all levels in the Structure and Content table, regardless of which level is currently selected. To insert subtitles, click the Options button on the Formatting tab, and then select Insert Subtitles between Text Elements from the menu that appears. The subtitles are visible in the Formatting Editor and can be formatted like any other element.

This function is most useful for rough drafts where you want to see extra elements alongside the title and text of your scenes or chapters.

Displaying notes after the main text

By default, when you choose to include notes for an item type, they appear before the main document text. This option allows you to move the notes text below the main text. Click the Options button on the Formatting tab, and then select Place Notes after Main Text from the menu that appears.

Removing first paragraph indents

Book formatting often has the first paragraph after a title or subheading not indented. To remove first paragraph indents from your manuscript, click the Options button on the Formatting tab, and then select Remove First Paragraph Indents from in the menu that appears. These three options are enabled:

- **On New Pages Only:** When a page break has been forced either in the Contents pane or the Separators pane.

  Choose this option when you want to remove the indent from the first paragraph of a chapter.

- **At the Start of Each Document:** On the transition to a new document.

  If you're using titles at the beginning of each scene — or prefer not to indent the first scene paragraph — choose this option to remove the first paragraph indent for each document.

- **After Empty Lines and Centered Text:** This option works within a document, stripping the paragraph indent after a blank line or after centered text, such as a heading or the # separator.

  Use this option if you have large documents that contain multiple scenes or sections separated by a blank line or by centered text on its own line.

Working with chapter titles and subtitles

Many Compile presets, such as Standard Manuscript Format, are set up to number your chapters automatically. But what if you want to use chapter names rather than numbers? Or you want to add subtitles? Or part numbers?

In the Formatting Editor header, the Section Layout button (formerly Level Settings on the Mac and Title Settings in Windows) provides options for changing the text and appearance of headings. You can create auto-numbered sections, add prefixes or suffixes to a heading, and change the formatting.

The Section Layout menu has three tabs:

- **Title Prefix and Suffix:** Shown in Figure 12-9, this tab lets you designate text to appear before or after the Binder item title. You can customize the text for every level, which allows different prefixes for parts, chapters, and sections.

✔ **Title Appearance:** Called Case in Windows, this tab provides options for changing the case of the title elements.

✔ **First Page:** Formerly called Text, this tab lets you designate a number of words to make uppercase at the beginning of a new section.

If you're getting strange output — such as two titles for each chapter or chapter numbers for each scene — check the settings for each level. Even if you have Title turned off for a level, a prefix or suffix designated for that level still appears in the compilation.

If a paragraph (carriage return) character is present in the Prefix text box on the Title Prefix and Suffix tab of the Section Layout menu (see Figure 12-10), the prefix text appears on the line above the item title in your compiled output. To put the chapter number and title on the same line, delete the paragraph mark. You can also add tabs, and you must include any spacing desired between the prefix or suffix, and the title.

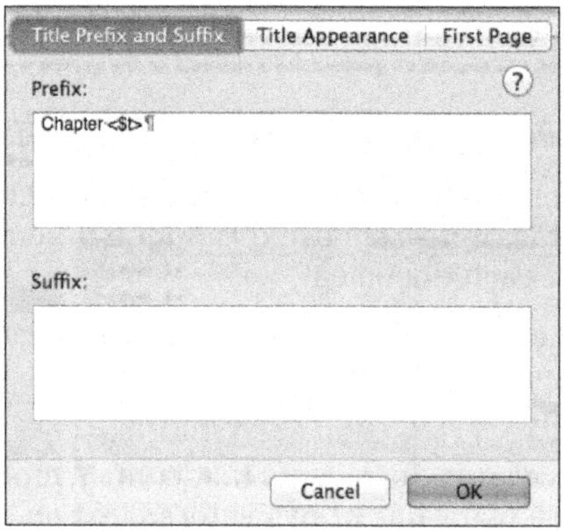

| Title Prefix and Suffix | Title Appearance | First Page |

Prefix: ⑦

Chapter<$t> ¶

Suffix:

Figure 12-10:
Setting up prefixes and suffixes.

Cancel   OK

Auto-numbering chapters, parts, and sections

To auto-number your items, you can use placeholder tags such as <$n> (for Arabic numbers, such as Chapter 1) or <$t> (for words, such as Chapter One). So, if you wanted output like Chapter One: Perfect Title (where Perfect Title is the title of the chapter in the Binder), type **Chapter <$t>:** (with a space after it) into the Prefix text box on the Title Prefix and Suffix tab of the Section Layout menu.

Auto-numbering is done sequentially by tag, so if you're trying to auto-number two different levels (for example, parts and chapters), you can either use a different tag type for each or refer to Help➪Placeholder Tags List for more options. The list also has options for restarting chapter numbering at the beginning of each book part.

Windows users can visit `https://scrivener.tenderapp.com/help/kb/windows/placeholder-tags-list` if the Placeholder Tags List doesn't appear in the Help menu.

To use auto-numbering, but not item titles, deselect Title for that level in the Structure and Content table.

Removing auto-numbered chapters, parts, and sections

By default, certain templates come preloaded with compile settings that add auto-numbered chapter titles to the compiled output.

If you want to use only the item titles you've used in the Binder — for example, because you have Prologue and Epilogue chapters — delete any text or characters in the Prefix or Suffix text box on the Title Prefix and Suffix tab of the Section Layout menu.

You can also exclude the prefix or suffix from specific documents, which I talk about in the "Excluding the prefix or suffix from the header of specific documents" section, later in this chapter.

Changing the letter case of titles

The Title Appearance tab (the Case tab in Windows), illustrated in Figure 12-11, lets you specify the case of each element of the title by selecting an option from the drop-down list next to each. Setting the letter case here means that you can use whatever case you want in the Binder.

You can choose from four case options:

- ✔ **Normal:** Uses the title as it appears in the Binder
- ✔ **Uppercase:** All capital letters
- ✔ **Faked Small Caps:** Mimics the look of small caps
- ✔ **Lowercase:** All lowercase letters

If you choose the Fake Small Caps option, the title appears in the Formatting Editor as full caps. Because many fonts don't have a small caps option, this setting mimics the look by reducing font size and capitalizing the text.

| Title Prefix and Suffix | Title Appearance | First Page |

Choose the text case for title elements.

Title: Normal

Title Prefix: Uppercase

Title Suffix: Normal

"Faked Small Caps" uppercases and reduces the font size of lowercase text in the compiled document (the preview shows plain uppercase text). "Real" small caps are only available for certain fonts (set via the Typography pane of the Font panel).

☐ Insert title as run-in head

If ticked, text following the title will be placed on the same line if possible in the final document.

Cancel   OK

Figure 12-11:
Choosing
the case for
titles.

Creating run-in headings

It might sound like a nasty collision, but a run-in heading is simply a heading that's on the same line as the main text, like the example shown in Figure 12-12. To create a run-in heading, follow these steps:

1. **Click the Section Layout button in the Formatting tab to open the Section Layout window.**

2. **Click the Title Appearance tab at the top of the window.**

3. **Select Insert Title as Run-In Head at the bottom of the window.**

   When the Insert Title as Run-In Head option is checked, any text immediately following the title (in Text, Notes, or Synopsis elements only) appears on the same line — unless the heading is too long — with a space between the title and text.

   The title retains all its character attributes, but the Text settings are used for paragraph-level settings such as indents and alignment.

Run-in headings don't appear in the Formatting Editor.

Figure 12-12:
A run-in
heading.

CHAPTER TWO

ₗSection 6.ₗI think the human brain is fascinating. As a writer who wants plot ideas on demand, it

can also be frustrating¹.

Run-in heading

Adding uppercase words at the beginning of a new section

Many novels capitalize the first word — or several words — of a new chapter or section. You can get the same effect in your compiled output. To start off each new section of text after a page break (for example, a new chapter) with uppercase words, follow these steps:

1. **From the Formatting tab of the Compile menu, click the Section Layout button.**

   The Section Layout window appears.

2. **Click the First Page tab at the top of the window.**

3. **In the Number of Words to Make Uppercase text box, type the number of words you want to capitalize.**

   For example, if you type **3** in the text box, the first sentence of a new section appears like THE SHRILL RING of the phone woke Bob from a deep sleep.

Excluding the prefix or suffix from the header of specific documents

Certain documents or folders might work best without the defined prefix or suffix. For example, if you have a Prologue or Epilogue chapter, you might want to forgo the auto-numbering and use just the document title for that chapter.

To leave off the prefix or suffix for one or more items, follow these steps:

1. **Click the Title Adjustments tab in the Compile window.**

   This tab is available only if at least one of your levels in the Formatting tab has a title prefix or suffix specified.

2. **Click the Choose button next to Do Not Add Title Prefix or Suffix to Documents.**

3. **From the drop-down list that appears, select the item to which you don't want the prefix or suffix to apply.**

4. **To pick more than one item, repeat Steps 2 and 3.**

To deselect a file, click the Choose button and click the item to remove the check mark.

Working with Some Helpful Format Options

You can find a nearly endless list of formatting options in the Compile window. The following sections highlight some of the commonly sought or misunderstood features.

Forcing one font for the entire compilation

Want to quickly change the entire compilation to a single font family (for example, Times New Roman) when you export? The quick font override lets you do just that, applying the chosen font to every element and level in the Formatting tab, the header and footer settings, footnotes, and even those documents marked to compile As-Is (which I talk about in the section "Preserving the format of a document," later in this chapter).

Overriding the font is especially useful if you like nearly everything about a Compile preset except for the font. Using this option saves you from having to make adjustments in the Formatting Editor and Page Settings just to change the font family.

Only blocks of preserved formatting remain unaffected. (I talk about preserving formatting in Chapter 6.)

The quick font override does *not* affect the font size or typeface (for example, italic or bold); therefore you may still have to adjust font size and typeface in the Formatting tab (see the section "Formatting the compiled output," earlier in this chapter).

To globally change the font for your final output, select Override All Fonts with Face in the Quick Font Override tab, and then select the desired font family from the drop-down list that appears.

Forcing a page break before a document

For non-repeating items that need to start on their own page, such as a title page, table of contents, or other front matter, follow these steps to insert a page break before the document:

1. **Click the Contents tab.**
2. **Select the Pg Break Before check box for the desired list item.**

To control the behavior for recurring items, such as chapter folders and text documents, use the Separators Option tab (covered in the "Customizing the transitions between Binder items with separators" section, later in this chapter).

It's best to force the page break only if you can't get results by using the Separators options (covered in the "Customizing the transitions between Binder items with separators" section, later in this chapter). If you save your compile format for use with other projects, the Pg Break Before settings aren't included.

Preserving the format of a document

If you have special formats applied to a document — for example, a table of contents or title page — selecting the As-Is check box on the Contents tab prevents the formatting in that item from being changed when you compile.

The one exception is if you override the font by using the Quick Font Override option (see the "Forcing one font for the entire compilation" section, earlier in this chapter).

This option tells Scrivener to ignore all the settings in the Formatting tab, so it's not intended for the entire manuscript.

You don't have to use this method for documents that have Preserve Formatting applied to a section. Scrivener doesn't override preserved formatting when you compile (see Chapter 6 for more on preserving formatting), even if you choose the Quick Font Override option.

Customizing the transitions between Binder items with separators

The Separators tab lets you choose what type of separator to include when your project transitions from one item to the next. By making selections in this tab, you only need to use the Pg Break Before option in the Contents pane for exceptions to these rules (see the "Choosing which Documents to Export" section, earlier in this chapter, for more information).

The Separators tab offers four transition types, depicted in Figure 12-13:

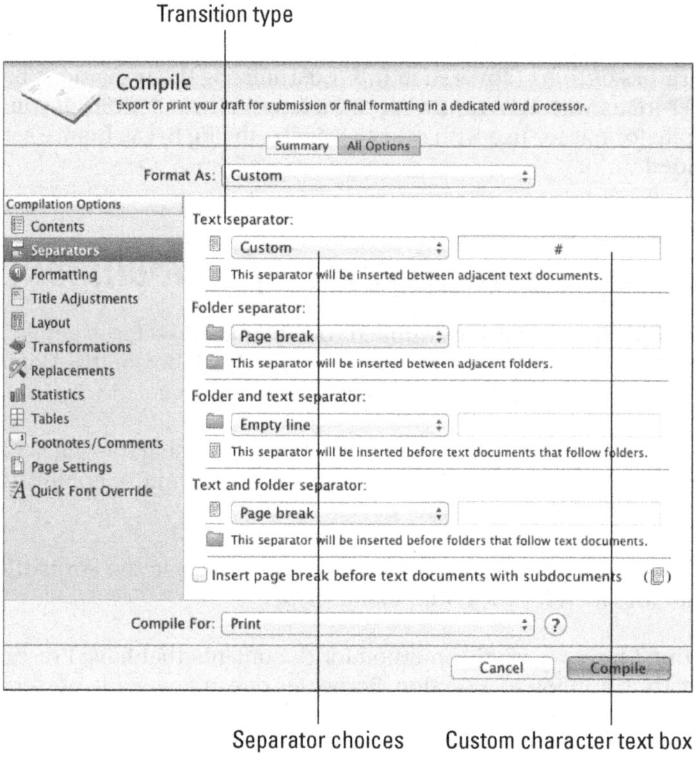

Transition type

Figure 12-13:
Specifing
transition
types in the
Separators
tab.

Separator choices   Custom character text box

- ✔ **Text Separator:** Specifies the separator for a text-type file (including file groups — text files with subdocuments) followed by another text item. For example, two scene documents in a row might require a custom character between them.

- ✔ **Folder Separator:** Designates the separator for a folder followed by another folder. A project might have a part folder followed by a chapter folder, which you want to separate with a page break.

- ✔ **Folder and Text Separator:** Lets you choose the separator for a folder followed by a text-type item. For example, a chapter folder followed by the first scene might require the seamless transition of only a single return.

- ✔ **Text and Folder Separator:** Sets up the separator for a text-type file followed by a folder. For example, the last scene in a chapter, followed by the next chapter folder, is often separated by a page break.

Each of the four transitions lets you choose the separator type from their drop-down lists. The drop-down lists offer four options:

- ✔ **Single Return:** Adds a single paragraph return, which provides a seamless transition from one item to the next with no visual break of any kind.

- ✔ **Empty Line:** Adds two paragraph returns, adding one blank line between the two items.

    If Remove First Paragraph Indents after Empty Lines and Centered Text is chosen in the Formatting options (see the "Removing first paragraph indents" section, earlier in this chapter), this option starts the second item with a non-indented paragraph.

- ✔ **Page Break:** Inserts a page break between the two items so that the following item starts on a new page.

- ✔ **Custom:** Centers the chosen character(s) on its own line between the two items.

    To add the # symbol between scenes of a book, select the Custom transition for the Text Separator, and then type # in the text box.

If you select the Insert Page Break Before Text Documents With Subdocuments check box at the bottom of the Separators pane, Scrivener inserts a page break before all file group items (meaning text-type files with subdocuments). This option is handy if you're using file groups for sections within a chapter because it allows you to force each section to start on its own page. You can also select this option if you're using file groups, rather than folders, to organize chapters or book parts, because it allows you to treat the file groups as folders, forcing a page break before each new file group.

Inserting a separator when an empty line falls on a page break

Sometimes, a scene separator falls on a page break, making it difficult to distinguish the scene break when you're using an empty line. For PDF and Print output, you can set up Scrivener to automatically insert characters on the empty line to make the scene break obvious (as shown in Figure 12-14). In the Layout tab, select Replace Empty Line Separators that Fall across Pages, and then change the characters in the text box, if you want.

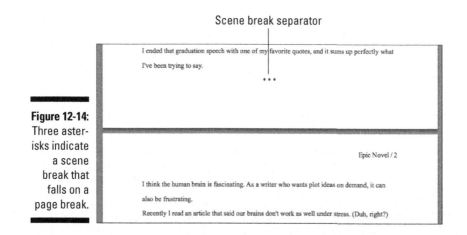

Scene break separator

Figure 12-14:
Three aster-
isks indicate
a scene
break that
falls on a
page break.

Adding an end-of-text marker

It's common practice to add some kind of marker to the end of your output. For a magazine article, you might use Ends. Scrivener's Novel format adds <<<<>>>> to the end of a manuscript.

If you want to use a character or set of characters to denote the end of the exported file, click the Layout tab (Transformations in Windows), select Mark End of Text With, and then enter the desired character(s) in the text box.

To remove an existing marker, deselect the Mark End of Text With check box.

Formatting your output into columns

Want your compiled document to be displayed in columns, much like a newspaper or magazine? If you're exporting to Rich Text (.rtf – Word Compatible) or Microsoft Word 97–2004 (.doc) output types, you can add columns by following these steps:

1. **Click the Layout tab, and then select Use Columns.**

2. **Click the Start Columns drop-down list and select where to start columns within your compilation.**

   You can choose from one of the following options:

   - *On First Page:* Start columns from the very first document.

   - *After First Document:* If your first document is a title page or other text that shouldn't be in columns, select this option.

   - *After Front Matter:* Select this option to start columns after the items in your Front Matter folder.

3. **Click the Number of Columns drop-down list, and then select the desired number of columns.**

4. **Click the Space between Columns drop-down list, and then select the desired amount of spacing between each column.**

Removing footnotes from compiled output

To remove footnotes (covered in Chapter 11) when compiling your manuscript, click the Footnotes/Comments tab (Footnotes/Annotations in Windows), and then select Remove Footnotes.

For output types that don't support footnotes, footnotes are converted to endnotes — or something approximating endnotes — when you compile, unless you remove them first.

Converting footnotes to endnotes

For output types that support it, you can convert footnotes of either type (inline or linked) to endnotes during the compile process. In fact, because they're treated separately, you can convert one type to endnotes and leave the other as footnotes (see Chapter 11 for more on footnotes). You might want to convert footnotes to endnotes if you want to use a word processor that doesn't support footnotes.

Converting footnotes affects only the compilation, not the footnotes within your Scrivener project. Convert them by following these steps:

1. **Click the Footnotes/Comments tab.**

   You click the Footnotes/Annotations tab in Windows.

2. **If necessary, deselect Remove Footnotes to enable the footnote options.**

3. **Choose an option, depending on which type of footnotes you used and what operating system you use.**

   Here are your options:

   - *Export Inspector Footnotes as Endnotes:* Mac only. For linked footnotes (those appearing in the Comments & Footnotes pane of the Inspector).

   - *Export Inline Footnotes as Endnotes:* Mac only. For inline footnotes (those embedded in the text in gray bubbles).

   - *Endnotes:* In Windows, select Endnotes in the Export to RTF drop-down list.

Exporting comments and annotations for use in Word

If compiling to Rich Text (.rtf – Word Compatible) or Microsoft Word 97–2004 (.doc) output types, you can turn linked comments and inline annotations into comments that are visible when in Microsoft Word. (See Chapter 10 for more about comments and annotations.)

For this conversion to work properly with the Microsoft Word 97–2004 (.doc) output type, the Microsoft .doc setting in the Scrivener Preferences Import/Export pane must be set to Export as RTF-Based .doc File, which is the default.

Make comments and annotations — which can be treated separately — compatible by following these steps:

1. **Click the Footnotes/Comments tab.**

   Windows users, click the Footnotes/Annotations tab.

2. **In the Comments and Annotations section, deselect the check boxes for the items that you want to retain.**

   Deselecting these options prevents the comments or annotations from being deleted from the final output during the compile process:

   - *Remove Inspector Comments:* Mac only

   - *Remove Inline Annotations:* Mac only

   - *Remove Annotations:* Windows only

3. **From the Export To RTF As drop-down list, select Margin Comments.**

   This option appears as simply Comments in Windows.

If for some reason the preceding steps don't work for you, try exporting as inline comments, as described in the following section.

Exporting comments and annotations as inline comments

Generally, you want Scrivener to strip the inline comments and annotations from your final output, especially for submissions, but if you want to include them, you can embed them directly into the text, surrounded by your choice of characters to set them off from the rest of the text.

For output types that support text color, the comments are colored to match the annotation or comment color in the manuscript.

To export inline comments and annotations, follow these steps:

1. **Click the Footnotes/Comments tab.**

   Windows users, select the Footnotes/Annotations tab.

2. **Deselect the check boxes for the items that you want to retain.**

   Deselecting these options prevents the comments or annotations from being deleted from the final output during the compile process:

   - *Remove Inspector Comments:* Mac only

   - *Remove Inline Annotations:* Mac only

   - *Remove Annotations:* Windows only

3. **From the Export to RTF As drop-down list, choose Inline Comments.**

   Windows users, choose Comments.

   Don't want comments and annotations inline with the text or in the margin, but still want them in your final output? Export them as footnotes or endnotes by choosing either Footnotes or Endnotes from the drop-down list.

4. **In the Enclosing Markers text boxes, enter the characters that you want to use to enclose the comments.**

   Windows users don't have this option. The comments are surrounded by square brackets and colored, if color is supported.

   If you're using Web Page (.html) or MultiMarkdown⇨LaTeX output types, you can insert open and close syntax for HTML comments as the enclosing characters.

Setting the margins

You can set the compilation's page margins as part of the compile settings if you're using one of the following output types: Print, PDF, either of the Rich Text options, both Microsoft Word options, or Open Office (.odt). Follow these steps:

1. **Click the Page Settings tab.**

2. **If necessary, deselect Use Project Page Setup Settings.**

This option appears only in the Mac version. When you deselect it, the Margins section is enabled.

3. **Enter the desired value for each margin in the corresponding text boxes: Top, Bottom, Left, and Right.**

4. **Select your measurement type from the drop-down list next to each margin text box.**

In Windows, select from the Units list at the bottom of the Margins section.

You can choose from centimeters, inches, or points.

Adjusting how word and character counts are calculated

Some project templates include a title page with a placeholder tag (see the following section for more on placeholder tags) that tallies the manuscript's word count when you compile. To adjust the text elements that are included in the word count, click the Statistics tab, and then select accordingly from the menu of elements to include.

Customizing Headers and Footers

Need to add a header or footer to your compiled file? Want to edit or delete one that's already specified by the compile format you chose?

The Header and Footer settings are available as long as you've chosen an output type that supports them: Print, PDF, Rich Text (.rtf), or Microsoft Word 97–2004 (.doc).

In addition to regular text, the header and footer allow the use of special character tags that are replaced with a value during the compile process. Here's a sampling of the special tags available for use (for more tags, choose Help➪Placeholder Tags List or consult the Scrivener User Manual):

✓ <$p>: Inserts the page number

✓ <$pagecount>: Inserts the total number of pages

✓ <$projecttitle>: Uses the title specified in Project Properties (shown in Figure 12-15), or if none is specified, uses the name of the Scrivener project file

✔ **<$surname>:** Takes the surname from the Project Properties or the author's Address Book entry

✔ **<$fullname>:** Inserts the full name from the Project Properties or the author's Address Book entry

For character-based tags (including Roman numerals), you can type them in all caps to get an uppercase result (for example, <$PROJECTTITLE> produces EPIC NOVEL).

Some of the information is pulled from the Project Properties window (shown in Figure 12-15), which you can access by choosing Project➪Meta-Data Settings➪Project Properties. Scrivener displays the default values in gray text, but you can click in any text box to overwrite the default. The tag next to each text box is the one that you can use in the Header/Footer section, if desired.

The benefit of using a tag in the header or footer, rather than just entering the actual value of something like the project title, is that if you change your project title at a later date, it automatically updates the header. It also updates the information if you decide to use a pseudonym or different version of your name.

Plus, if you set up and save your own Compile format (covered in Chapter 13), using tags prevents you from having to edit the settings when you use the saved Compile format in a different project.

Property value   Tag

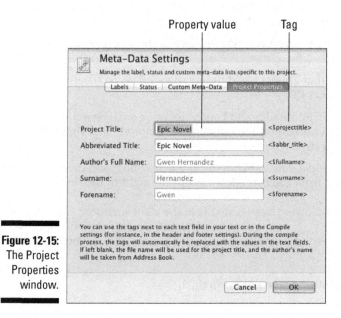

Figure 12-15:
The Project
Properties
window.

You can also format the header and footer text by bracketing it with special characters:

- **Italic:** asterisk (*); typing `*text*` produces *text*
- **Bold:** double asterisk (**); typing `**text**` produces **text**
- **Underline:** underscore (_); typing `_text_` produces <u>text</u>

Adding or modifying a header or footer

Follow these steps to add a header or footer, or modify the existing one, in the Compile settings:

1. **Click the Page Settings tab.**

2. **If the Header/Footer section isn't visible, change your output type to one of the compatible types.**

   Compatible types include Print, PDF, Rich Text (.rtf), and Microsoft Word 97–2004 (.doc).

   Figure 12-16 shows the Header/Footer section.

3. **Click the Header and Footer button to view header and footer options.**

   This button appears only in the Mac version. The grayed out text within the text boxes doesn't appear in the final output, it's just there to remind you how to format the text or add special tags, such as page number. Any text in black will print.

4. **Enter or edit the desired text and/or tags in the appropriate text boxes.**

   The text boxes that appear are different, depending on whether you use a Mac or Windows PC:

   - *Mac users:* The Header and Footer sections each have three text boxes that correspond to left-aligned, centered, and right-aligned text, respectively.

   - *Windows users:* Enter text in the single text box, and then select the alignment from the drop-down list to the right of the text box.

In Figure 12-16, the following header text is in the right text box: `<$surname>` / `<$PROJECTTITLE>` / `<$p>`. Based on the data in the Project Properties, the header on the second page of the compiled manuscript will be Hernandez / EPIC NOVEL / 2.

For no header or footer, delete all text in the boxes.

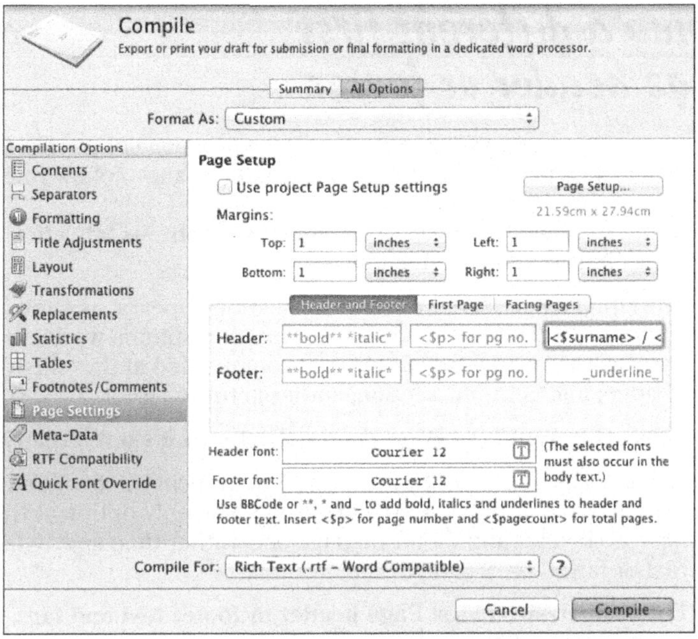

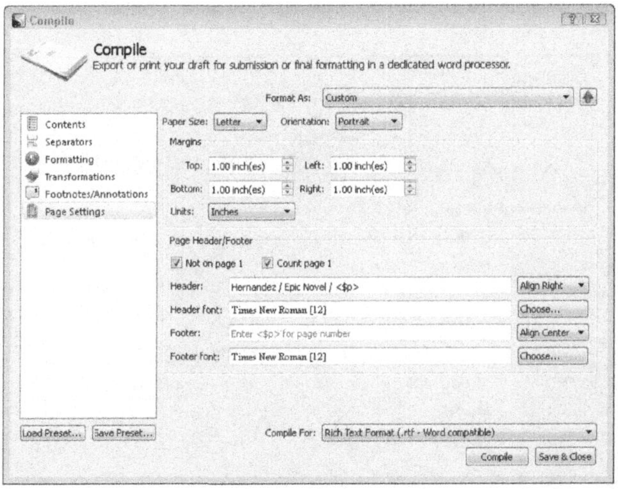

Figure 12-16:
Specifying a right-aligned header on the Mac (top) and in Windows (bottom).

Using a different first page header or footer

To create a different header or footer on the first page of your compilation — even if it's just a page with no header or footer at all — follow these steps:

1. **In the Header/Footer section of the Page Settings tab, click the First Pages button (on the Mac only).**

   The First Pages Header and Footer section appears, as shown in Figure 12-17. The text boxes and formatting options work exactly the same as the Header and Footer section outlined in the "Customizing Headers and Footers" section, earlier in this chapter.

2. **Select Different First Page Header/Footer, if it's not already checked.**

   Windows users, select Not on Page 1 to prevent the header and footer settings from applying to the first page. The only option at this time is to have no header and footer on page one, rather than specifying different text or tags.

3. **Enter the desired First Page header or footer text and tags, or leave them blank to have no header or footer on the first page.**

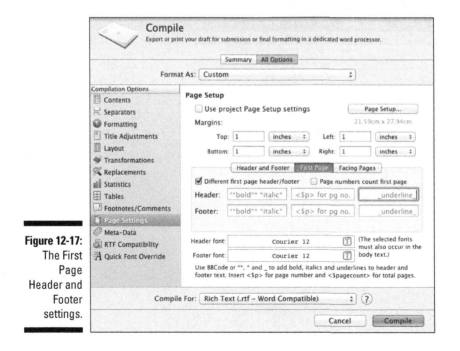

Figure 12-17:
The First Page Header and Footer settings.

Starting the page count on the first page

If you're using a different header or footer for the first page but you still want the page count to start with the first page of the first document — even if you don't want a page number to appear — follow these steps:

1. **If you're using a Mac, click the First Pages button in the Header/Footer section of the Page Settings tab.**

2. **If it's not already checked, select Different First Page Header/Footer.**

   Windows users, select Not on Page 1.

3. **Select Page Numbers Count First Pages.**

   Select Count Page 1 in Windows.

For page numbers to show up on any of the pages, you must have specified them in the Header and Footer section, as described in the "Customizing Headers and Footers" section, earlier in this chapter.

Making Text Conversions

Not all software programs play nicely with Rich Text, and some publishers have strict guidelines regarding the use of special characters (for example, em-dashes and ellipses) and formatting (such as italics).

By dealing with these differing needs in Compile, you can write the way you want because these options affect only the compiled output, not your writing in Scrivener.

The following sections run through the options for converting special characters and formats during the compile process so that you don't have to worry about it while writing. You can make all these changes in the Transformation tab.

Converting special characters to plain-text versions

Some special characters — such as em-dashes, smart (curly) quotes, and ellipses — aren't compatible with plain text editors or the Plain Text Screenplay Compile format that you can use to export to Celtx or Movie Magic Screenwriter.

If you're outputting to a plain text format, or even to Rich Text Format, you can convert special characters to their plain text–friendly counterparts. Just select the desired conversions from the options that appear in the Transformation tab.

If you select the Convert to Plain Text option, Scrivener enables a drop-down list that lets you substitute spaces and carriage returns for indents and paragraph spacing:

- ✔ **Paragraph Spacing:** Approximates paragraph spacing by inserting carriage returns.

  The number of carriage returns to insert is determined by dividing the paragraph spacing value by the base font size and then rounding to the nearest whole number. So, if the base font is 12 and the paragraph spacing is set to 22, two carriage returns are inserted between paragraphs (22 ÷ 12 = 1.8, rounded to 2).

- ✔ **Paragraph Spacing and Indents:** Adds paragraph spacing, as well as inserting spaces in place of indents.

  This feature works only with first-line indenting and can't simulate block quotes or hanging indents. For more complicated indents and formats, use one of the following options.

- ✔ **All Whitespace:** Except in full justification alignment, this setting attempts to maintain all whitespace, including alignment; all types of indents (left and right); block quotes; and so on.

- ✔ **All Whitespace (Add a One Inch Margin):** Does the same as the All Whitespace option, but adds ten spaces to the left of every line.

Changing character formatting

Does the publisher you're submitting to require you to change italics into underlined words? Want to remove hyperlinks from Internet addresses? Need to strip out highlighter colors? This list covers these and other options for modifying character formatting during the compile process:

- ✔ **Deleting struck-through text:** If you used strike-through formatting to denote text to delete, either by using revision marking (see Chapter 20 for more on revisions) or on your own, you can force Scrivener to strip it out during the compile process by selecting Delete Struck-Through Text.

- ✔ **Converting italics to underlines:** Want to use italics while writing, but need to submit them as underlined text? Let Scrivener convert them for you. You must be using a Rich Text output type (all except Plain Text, Final Draft 5–7, and the MultiMarkdown types). You simply select Convert Italics to Underlines.

✓ **Converting underlines to italics:** If you've been using underlines to represent italicized words but want the compiled output to use italics, select Convert Underlines to Italics. This option is available for Rich Text output types (all except Plain Text, Final Draft 5–7, and the MultiMarkdown options).

✓ **Removing highlighter colors:** If you've been marking up your text with highlighter colors but don't want the color to appear in the compiled output, select Remove Highlighting. This option is available for Rich Text output types (all except Plain Text, Final Draft 5–7, and the MultiMarkdown options).

✓ **Converting hyperlinks to standard text:** Got hyperlinks? Want them to print out as normal text, like the rest of the compilation? Set Scrivener to remove the hyperlinks from the text during the compile process by selecting Remove All Hyperlinks. This option works for Rich Text output types (all except Plain Text, Final Draft 5–7, and the MultiMarkdown options).

Formatting Your E-Book

The compile options in the following sections are specific to the ePub and Kindle output types.

Adding a cover

Despite advice to the contrary, books are always judged by their covers. Luckily, Scrivener makes it easy to insert cover art for your e-book. The design is up to you.

The cover image is displayed at the beginning of the book, before the table of contents or any other front matter, and as a thumbnail on the virtual bookshelf on most e-readers.

The image you plan to use must be imported into the Scrivener project before you can add it as a cover (see Chapter 2 for more on importing).

Keep in mind a couple of things when choosing or creating cover images:

✓ **Image Type:** The image should be an RGB-based raster format (for example, PNG, TIFF, or JPEG), not a vector format (such as EPS). Also, don't use the CMYK color model, which is better for high-quality printing.

✓ **Image Size:** 800 pixels tall by 600 pixels wide at 72 DPI is ideal for a clean display without unnecessarily inflating the e-book size. Large files can cause memory problems for e-reader devices and make the file difficult to send via e-mail.

To add a cover to your e-book, click the Cover tab and click the Cover Image drop-down list to view all images located in your Binder. You must import the desired image to the Binder if you want it to appear in the list.

The following options appear only for ePub output:

- **For Reading in iBooks Only:** Select this option if you're compiling for use in iBooks (but not delivering via iTunes Producer). This option adds additional information that iTunes needs to create the thumbnail for the bookshelf.

  This is a good option for proofreading your work on the iPad, but if you're submitting your work to iTunes Producer, leave it unchecked so that Producer can create its own thumbnail information.

- **Cover Page Title:** Enter the title of the cover page as you want it to appear in the table of contents (not the title of your book). The default is Cover.

- **SVG (Advanced):** Click this button to insert SVG code that can be used with or rather than a bitmap image. Be sure to maintain the correct aspect ratio to avoid a distorted image. SVG isn't compatible with iBooks. If you don't know what SVG code is, you can safely ignore this option.

Adding document properties for e-books

Document properties added for e-books populate the description fields used by most e-readers. Some readers take only Title and Author, but many desktop readers and services (such as Adobe Digital Editions and Calibre) use all the data you provide.

Add the properties by clicking the Meta-Data tab and then entering the desired data into the appropriate text boxes. Keep in mind these tips:

- **Authors:** Enter the author name(s). The EPUB format supports multiple authors and individual author searches on books with more than one author. If the book has more than one author, separate them by a semicolon so that each is registered separately.

  The Kindle exporter exports only the first author name if you separate the names with semicolons. To include all author names, insert a space or comma between each name, rather than a semicolon.

- **Language Code:** Be sure to use the correct ISO standard two-letter language code. For English, it's **en**. (Windows users, select the correct language from the drop-down list.)

  Find the list of language codes at www.loc.gov/standards/iso639-2/php/code_list.php.

> ✓ **Custom Identifier:** If you have a custom identifier from your publisher (for example, an ISBN), select Use Custom Unique Identifier and enter it in the text box. Otherwise, Scrivener creates a unique identifier — required for published e-books — when you compile.

Increasing the navigation dots on the Kindle progress bar

The Kindle uses the top levels of the table of contents to create the navigation dots in the progress bar. To create more navigation dots (one for each item in the Binder), you must flatten the list so that every item is considered a top-level file.

To create a flat (nonhierarchical) list of the Binder items, click the Layout tab, and then select Use Flat List of Contents in Navigation Controls (NCX).

Setting Up Scripts for Export

If you're exporting a screenplay or script for use in Final Draft 8 (.fdx) and the first document is a title page without script formatting, you can assign the document to Final Draft's Title Page window, keeping it separate the from the rest of the script. Just click the Script Settings tab, and then select First Document Is Title Page.

If you're not using a title page and the first page of your script is missing when you open the FDX file in Final Draft, deselect this option.

You can convert inline and linked footnotes, as well as inline annotations and linked comments, to Final Draft 8 script notes. If you don't convert them, they're stripped from the compiled document. Simply select an option in the Script Settings tab to specify the conversion:

> ✓ **Footnotes:** Select Include Footnotes as Script Notes.
>
> ✓ **Annotations and comments:** Select Include Comments and Annotations as Script Notes.

Chapter 13

Exporting Your Project with Compile

. . . .

In This Chapter

▶ Choosing a compile method

▶ Looking at your output

▶ Preserving the latest compile settings

▶ Customizing compile format presets

▶ Setting up an e-book for export

▶ Creating other types of output

. . . .

*A*fter you pick out the compile settings — as covered in Chapter 12 — compiling is a simple matter of clicking a button. But what about next time? You don't want to go through all those options again, right? And after your work is transformed, then what?

This chapter walks you through the act of compiling and viewing your work, shows you how to save your settings for future use, helps you set up your project to export as an e-book, and reviews other output options.

Compiling Your Project

Compiling is simply taking the many items in your Binder — those in the Manuscript (Draft) folder — and turning them into a single, polished file in the output type of your choice. You can make that happen in a couple of ways:

✔ **Summary mode:** The simplest way to compile your project is with the Summary option, shown in Figure 13-1. The Summary tab is set up to let you output your project with a minimum of fuss or adjustments, so it contains a limited number of settings.

On the flip side, using the Summary option precludes most customization, so you may not get exactly what you're looking for.

If you're more comfortable playing with the final format in your word processor, Summary mode can get you close to what you want, and then you can tweak it in your word processor.

✔ **All Options mode:** If you want to have more control about how your file looks after the compile process, you need to work with the compilation options in the All Options mode.

Follow these steps to compile:

1. **Choose File➪Compile.**

   The Compile window opens.

2. **Click the appropriate button to view the options you want to see.**

   On a Windows PC, you click the Expansion button to view or hide the options.

   If you click Summary, your window should look like Figure 13-1. If you click All Options, you see a window like in Figure 13-2, but the available choices vary depending on your format and output types selections.

3. **Select the desired format from the Format As drop-down list and the output type from the Compile For drop-down list at the bottom of the window.**

4. **If you're in All Options mode, configure your project by using the Compilation tabs along the left side of the window.**

   See Chapter 12 for more on formats, output types, and compilation options.

5. **Click Compile.**

   The Export window appears. Or, if you chose the Print output in Step 3, the Print window appears.

6. **Choose the desired location from the file list at the left, enter a filename in the Save As text box, and then click Export.**

Figure 13-1:
The Compile window in Summary mode on the Mac (top) and in Windows (bottom).

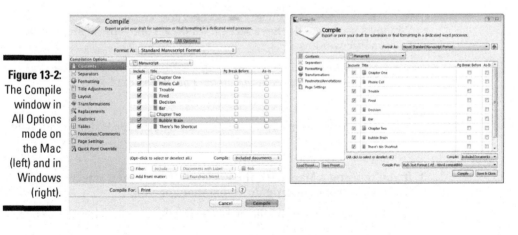

Figure 13-2:
The Compile window in All Options mode on the Mac (left) and in Windows (right).

Viewing and Previewing the Output

After your project is compiled and saved, you can view it in a program compatible with the output type you selected.

But what if you want to see the results of your settings before you export? You may want to double-check your output, especially if you're going to print. No need to waste all that paper, or keep creating and overwriting files on your hard drive.

Scrivener has a kind of try-before-you-buy option that lets you take a look before you commit. It works only for settings compatible with the Print output type, but that still covers most of the format, layout, and page settings, as well as footnotes, separators, and text conversions.

Follow these steps to preview your work after you specify the compilations options (as described in Chapter 12):

1. **Select the Print output type from the Compile For drop-down list in the Compile window.**

   Windows users, select the PDF output type.

2. **Click Compile.**

   The Print window opens on the Mac.

   Windows users see the Save As PDF window. Follow these steps in the Save as PDF window:

   a. Choose a location to save your file from the list on the left, and then type the desired name in the File Name text box.

   b. Click Save.

   A window pops up to notify you when the file is done compiling.

   c. Click OK.

3. **If you're using a Mac, click the PDF button, and then select Open PDF in Preview from the drop-down list that appears.**

   Windows users, open the file in Adobe Reader X or another PDF reader program of your choice.

   The Preview program opens to display your output.

If you're a Windows user, you can compile to the Preview output type for a quick view of your compilation without saving to a file, but the Preview option doesn't display elements such as headers and footers, page breaks, or margins.

Saving and Resetting Compile Settings

You've worked really hard to get your output absolutely perfect, but if you close the Compile window without compiling (or saving), your settings revert back to what they were when you first opened the window.

The good news is you can save your settings so that they'll be there the next time you open the Compile window.

Saving compile settings without compiling the project

The Compile window defaults to the last compiled settings, but if you make changes and then exit without compiling, the changes you made during the session are lost. (See the section "Compiling Your Project," earlier in this chapter, for how to specify these settings.) No worries, though. You can save the settings without compiling.

Press and hold the Option key to make the Compile button change to a Save button (the Cancel button also changes to Reset), and then click Save. Windows users, click Save & Close.

The Compile window closes, but next time you open it, your settings will still be there, even though you didn't compile the project.

Resetting the compile settings

Been fooling around with the compile settings and wish you could just go back to what you had when you opened the window? No problem, you can roll things back, even if you don't remember which preset you originally had.

Press and hold the Option key to change the Cancel button to Reset (the Compile button also changes to Save). Click the Reset button.

Your changes revert back to the last saved compile settings (saved either manually or by running compile, as discussed in the section "Compiling Your Project," earlier in this chapter).

At this time, there's no easy way to roll back the changes in Windows unless you remember the format preset you started with; however, a Cancel button is in the works for a future version.

If you remember the format preset you started with, you can just choose that preset again to reset the settings. Or click Cancel to close the window without saving your changes, and then reopen it.

Creating and Deleting Compile Format Presets

Scrivener comes preloaded with a nice selection of compile format presets (covered in detail in Chapter 12), but you can also add (and delete) your own.

If you spent a lot of time getting the settings just right — and maybe you can't remember all the steps you took to get there — you probably want to avoid starting over next time you want the same format. That's when saving your own format preset comes in handy.

The best part is that your saved presets are available for all your Scrivener projects.

Saving your compile settings as a custom format

A *format preset* is basically a saved setting that includes all the compilation options and the output type.

If you have your compile settings perfectly tuned and don't want to lose them, you can go beyond the basic save-for-next-time approach outlined in the "Saving compile settings without compiling the project" section, earlier in this chapter. Instead, you can create your own preset with exactly the settings you want and use it again any time on any project.

Follow these steps to create your own compile preset in the Compile window:

1. **From the Format As drop-down list select Manage Compile Format Presets.**

2. **Click the plus sign (+) button in the bottom-right corner of the window that appears.**

   Windows users, simply click the Save Preset button at the bottom-left of the Compile window.

   A small pop-up window appears.

3. **Type a descriptive name in the Enter a Name for This Compile Format text box, and then click OK.**

   The pop-up window closes.

4. **If you're a Mac user, click OK to close the Manage Compile Format Presets window.**

   Scrivener saves the current settings with the name you entered.

5. **Click the Format As drop-down list.**

   The preset appears in the My Formats section of the list that opens, and it's now available for all projects.

Deleting a custom compile format

Did you get a little too preset-happy? Need to delete an old format you never use? No worries. Just follow these steps:

1. **In the Compile window, click the Format As drop-down list, and then select Manage Compile Format Presets.**

   Windows users, click the Load Preset button at the bottom-left of the Compile window.

   The Presets window opens.

2. **Select the preset that you want to delete.**

   Mac users, click the text to highlight the line, not the check box.

3. **Click the minus sign (–) button at the bottom-right of the Presets window, and then click OK.**

   Windows users, click the Delete button, and then click Yes.

   A warning window appears asking if you really want to delete the preset.

4. **Click OK.**

   Windows users, click Yes.

   The preset is removed from the list.

5. **Click OK to close the Presets window.**

6. **Click the Format As drop-down list in the Compile window.**

   The preset no longer appears on the list that opens.

You can delete only the presets you created, not those installed with Scrivener. However, the following section shows you how to hide presets.

Revealing or hiding compile presets

Scrivener offers even more compile presets than you see on your list in the Compile window. Some of them are presets from earlier Scrivener versions, and some of them are simply less popular. And although you can't delete the predefined presets that came with the program, you can hide the ones you don't use. You can also hide presets that you've created, instead of deleting them.

Follow these steps to reveal or hide a compile preset:

1. **In the Compile window, click the Format As drop-down list and select Manage Compile Format Presets.**

   The Manage Compile Format Presets window appears.

2. **Select or deselect a preset from the list of presets to show or hide it, respectively.**

3. **Click the OK button to save your changes and close the window.**

4. **Click the Format As drop-down list to see your changes.**

Exporting for E-Books

Thinking of self-publishing? Want to do a read-through of your manuscript on your Nook? Maybe your critique partner wants to read your next chapter on her Kindle.

Scrivener has you covered with output options for ePub (Nook, iPad, Sony, and other popular e-readers) and MOBI (Kindle) formats. During the compile process, Scrivener even generates a table of contents, including all items that have a section break (for example, a page break before a new chapter).

Compiling for ePub

ePub is the most popular format for non-Kindle e-books, and it's compatible with most e-reader devices and desktop reading software programs. Follow these steps to create an EPUB file from your manuscript:

1. **Choose File⇨Compile.**

   The Compile window opens.

2. **If necessary, click All Options to see the compilation options tabs.**

   On a Windows PC, click the Expansion button.

3. **Select E-Book from the Format As drop-down list.**

   The Compile For output type changes to ePub eBook (.epub), and the relevant compilation options tabs appear along the left side of the Compile window.

4. **In the Contents tab, choose the content to include (as outlined in Chapter 12).**

5. **Adjust the other options, as desired.**

   See Chapter 12 for more on compile options.

   Some key options tabs that you may want to make adjustments in are Separators (to add transitions between item types), Cover (because readers will judge it), Formatting (to determine the format of titles and text), Layout (if you want an additional HTML table of contents that includes hyperlinks), and Meta-Data (to fill in the book's title, author, and other information).

6. **Click Compile.**

   The Export window opens.

7. **Choose the desired location from the file list at the left, enter a filename for your e-book in the Save As text box, and then click Export.**

Validating your ePub file

No need to guess if your shiny new EPUB file works. You can validate the file to make sure it adheres to the ePub standards by following these steps:

1. **Go to** `http://validator.idpf.org`.

2. **Click Choose File.**

3. **In the File Upload window that appears, select the EPUB file you just compiled, and then click Open.**

   The filename appears in the text box below Submit an EPUB Document for Validation, as shown in Figure 13-3.

4. **Click Validate.**

   After a few seconds (or longer for a larger file or slower connection), a Results page appears, showing whether the file has any problems.

Uploaded file

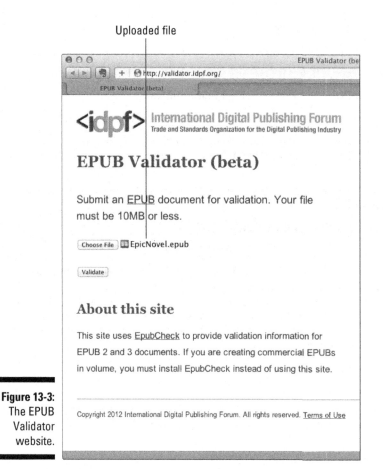

Figure 13-3:
The EPUB
Validator
website.

Keep in mind that the validator doesn't tell you whether the formatting will look good on e-reader devices. If you don't have an e-reader, download software such as Adobe Digital Editions (www.adobe.com/products/digitaleditions), shown in Figure 13-4, so that you can get a feel for the format of your book — and make changes to the compile settings, if necessary — before you send it out.

Chances are you'll have to go back to Compile a few times and make some adjustments to get exactly the look you want. Just remember that your book may look slightly different on each e-reader.

To view your EPUB file on your iPad, simply drag the file into iTunes.

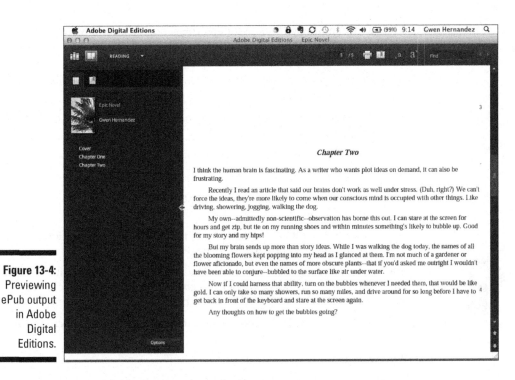

Figure 13-4:
Previewing
ePub output
in Adobe
Digital
Editions.

Compiling for Kindle

Amazon's Kindle has its own proprietary file type: `.mobi`. Follow these steps to create a MOBI file from your manuscript:

1. **Choose File⇨Compile.**

   The Compile window opens.

2. **If necessary, click All Options (Mac) to see the compilation options tabs.**

   Windows users, click the Expansion button.

3. **From the Format As drop-down list, select E-Book.**

   The Compile For output type changes to ePub eBook (.epub), and the relevant compilation options tabs appear along the left side of the Compile window.

4. **From the Compile For drop-down list, select Kindle eBook (.mobi).**

You can't compile without installing the KindleGen tool, which lets Scrivener convert your file to the MOBI format. If you haven't installed KindleGen, follow these steps:

a. *Go to* www.amazon.com/kindlepublishing *and download the KindleGen version appropriate for your computer.*

   Save the downloaded file somewhere safe and appropriate, such as the Applications or Program Files folder.

b. *From the KindleGen tab in the Compile window, click Choose.*

   The Open window appears.

c. *Navigate to the KindleGen executable file you just downloaded, and then click Open.*

   The KindleGen pane displays the location of the KindleGen executable, as shown in Figure 13-5.

Mac users: KindleGen runs only on Mac computers running Intel processors and Mac OS X 10.5 or higher. To check whether your machine has Intel, choose ⌘⇨About This Mac, and then look next to Processor.

5. **Choose the content to include from the Contents tab (as discussed in Chapter 12).**

6. **Adjust your settings, as desired.**

   See Chapter 12 for more on the settings you can change.

   Some key options tabs that you may want to make adjustments in are Separators (to add transitions between item types), Cover (because every book needs a cover), Formatting (to determine the format of titles and text), and Meta-Data (to fill in the book's title, author, and other information).

   If you want to adjust the number of navigation dots that appears on the Kindle progress bar, check out Chapter 12.

7. **Click Compile.**

   The Export window opens.

8. **Choose the desired location from the file list, enter a filename for your e-book in the Save As text box, and then click Export.**

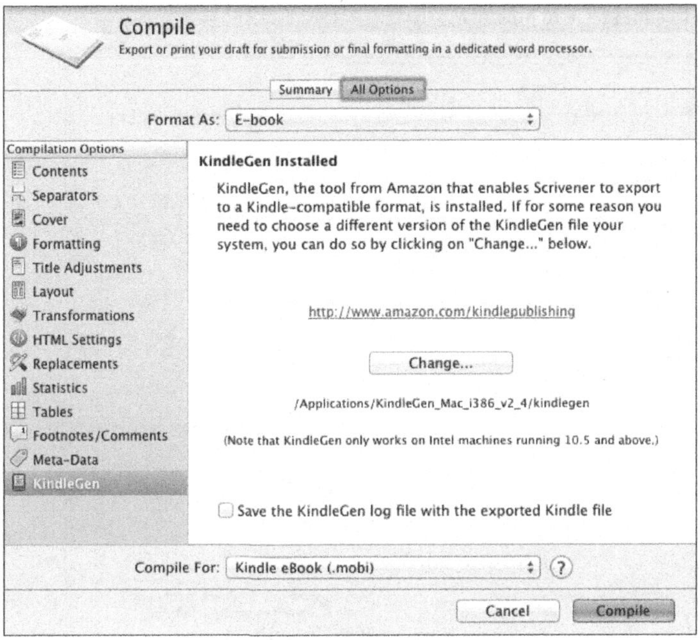

Figure 13-5:
The
KindleGen
pane.

Previewing your Kindle file

To ensure that your MOBI file is properly formatted, you can use the Kindle Previewer to see how your book appears on Kindle devices and apps. Just follow these steps:

1. **Go to** www.amazon.com/kindlepublishing.

2. **In the Resources section, click Kindle Previewer.**

3. **On the Kindle Previewer page that appears, click the appropriate button to download the version for your computer.**

4. **Save the application to your hard drive.**

   I recommend you save in Applications or Program Files because this application is a piece of software.

5. **Open the Kindle Previewer.**

   A window like the one shown in Figure 13-6 appears.

Click to choose file to preview

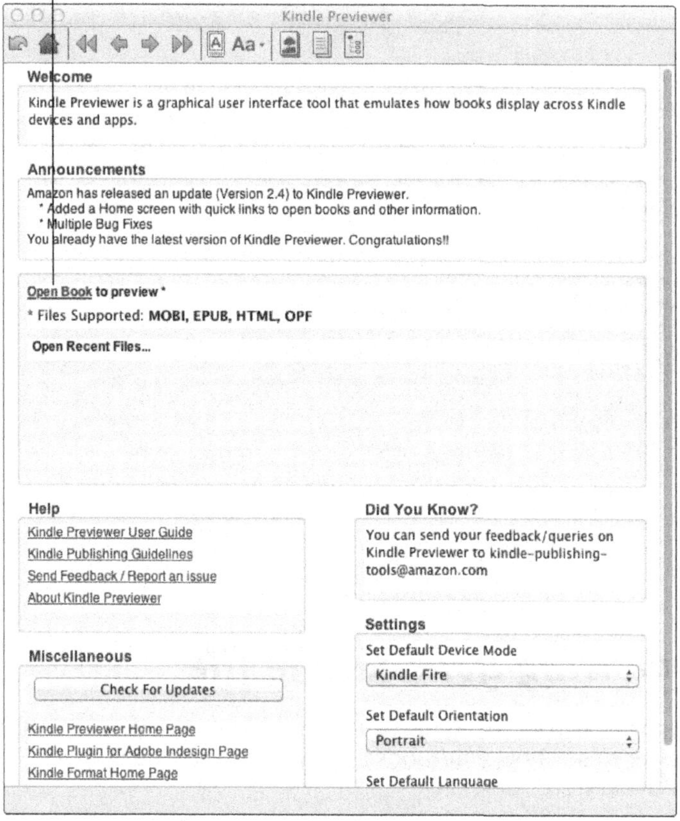

Figure 13-6:
The Kindle
Previewer
main
window.

6. **Select the device to preview from the Set Default Device Mode drop-down list, in the Settings section.**

7. **Click the Open Book to Preview link in the middle of the window.**

8. **Choose the MOBI file you created from Open Kindle Book window that appears, and then click Open.**

    Your book opens in the Previewer, like in Figure 13-7. Use the arrows at the top to navigate through the file, and the Home button to return to the main window (refer to Figure 13-6).

9. **If you see any formatting problems, you can go back into Compile to fix them and then preview again.**

10. **Repeat Step 9 until your book looks good on all the desired Kindle devices and apps.**

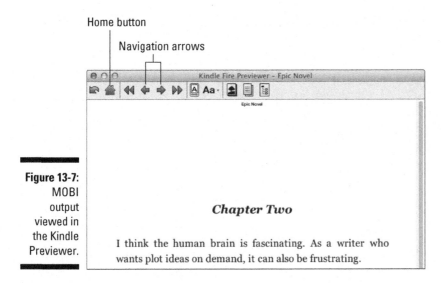

Home button

Navigation arrows

Figure 13-7:
MOBI
output
viewed in
the Kindle
Previewer.

Exporting Special Types of Output

In addition to exporting your project file as a compilation of your writing, you can create outlines, a Synopsis list, or a collection of document notes in the Compile window (which you can open by choosing File➪Compile).

Follow these steps:

1. **From the Format As drop-down list, select the appropriate option.**

   Here are your choices:

   - *Enumerated Outline:* A numbered list of documents in hierarchy fashion; see Figure 13-8

   - *Synopses and Titles:* A list of Binder items and their Synopses, shown in Figure 13-9

   - *Synopsis Outline:* Similar to Synopses and Titles, but the outline doesn't include the underlined document titles

2. **In the Contents tab, choose the items that you want to include in the numbered list.**

   See Chapter 12 for more on selecting items to include in compiled output.

3. **From the Compile For drop-down list, select the desired output type.**

4. **Click Compile.**

You can change how the outline appears in the Formatting tab (covered in Chapter 12).

Chapter title (Level 1)

Text document title (Level 2)

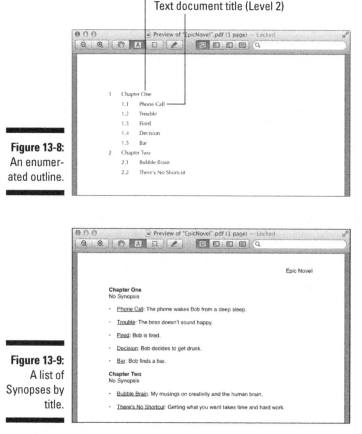

Figure 13-8: An enumer- ated outline.

Figure 13-9: A list of Synopses by title.

All of these presets are creating by changing the selections in the Formatting tab. You can modify them or create your own. See the following sections and Chapter 12 for more information about the Formatting options.

Creating an outline without numbering

You can modify the Synopsis Outline format (discussed in the preceding section) to create a list of chapters, with each subdocument in a bulleted list appearing below the chapter in which it falls. Follow these steps:

1. **Click the Formatting tab.**

2. **In the Synopsis column, deselect all the check boxes.**

   This step excludes the Synopses from the list.

   Option-click (Alt-click in Windows) any check box in a column to select or deselect that column for all rows.

3. **Make sure Title column check boxes are selected for all levels and items.**

   By default, the text document Levels 2 through 5+ are unchecked in the Synopsis Outline preset.

4. **(Optional) Remove the Title underline to help declutter the outline.**

   If you want to neaten up your outline, follow these steps:

   a. *Select Level 2, as shown in Figure 13-10.*

   b. *Click Title in the Formatting Editor to activate the Format bar.*

      Windows users, click the Modify button to access the Editor first.

   c. *Click the Underline button in the Format bar to remove the underline.*

   d. *Repeat Steps b and c for Levels 3 through 5+.*

5. **From the Compile For drop-down list, select the desired output type.**

6. **Click Compile.**

   The final output should look similar to the one in Figure 13-11.

Compiling a list of document notes

Want to capture all your document notes — those notes you entered in the Document Notes pane of the Inspector — in one place?

Follow these steps to modify the Synopsis and Titles format (discussed in the section "Exporting Special Types of Output," earlier in this chapter) to create a Notes outline, instead:

1. **Select the Formatting tab.**

2. **In the Synopsis column, deselect all the check boxes.**

   This step excludes the Synopses from the list.

   Option-click (Alt-click in Windows) any check box in a column to select or deselect that column for all rows.

3. **In the Notes column, select the check box for each item level.**

4. **From the Compile For drop-down list, select the desired output type.**

5. **Click Compile.**

Your output should look similar to Figure 13-12. Notice that even if a document has no notes, the title still appears in the outline.

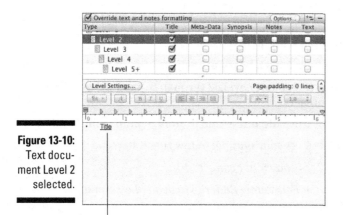

Figure 13-10:
Text document Level 2 selected.

Click here to activate the format bar

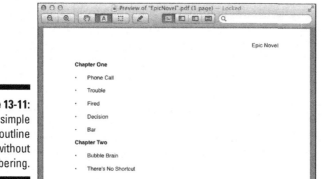

Figure 13-11:
A simple outline without numbering.

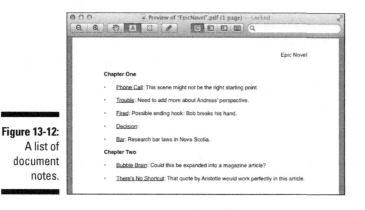

Figure 13-12:
A list of document notes.

Part V
Customizing Your Scrivener Experience

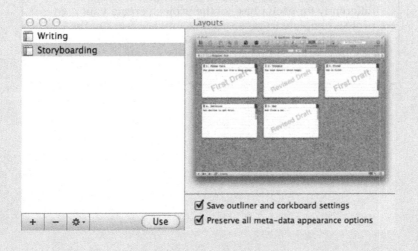

In this part . . .

This part takes you deep into features that keep you on track, save you time, and let you further customize your writing experience.

Got a word count goal? Want to check whether you're overusing a word, organize your Scrivener workspace differently for each phase of the project, create your own project template to save you time, or keep track of the same information for every character, setting, automobile, or interviewee? Scrivener offers tools to help.

Chapter 14

Setting Word Count Goals and Checking Progress

*W*ant to know how many words you added (or subtracted) from your draft today? Trying to meet a goal of 5,000 words by next Tuesday? Need to know how close you are to completing your 80,000-word manuscript?

Scrivener has several features that let you set targets and monitor your progress. In addition, you can look at statistics about your project or an individual document, including an estimated page count and a histogram of word frequency so that you can spot those overused words. (I don't know about you, but the geek in me just got excited.)

This chapter shows you how to set your own targets, view the stats, and get a handle on your productivity.

Working with Project Targets

Writing into the fog is fine, but sometimes you need to shoot for a specific goal. Scrivener's project targets provide visual feedback on how you're doing, and you can set them up to calculate the number of words you need to write daily to meet a deadline.

Whether you have a 400-page novel due in six weeks, want to write 50,000 words for National Novel Writing Month (NaNoWriMo) this year, or are just trying to practice your discipline by writing 500 words each day, project targets can help.

Setting a draft and session target

A *draft target* is the total word count goal for the project. A *session target* is specific to your current writing session, and you can use it in addition to a draft target. Even though you might be working toward an ultimate goal of 50,000 words for your manuscript, if your target for the day is 1,000 words, then 1,000 is your session target.

Note: In the Novel template that I used for the examples in this book, the Draft folder is called Manuscript, so the draft target is called the manuscript target. To be consistent with the figures, I call it the manuscript target from here forward.

By default, your session resets at midnight, but if you choose a different reset option (covered in the "Adjusting the target options" section, later in this chapter), a session can encompass more than one day.

Only items in the Manuscript (Draft) folder count toward your manuscript target, and by default, Scrivener calculates the words written toward your target from documents for which you have selected Include in Compile (see the section "Adjusting the target options," later in this chapter).

Imported documents or documents moved into the Manuscript folder from elsewhere in the Binder don't increase the session count, just like documents removed from the Manuscript folder don't detract from it. (Documents added or removed affect the manuscript target progress, though.)

You can easily set a manuscript or session target by following these steps:

1. **Choose Project⇨Show Project Targets.**

   You choose Project⇨Project Targets on a Windows PC.

   The Project Targets window opens. It's broken into two sections, with Manuscript Target settings in the top half. (I show working with these settings in Figure 14-1.) The Session Target section appears in the bottom half. The bars in both sections are progress meters that fill with color in graduating shades from red to green while you get closer to meeting the goals.

   The number on the left shows how many words are in the manuscript, and the number in the text box to the right is the goal amount.

2. **(Optional) Change the progress bar colors by choosing Scrivener⇨Preferences, clicking the Appearance button at the top of the window that opens, and choosing Target Progress Bars in the Customizable Colors section.**

3. **Click the goal number to activate the text box.**

   If you set up the session target to calculate automatically from a deadline (see the "Adjusting target options" section, later in this chapter), you can't edit this number for the session target.

4. **Type the desired number.**

5. **Mac users, click Apply.**

   The option is a standard text box in Windows, so you don't have an Apply button to click.

   If you have any text already entered in the manuscript, the progress bar fills — and is colored — according to how much of the goal you've met.

   If you need to cut words, you can set a negative session target. The count appears correctly if you change the settings to allow negatives (see the section "Adjusting the target options," later in this chapter), but the progress bar doesn't show progress.

6. **From the Words drop-down list, select whether you're measuring Words, Chars (characters), or Pages.**

   The Pages option is available only for the manuscript target.

7. **Click the X in the upper-left corner of the window to exit.**

   Alternatively, Mac users can press Esc.

To view your progress, open the Project Targets window. You can adjust the manuscript or session target at any time by repeating the preceding steps. If you want, you can even leave the window open while you work so that you can keep track of your progress in real time.

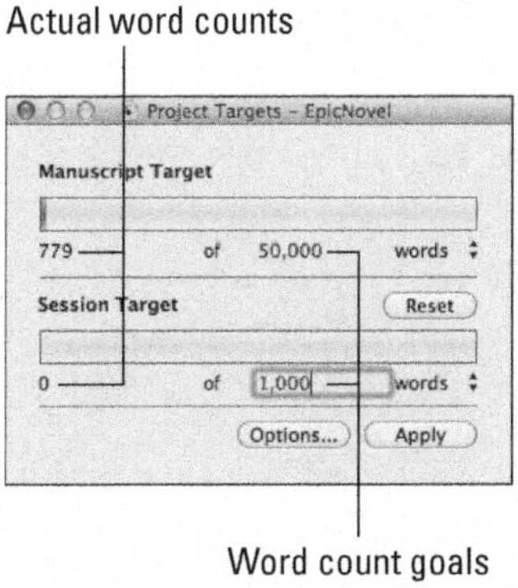

Actual word counts

Figure 14-1:
Setting a
session
target.

Word count goals

Resetting the session count

Did you read through yesterday's work and delete a few lines, but you don't want that to count against today's writing?

Whatever the reason, you can easily reset the session count. Just open the Project Targets window by choosing Project➪Show Project Targets, and then click the Reset button (refer to Figure 14-1).

The session progress resets to zero.

Adjusting the target options

The Targets Options window allows you to modify the way Scrivener calculates progress for manuscript and session targets, change when it resets session counts, set deadlines, and more.

To open the Project Targets Options window, choose Project➪Show Project Targets, and then click the Options button. (Windows users, choose Project➪Project Targets.)

The Project Targets Options window appears, as shown in Figure 14-2. The first three options apply to manuscript targets, the rest apply only to session targets.

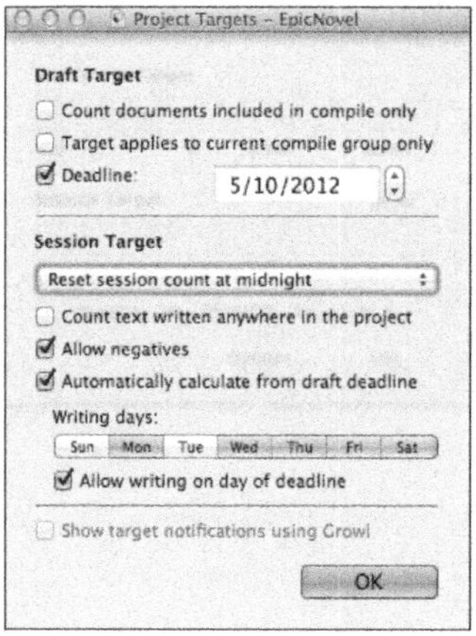

Figure 14-2:
The Project
Targets
Options
window.

Count Documents Included in Compile Only

If this option is selected, only words added to documents that are marked to Include in Compile — either in the Compile window (see Chapter 12) or in the General Meta-Data section of the Inspector pane (see Chapter 4) — count toward target progress.

So, if you recently compiled the first three chapters of your manuscript, the progress toward your goal might suddenly look much smaller because only those documents are being used to count words added.

Figure 14-3 shows the Compile window with only Chapter Two files selected for inclusion. The progress bar in the Project Targets window shows the 680 words contained in Chapter Two, but this manuscript actually has 779 total.

To prevent compile options from affecting your progress count, I recommend deselecting this option unless you plan to work in files within your Manuscript (Draft) folder that you don't want to count toward your goal.

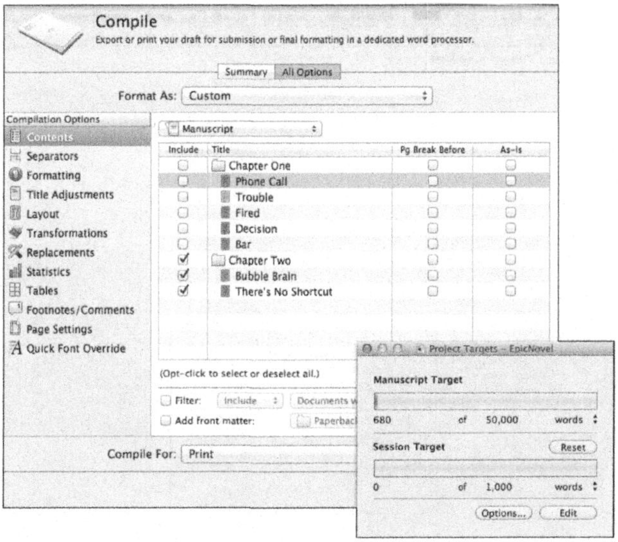

Figure 14-3:
The Manuscript Target progress bar reflects only those items selected to include in Compile.

Target Applies to Current Compile Group Only

If this option is selected, only those files currently listed in the Compile window's Contents pane count toward your goal (see Chapter 12), regardless of their Include in Compile status.

Front matter that you add to the compile group isn't counted, but items removed via filter are.

Figure 14-4 shows how this option works. Even though none of the documents are marked for inclusion, those in Chapter One — all 99 words — are still counted in the Project Targets window because they're listed in the Compile group. Words in Chapter Two aren't counted because they're not part of the group.

If you used this option in conjunction with Count Documents Included in Compile Only, the progress count in Figure 14-4 would be zero because none of the files have Include in Compile selected.

This option is best left blank if you don't want the compile settings messing with your progress counts.

Compilation group

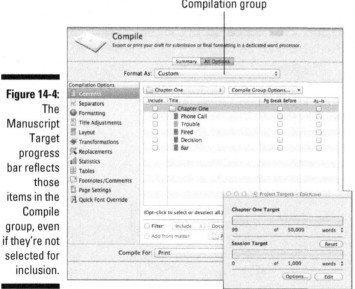

Figure 14-4:
The
Manuscript
Target
progress
bar reflects
those
items in the
Compile
group, even
if they're not
selected for
inclusion.

Deadline

Select this option to enter a deadline that can be used to automatically calculate your daily writing goals (see the section "Setting a draft and session target," earlier in this chapter).

Reset Session Count

This drop-down list lets you choose when Scrivener resets the session count to zero. If you don't want Scrivener to reset the session count automatically, even on project open or close, choose Never Automatically Reset Session Counts.

By default, Scrivener resets the session count at midnight.

Count Text Written Anywhere in the Project

Choosing this option forces Scrivener to count all text written, regardless of location, even in documents outside the Manuscript (Draft) folder.

You might use this option if you want to work on a scene but aren't yet ready to include it in the manuscript, or when you want to count the words written in your notes or research.

Words written outside the Manuscript (Draft) folder don't count toward the manuscript target progress, even if this option is selected.

Allow Negatives

Selecting this option allows the session count to go below zero. If you leave it unchecked, the count doesn't go negative, even if you delete more words than you add.

If this option is deselected, Scrivener doesn't keep track of how negative you are, so any words added when you're at zero increase your session target progress. If you want a more accurate reflection of your net word count, select this option.

Automatically Calculate from Draft Deadline

This option uses the deadline date (see the "Deadline" section, earlier in this chapter) to determine the daily target needed to meet the deadline.

If this option is selected, the session target can't be edited.

Writing Days

Select the buttons for the days of the week you plan to write so that Scrivener can more accurately calculate the daily session goal. Otherwise, it assumes seven days per week. Chosen days turn blue.

Allow Writing on Day of Deadline

Select this option if you can work on the deadline day. If this option isn't selected, Scrivener doesn't include the deadline date when making calculations.

Show Target Notifications

This Mac-only option applies to both target types. If you have Growl installed on your computer (go to `http://growl.info` to find out more), selecting this option triggers a Growl notification when you reach either your session or manuscript target, or fall below a target (useful when cutting words). This option eliminates the need to open the Project Targets window to see whether you've reached your goal.

Don't want to use Growl? Target notifications also work with Apple's notification system for Mac OS X Mountain Lion.

Adding Targets to a Document

Need to produce a 1,000-word article? Shooting for 3,500 words in your next scene? Consider setting a document target. A document target tracks progress for the specific document in which it's set.

Follow these steps to set a document target:

1. **In the Binder, select the document for which you want to set a target.**

2. **Click the Set Target button on the Status bar, shown in Figure 14-5.**

   A Target window appears.

3. **Enter the desired count in the Target For This Document text box, and then select Words or Chars (characters) from the Words drop-down list.**

4. **If you want a notification when you meet, or fall below, your document target, select the Show Target Notifications option.**

   This option works the same as described in the preceding section.

5. **Click OK.**

   A progress bar appears in the Status bar, shown in Figure 14-5. Just like with manuscript and session targets, the progress bar changes color from red to green while you move closer to your target.

   The progress bar colors can be changed as outlined in the "Setting a draft and session target" section, earlier in this chapter.

   The word count in the status bar changes to display the target amount, changing from 15 to 15/100 in the example in Figure 14-5.

Figure 14-5:
Adding a
document
target.

Set Target button

125%   Words: 15/100   Chars: 86

Document target progress bar

 You can sort documents by Progress in the Outliner (covered in Chapter 9) to quickly see which items need more work. Document targets can also be edited in the Outliner by double-clicking the value in the Target column.

Checking Project Statistics

The Project Statistics window provides word, character, and page counts for contents of the Manuscript (Draft) folder based on the compile settings. Basically, the Compile function runs in the background to determine the numbers.

So, even if you have documents selected, if you have the Text element deselected in the Formatting tab of the Compile window, the text isn't counted (see Chapter 12 for more about Compile options). This is where the ability to change and save the compile settings without running the Compiler comes in handy (see Chapter 13).

You can also view the same information for the current Binder selection. Unlike the Manuscript (Draft) Statistics, Selection Statistics apply to all files selected in the Binder, regardless of their location within the project or their compile status.

Check your stats by choosing Project➪Project Statistics. The Project Statistics window opens, as shown in Figure 14-6. The upper half applies to all files in the Manuscript (Draft) folder, and the lower half applies to the item(s) selected in the Binder.

 The Pages (Paperback) count is calculated by using the industry standard of total character count divided by the product of the word count per page and the average number of characters per word. Pages = Total Chars ÷ (Words per Page × Chars per Word). You can change the Words per Page value in the Project Statistics Options window (see the following section).

The Pages (Printed) count is calculated based on your Compile settings. If the project is large, this calculation can take a minute because Compile has to run in the background. Projects over 100,000 words don't Compile every time you open Project Statistics and aren't up to date unless you click the Update Printed Counts button that appears for large projects.

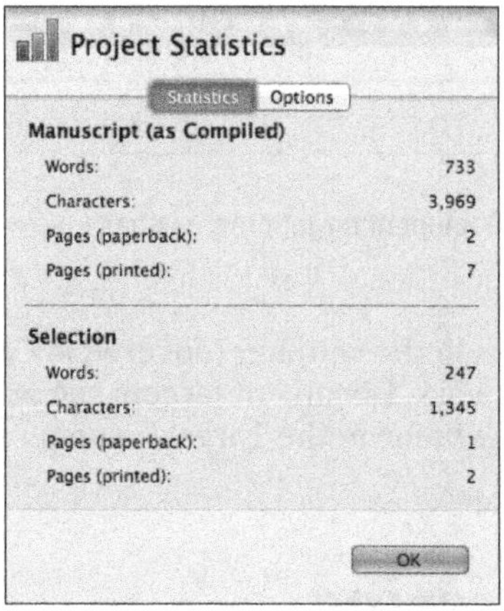

Figure 14-6:
The Project
Statistics
window.

Changing Project Statistics Options

The Project Statistics Options tab lets you modify how statistics are calculated. Follow these steps to access the options:

1. **Choose Project⇨Project Statistics.**

   The Project Statistics window opens.

2. **Click Options at the top of the window.**

   The Project Statistics Options window appears, as shown in Figure 14-7. The top portion of the window, called Draft Statistics, applies to manuscript stats, the center section is for selection stats, and the last section lets you adjust how paperback pages are calculated.

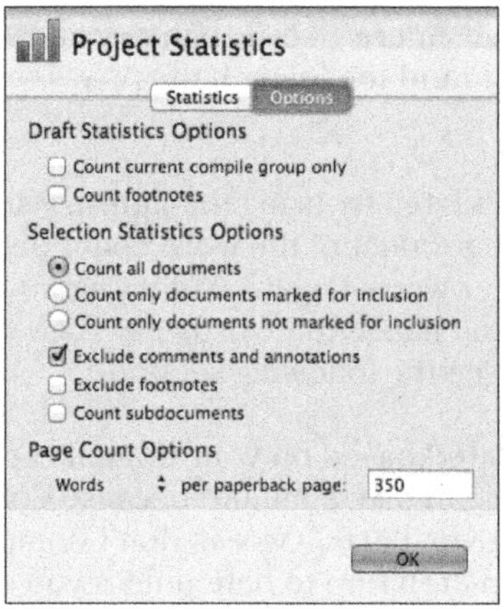

Figure 14-7:
The Project
Statistics
Options
window.

The two options in the Draft Statistics section let you choose what to include in the manuscript word count. Here's a description of each option:

- ✓ **Count Current Compile Group Only:** If selected, the statistics are calculated based on only the documents listed in the Contents pane of the Compile window (see Chapter 12 for more on the Compile window).

- ✓ **Count Footnotes:** Includes footnotes in the word and character count.

The Selection Statistics Options section has six options, which apply only to the current writing session. (The first three are radio buttons, which means you can choose only one of them.)

Here's what each option does:

- ✓ **Count All Documents:** Counts all selected documents, regardless of their Include in Compile status.

- ✓ **Count Only Documents Marked for Inclusion:** Counts only those documents for which you've selected the Include in Compile option (either in the Compile window, covered in Chapter 12, or in the General Meta-Data pane of the Inspector, which I discuss in Chapter 4).

- ✓ **Count Only Documents Not Marked for Inclusion:** Counts only documents for which you didn't select Include in Compile.

- ✓ **Exclude Comments and Annotations:** Comments and annotations are counted in the document and manuscript word counts, but you can exclude them from the selected document count by choosing this option.

  If you exclude comments and annotations from the manuscript word count on the Statistics options pane in the Compile window (see Chapter 12), they won't be counted here.

- ✓ **Exclude Footnotes:** When this option is selected, footnotes aren't included in the selected documents counts.

- ✓ **Count Subdocuments:** Select this option if you want to select a container and have Scrivener calculate selection statistics for all its subdocuments. Otherwise, the count applies only to text within the container.

The Page Count Options section lets you set how many words or characters per page you want Scrivener to use to calculate paperback pages.

For more on how Scrivener calculates pages, see the preceding section.

When you're done with the Options window, you can either click the Statistics button to see the effect of your changes or click OK to exit the Project Statistics window.

Using Text Statistics to View Word Frequency

Most writers have words that they overuse in their writing — just, back, really, it. Those are just a few of the words I really misuse, when I look back on it.

Scrivener has a built-in Text Statistics feature that can help you catch your own worn-out word choices. (In order to access Text Statistics, a document must have the keyboard focus, meaning the cursor must be blinking in the Editor pane.) Follow these steps:

1. **Select the desired item in the Binder.**

   You can select more than one item, but if you get the Corkboard or Outliner, choose View⬂Scrivenings to see the Editor.

2. **Choose Project⬂Text Statistics.**

   If the menu option is grayed out, go back and make sure the Editor pane is active by clicking in it, and then try this step again.

   The Statistics window appears, displaying counts for words, characters, paragraphs, and lines, as well as a Word Frequency section.

3. **To view the word frequency statistics, click the triangle next to Word Frequency to expand it.**

   Figure 14-8 shows the Word Frequency count and bar graph, sorted in descending order by Count to show the most-used words at the top. Pronouns, prepositions, and conjunctions generally show up first, but scroll down to see other words that appear frequently in your work.

4. **(Optional) Sort the Word Frequency by clicking the desired column heading.**

   A sort triangle appears in the heading, pointing up to indicate the column is sorted in ascending order.

5. **(Optional) Click the heading again to sort in descending order.**

   The triangle now points down.

6. **Click OK when you're done viewing the statistics.**

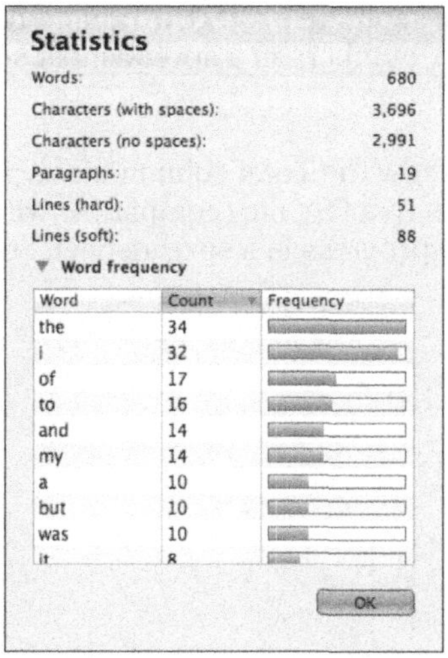

Statistics

Words:	680
Characters (with spaces):	3,696
Characters (no spaces):	2,991
Paragraphs:	19
Lines (hard):	51
Lines (soft):	88

▼ **Word frequency**

Word	Count ▼	Frequency
the	34	
i	32	
of	17	
to	16	
and	14	
my	14	
a	10	
but	10	
was	10	
it	8	

OK

Figure 14-8:
The Text
Statistics
window.

Tracking Productivity

All these statistics are great, but what can you do with them? Well, if you're like me — you have my sympathies — you record the numbers, and then graph them at the end of the year.

Yes, it's a sickness.

But seriously, it's a good idea to track your daily work, if for no other reason than to convince the IRS you're really working next time you get audited.

It's also helpful to go back and see how long it really took you to finish that last project, and where you had long lags in productivity. That way, when a publisher asks you how quickly you can write a book, you'll have some numbers on which to base your guess.

I keep a file called Productivity within each project where I enter the date, hours worked, and words written, plus any notes about the type of work I did on the project that day (writing, revisions, query letters, plotting, and so on) and sometimes what part of the manuscript I worked on.

At the end of each day, I enter all the separate project word and time counts into a calendar, and then compile the numbers in a spreadsheet so that I can look at my month and year as a whole.

You can set up the Outliner view to show the Total column for each chapter, and then export the Outliner contents to a CSV file (compatible with most spreadsheet programs) to track your progress in a spreadsheet. See Chapter 9 for details.

Chapter 15

Saving Time with Custom Layouts and Project Templates

I don't know about you, but I'm inherently lazy. If there's anything I can do to save time and avoid repeating work that I've already done, I'm all over it. Which is why I love this chapter. It's all about saving your workspace and your project templates just the way you like them so that you don't have to start from scratch when you want to switch layouts or begin a new project.

Customizing Your Workspace with Layouts

One of my favorite things about Scrivener is the easily overlooked — but imminently helpful — way that every time you open a project, it takes you to the exact position where you left off.

Scrivener also remembers each project's *layout:* the position and status of each element of the workspace. For example, the layout might have the Binder visible, Editor split horizontally, and Inspector closed.

Beyond that, you can save layouts for different stages of your writing process or for different types of writing, and switch to them quickly, saving time when you want to rearrange your workspace.

You could have one layout for writing your novel, one for revisions, one for storyboarding, and one for writing blog posts. When you save a layout, it's available to all projects, thus saving you even more time.

I like to think of saved layouts like a magic Rearrange button. A couple of clicks, and your workspace is just the way you want it; a couple more, and it's changed again.

Here's a sample of elements that get saved in a layout (for a complete list, check the Scrivener User Manual):

✔ Visible or hidden status:

   • Binder

   • Collection tab interface

   • Inspector

   • Header and Footer bars

   • Ruler and Format bar

   • Toolbar

✔ Split type (horizontal, vertical, or none)

✔ Window size and position

✔ Toolbar view mode (such as icon size and text)

✔ Corkboard, Outliner, or Scrivenings mode for each split

✔ Page View or standard Draft view for each split

✔ Mac Full Screen status (Mac OS X 10.7 Lion only)

To open the Layouts window, choose Window➪Layouts➪Manage Layouts. (Windows users, choose View➪Layout➪Manage Layouts.) The following sections explain what you can do in this window. (To close the window when you're done, just click the red X button.)

Saving the current layout

When you have your layout just the way you want it, you can save it so that no matter what you do to your workspace, you can always get back to your favorite layout. Not only that, you can use your saved layout in future projects. Follow these steps to save your layout:

1. **Click the plus sign (+) button at the bottom-left of the Layouts window to add a layout based on your current Scrivener setup.**

   A text box appears with the words New Layout ready to be overwritten, and a snapshot of the current layout appears in the right half of the Layouts window.

2. **Type the name of the new layout, and then press Return.**

   In Figure 15-1, I created a new layout called Writing. The snapshot in the right pane provides a visual preview of the saved layout.

3. **(Optional) Select the two checkboxes at the bottom of the Snapshot pane.**

   These options provide additional control over how much is saved in the layout:

   - *Save Outliner and Corkboard Settings:* Ensures that settings such as index card size and Outliner columns are saved

   - *Preserve All Meta-Data Appearance Options:* Saves settings such as tinted Binder icons (covered in Chapter 4) and keyword chip visibility (find more in Chapter 8)

Saved layout

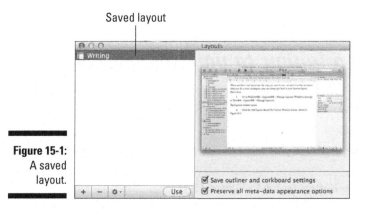

Figure 15-1:
A saved
layout.

Creating a new layout

Anytime you want to create a new layout, just make your adjustments to the project you're working on, and then save the layout, as outlined in the preceding section.

For example, if you want to save the layout that you like to use for brainstorming and storyboarding, you might hide the Inspector, select a container and switch to Corkboard view, adjust the Corkboard settings (which I talk about in Chapter 8), and hide the Binder. Then, save it as something brilliant, such as Storyboarding, as I did in the example in Figure 15-2.

Notice how the layout preview shows the Corkboard view so that you can easily tell what the layout looks like.

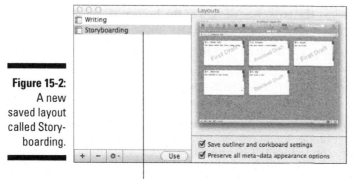

Figure 15-2:
A new
saved layout
called Story-
boarding.

New layout

Applying a layout to your workspace

Okay, so creating layouts is cool and all, but how do you apply a layout to your workspace? Just follow these steps, and Scrivener will make all the changes for you:

1. **Select the layout that you want to use from the list in the Layouts window.**

2. **Click the Use button (refer to Figure 15-1).**

    The workspace switches to the chosen layout. Pretty nifty, huh?

To apply a layout without opening the Layouts window, choose Window⇨Layouts⇨Manage Layouts (Windows users, choose View⇨Layout⇨All Layouts), and then choose the desired layout from the submenu that appears.

Mac users also have a Layouts button on the standard toolbar, which you can click to access the Layouts window. Click and hold the Layouts button for a list of layouts.

Windows users can add the Layouts button to the toolbar by following these steps:

1. **Choose Tools⇨Customize Toolbars.**

2. **In the window that opens, select Main Toolbar from the list at the top-right.**

3. **Select the Manage Layouts button from the list along the left side, and then click the right-arrow button.**

   The Layouts button is added to the toolbar.

4. **Click OK to close the Customize Toolbars window.**

Modifying a layout

Okay, so you have your layouts all set up, but while working on your project, you realize the layout needs some tweaking. No problem. Just follow these steps:

1. **Make the desired changes to your Scrivener setup.**

2. **In the Layouts window, select the layout that you want to modify.**

3. **Click the gear button at the bottom of the window.**

4. **From the pop-up menu that appears, select Update Selected Layout.**

   The layout preview updates to reflect the changes you made.

Deleting a layout

If you've created a layout that you never use, it's simple to delete it by following these steps:

1. **In the Layouts window, select the layout that you want to remove.**

2. **Click the minus sign (–) button.**

   On the Mac only, a message appears, reminding you that the action can't be undone.

3. **If you don't want the message to warn you anymore, select the Do Not Show This Message Again check box.**

4. **If you're sure you want to delete the layout, click OK.**

   The selected layout is removed from the list.

Exporting a layout

Want to share a layout with a friend or add it to another computer where you use Scrivener? Exporting is the answer. *Note:* Layouts aren't compatible between Mac and Windows.

Follow these steps to export a layout:

1. **In the Layouts window, select the layout you want to export.**

2. **Click the gear button, and then select Export Selected Layout from the pop-up menu that appears.**

3. **Choose a location from the file list, type a name for the exported layout in the Save As text box, and then click Save.**

   The file saves as a `.scrlayout` (Mac) or `.scrivlayout` (Windows) file.

Importing a layout

If you have a layout to import, the file must be accessible from your computer before you can import it. When you have the file ready, follow these steps:

1. **In the Layout window, click the gear button, and then select Import Layout from the pop-up menu that appears.**

   The Import window opens.

2. **Select the desired file.**

   The file will have a `.scrlayout` (Mac) or `.scrivlayout` (Windows) extension.

3. **Click Open.**

   The imported layout appears in the Layouts window.

Saving Time on Future Projects with Custom Project Templates

It wouldn't surprise me if this section were the reason you bought this book. I get more questions about project templates than any other topic in Scrivener, by a landslide.

Why are people so interested in finding out all about project templates? Because creating your own saves time and hassle.

When you first opened Scrivener, you had to choose a project template before you could even start working. Those templates were included with Scrivener for your convenience, but while you became familiar with the program, you probably made changes to the template so that it would work better for you.

Did you add or change root folders? Include an oft-viewed writing reference? Change the Label or Status fields? Add keywords?

Wouldn't you like to save this new, improved version of the template so that the next time you start a project, you don't have to make all those changes again? Then you're in the right place because creating a custom project template is what the following sections are all about.

Creating and saving a custom project template

The key thing to remember when creating a project template is that *everything* gets saved, including Label and Status settings, keywords, collections, initial Compile settings, initial layout, and every item in the Binder. Project-level settings such as tinted icons, text preferences, project targets, and statistics settings are included, too.

Basically, the entire project gets copied as-is, so if you don't want an item or setting in the template, you need to strip it out or turn it off. The safest way to do that is to make a copy of your project, remove everything that doesn't apply to all future projects of that type, and then save the template.

And don't worry, you can create more than one template to suit all your writing needs.

You can either start with a copy of an existing project and strip everything out, or start with a new project based on an existing template and make the desired changes.

Before making any changes to your project, save a copy of it as outlined in the following steps. Unlike a standard word processor, Scrivener auto-saves every few seconds, which means that you can't make all your changes and then select Save As after the fact. Don't do anything until you've made a copy.

Follow these steps to create your own custom template:

1. **Choose File⇨Save As.**

   The Save As window appears.

2. **Select a location from the file list, and then type a name for the project copy into the Save As text box.**

   If you want, you can just save it to the Desktop for easy deleting when you're done. This is a throwaway file that you're using to create the template. After that, you won't need it anymore.

After the copy is saved, the original project file closes, and the copy opens in Scrivener. (You can tell because the title bar at the top of the window displays the new project name.)

3. **Get the project set up exactly the way you want it for future projects of this type.**

   Parts II and III of this book cover most of the project customization options.

   Don't worry too much about getting everything just perfect. I show you how to modify your template in the section "Editing a project template," later in this chapter.

4. **Choose File⇨Save as Template.**

   If you have personal data in the project, you may get a message warning you about it. If you're saving it only for your own use, click Continue; otherwise, click Cancel and remove any personal data before trying this step again.

   The Save as Template window opens, as shown in Figure 15-3.

5. **Enter the desired template name in the Title text box.**

   I suggest using something descriptive, maybe even including your name or initials, to differentiate your template from the built-in ones.

6. **Choose a category from the Category drop-down list.**

   The category determines where in the Templates window your template is grouped.

7. **In the Description field, provide a detailed description of the template to help you remember what's in it.**

   This information is especially important if you plan to share the template with others.

8. **Choose an icon from the Icon drop-down list in the Icon section.**

   If you have a picture that you want to use to represent your template, you can choose Custom from the list and select the desired photo. In Figure 15-3, I used a screenshot of Scrivener in a layout similar to my template.

9. **Click OK.**

   The template is saved.

10. **Close the project copy you used to make the template by clicking the red X button.**

11. **If you want, locate the project copy in Finder or My Computer, and then delete it.**

Figure 15-3:
Saving a
custom
template.

TIP

What to toss from your template

When you create a custom template, remember to delete any documents, keywords, research files, images, Label and Status values, custom metadata fields, internal and external references, and project notes that you don't want to carry over.

If you might share the template with others, be sure to strip out the personal data from the Project Properties (accessible via Project⇨Meta-Data Settings), the Title page, and other front matter before continuing on. You should also check the Page Setup tab of the Compile window (covered in Chapter 12) for personal data.

Don't want to worry about embedded personal data? Use template placeholder tags for things such as author name and address, rather than the actual information. The tags pull the data from your address book whenever you create a new project based on the template. Choose Help⇨Placeholder Tags List for more information. Windows users can visit `https://scrivener. tenderapp.com/help/kb/windows/ placeholder-tags-list` if Placeholder Tags List doesn't appear in the Help menu.

Of course, some of these items are exactly what you want to keep. Just make sure they're generic enough to apply to the type of project for which you plan to use the template.

You might want to keep the chapter folders and customized Label values, as well as any files you imported that you want to have in the template. For my novel template, I like to include empty documents called Productivity (mentioned in Chapter 14), Ideas, Change Log, Outline, and Pitch/Blurbs. I also include a reference on story structure, tips on keeping up the suspense, and a list of words I tend to overuse.

In addition, I strip out the Label and Status values, but I keep the fields renamed to POV and Day (see Chapter 4 for more on working with metadata).

Working with project templates

After you create a template, you can use it to create new projects. And after you start using it, if you find the template isn't quite to your liking, you can edit or delete it. All these actions start in the Project Templates window.

To open the Project Templates window, choose File➪New Project. (Click Cancel to close the Project Templates window.)

Creating a new file from your project template

After you create a template (as described in the section "Creating and saving a custom project template," earlier in this chapter), how do you use it when you're ready to start your next project? Just follow these steps:

1. **In the Project Templates window, click the category to which you saved your template.**

   Mine was saved under Fiction, which I've selected in Figure 15-4.

My custom template

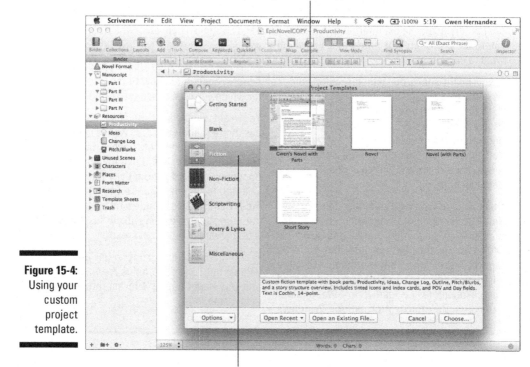

Figure 15-4:
Using your
custom
project
template.

My template's category

The templates in the selected category appear in alphabetical order, including the template you created.

2. **Select your template.**

   The chosen template is highlighted, and the description appears in the box below the list of templates.

3. **For Mac users only, click Choose.**

   The Save As window appears.

4. **Enter the desired project name in the Save As text box, and then select a location for the new project from the file list.**

   Windows users, select a location from the Where drop-down list.

5. **Click Create.**

   The new project opens, ready for you to write.

Setting a template as the default

Want to have the Project Templates window display your custom template as the preselected option whenever you open the window? Follow these steps to set the default template:

1. **In the Project Templates window, click the category to which you saved your template.**

2. **Select your template.**

   The chosen template is highlighted.

3. **Click the Options button at the bottom of the window (refer to Figure 15-4).**

4. **Select Set Selected Template as Default from the drop-down list that appears.**

Next time you create a new project, the Project Templates window opens directly to the template you set as the default.

The preceding steps also work for setting a built-in template as the default if you don't have — or don't want to use — one of your own.

Editing a project template

Say you've been working in a project based on your custom template for a while, and you realize you want to change some things about the template before you create another project from it.

Although you can't directly edit a template, you can replace it with a new version without having to re-enter the name, description, and other information. The easiest way is to create a throwaway project based on the template, make your changes, and save it as the new template. Follow these steps:

1. **If needed, in the Project Templates window, click the category to which you saved your template.**

2. **Select your template.**

3. **Mac users only, click Choose.**

Mac users, Option-click the Choose button to keep Scrivener from replacing placeholder tags with information from your address book. This leaves the placeholder tags intact, which is especially important if you plan to share the template with other users. Choose Help⇨Placeholder Tags List for more information.

The Save As window appears.

4. **Enter the desired project name in the Save As text box, and then select a location for the new project from the file list.**

Windows users, select a location from the Where drop-down list.

Because you're going to delete this project when you're done, I recommend saving it to the Desktop so that it's easy to find and maybe naming it something like DeleteMe.

5. **Click Create.**

The new project opens.

6. **Make the desired changes to the project.**

Did you forget to empty the trash? Are there files you forgot to include, keywords you didn't remove, or references you wanted to add? Maybe you don't want those Chapter folders, after all. Make all your changes before moving on.

7. **Choose File⇨Save as Template.**

8. **If necessary, click Continue to bypass the warning about personal information.**

The Save As Template window opens, with the current template's data already filled out.

9. **Modify any of the settings, such as the Description, if desired.**

   To overwrite the existing template, keep the name the same.

   You can't overwrite Scrivener's built-in templates. If you chose a built-in template in Step 2, you must give the template a new name.

10. **Click OK.**

    The old version of the template is replaced with the new one.

This process also works for creating a new template based on an existing one. To keep the original, follow the preceding steps, but in Step 9, enter a new name. (You'll probably want to change the Description, too.)

Deleting a project template

Got a custom template you never use anymore? Annoyed by the clutter? Deleting a template is simple. Just follow these steps:

1. **In the Project Templates window, click the category to which you saved your template.**

2. **Select your template.**

3. **Click the Options button at the bottom of the window.**

4. **Select Delete Selected Template from the pop-up menu that appears.**

   A window appears, warning you that this action can't be undone.

5. **Click OK.**

   Click Yes on a Windows PC.

   The template is removed from the Project Templates window.

You can delete only templates that you've created or imported, not the built-in templates that came with Scrivener.

Exporting a project template

If you want to share a template with another Scrivener user or transfer it to another computer on which you use Scrivener, you can export it by following these steps:

1. **In the Project Templates window, click the category to which you saved your template.**

2. **Select your template.**

3. **Click the Options button at the bottom of the Project Templates window (refer to Figure 15-4).**

4. **Select Export Selected Template from the pop-up menu that appears.**

   The Export window opens.

5. **Select a location for the new project from the file list, type the template name in the Save As text box, and then click Export.**

   Windows users, enter the name in the File Name text box and click Save.

   The file is saved with a .scrivtemplate extension.

Importing a project template

Does a friend have a really cool template you want to try? Did you create a template on a different computer, and now you want to have access on the one you're currently using? You're in luck. Templates can be shared across the Windows and Mac versions of Scrivener, and importing templates is as simple as following these steps:

1. **Copy the .scrivtemplate file to your computer.**

   Or make sure the file is accessible (for example, via a flash drive or Dropbox).

2. **Click the Options button at the bottom of the Project Templates window.**

3. **Select Import Templates from the pop-up menu that appears.**

   The Import window opens.

4. **Choose the template file that you want to import, and then click Import.**

   The new template appears in the category assigned when it was originally created, with the name it was given when created (not the name of the .scrivtemplate file).

5. **Click Cancel to close the window.**

Hiding the Getting Started category

If you don't want the Getting Started category to appear when you open the Project Templates window, you can hide it. But don't worry, you can always get it back if you want quick access to the Interactive Tutorial or the Scrivener User Manual. Plus, both features are available from the Help menu, as well.

Follow these steps to hide Getting Started:

1. **Click the Options button at the bottom of the Project Templates window (refer to Figure 15-4).**

2. **Select Hide "Getting Started" from the pop-up menu that appears.**

   Getting Started disappears from the category list.

3. **Click Cancel to close the window.**

To show Getting Started in the category list after hiding it, follow the preceding steps, but select Show "Getting Started" in Step 2.

Chapter 16

Creating Useful Forms with Document Templates

. . . .

In This Chapter

▶ Working with existing document templates

▶ Modifying a document template

▶ Making your own document template

▶ Removing and creating the Document Templates folder

. . . .

ocument templates are preformatted documents that you use to create new documents within your project. They're basically ready-to-go forms. When you create a document based on a template, you're making a copy of the template, thus preserving the original so that you don't have to worry about overwriting it.

In Scrivener, project templates in the Fiction category come with document templates, but even if the project you choose doesn't have any document templates, you can create your own.

Document templates are perfect for creating forms to capture information about characters, settings, automobiles, interviewees, animals, or whatever else you can think of. This chapter covers how to use, edit, and create them.

Viewing Existing Document Templates

If your project template came preloaded with document templates, they're located in a folder called Template Sheets — although you can rename it, if desired — and marked with a small T, as shown in Figure 16-1. (The project shown in Figure 16-1, which displays the Character Sketch document template, was based on the Novel project template.)

If your project doesn't have the Template Sheets folder but you want to add your own, see the section "Working with the Document Templates Folder," later in this chapter.

To view a document template, expand the Template Sheets folder to view its contents, and then click the desired template to view it in the Editor pane.

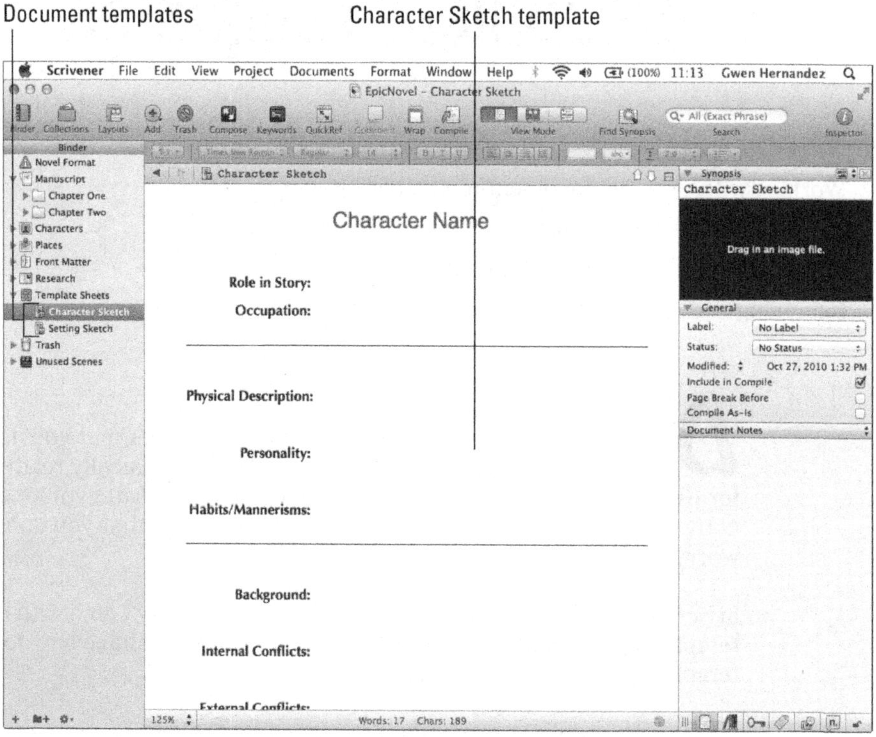

Document templates   Character Sketch template

Figure 16-1:
A document
template.

Creating a Document from a Document Template

You aren't supposed to fill in the template itself; rather it's the original that gets copied to make a new document. With a template, you don't have to remember to make the copy, you just add a new document, and you're ready to go. Follow these steps:

1. **Select the folder in which you want to place your new document.**

2. **Click and hold the Add button in the toolbar to open a drop-down list, as shown in Figure 16-2.**

Add button   Template choices

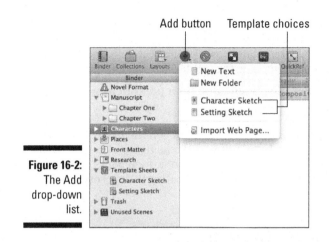

Figure 16-2:
The Add
drop-down
list.

3. **Select the template that you want to use from the list.**

   A new document based on the template appears in the folder you
   selected, its name ready to be overwritten, as shown in Figure 16-3,
   where I'm adding a new Character Sketch sheet.

New document from a template

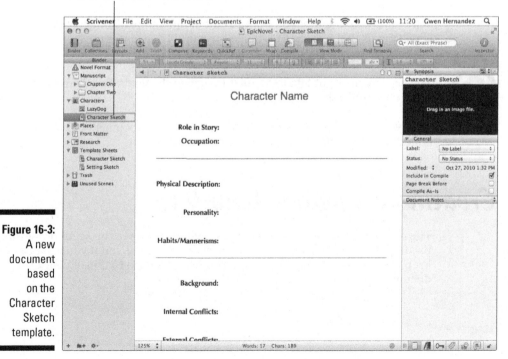

Figure 16-3:
A new
document
based
on the
Character
Sketch
template.

You can also add a document based on a template by right-clicking the folder to which you want to add the document, choosing Add⇨New from Template, and selecting a template from the list that appears. The same menu is also available by choosing Project⇨New from Template.

4. **Type a name for the new document, and then press Return.**

Now you're ready to fill in the information.

Nothing in the document auto-populates, not even the name. You can't tab through it like an online form, but you can navigate with your arrow keys. Document templates are really just regular documents that have a custom icon and prefilled text to make duplicating your forms easier.

Editing a Document Template

So you think the document templates are the best invention since chocolate and hazelnuts got together, except you want to make a few changes to a template. Add a few items here, take out a few there — make it work for you.

No problem. It's easy to modify a template so that all future documents created from it have the changes. The only downside is that changes to the template don't affect documents you've already created.

Select the template that you want to edit in the Template Sheets folder, which opens that template in the Editor pane. Then, make the desired changes to the template in the Editor.

You can use the right tab in the ruler to line up the fields. See Chapter 6 for more on setting tabs.

After you make your changes, when you add a new document based on the edited template, the changes appear in that document.

Creating a Custom Template

The character and setting sketches are a good start (see the section "Viewing Existing Document Templates," earlier in this chapter), but if you want to keep track of something else in your project, you need to create your own document template.

You can make a document template easily, but I do have one caveat: You must have a designated templates folder to put it in. If you don't, skip to the following section, and then come back to create your template.

Follow these steps to design your very own template:

1. **Select the Template Sheets folder in the Binder.**

2. **Click the green Add button in the toolbar.**

   Alternatively, you can right-click the Template Sheets folder and choose Add⇨New Text from the contextual menu that appears.

3. **Type over the highlighted filename to rename it.**

   The document appears in the folder, and is marked with a small T to designate it as a template. (This designation happens automatically when you add a document to the Template Sheets folder.)

   If you already have a document elsewhere in the project that you want to use as a template, simply drag it to the Template Sheets folder.

4. **Add the desired text to your template.**

   Designate the Label and Status fields (probably No Label and No Status) to prevent the default Label and Status from being applied to documents created from the template.

   When you finish customizing your template, you can start creating documents from it, as described in the section "Creating a Document from a Document Template," earlier in this chapter.

Working with the Document Templates Folder

Each project can contain only one Document Templates folder, named whatever you want. In the following sections, I show you how to remove the template designation from an existing templates folder and add it to a folder of your choosing.

If you already have a set of templates from another project that you want to copy over, you need to remove the existing folder's Template Folder designation before you can assign a new template folder.

Removing the template folder designation

To remove the template folder designation, follow these steps:

1. **Choose Project⇨Clear Templates Folder.**

   A warning window appears.

2. **Read the warning spiel, and then click OK.**

   As shown in Figure 16-4, the Template Sheets folder loses its special icon, and the documents within lose the T that identified them as templates. The templates no longer appear in the Add menu.

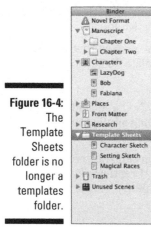

Figure 16-4:
The Template Sheets folder is no longer a templates folder.

Designating a templates folder

To designate a folder as the templates folder, follow these steps:

1. **Select the desired folder.**

2. **Choose Project⇨Set Selection as Templates Folder.**

   The icon of the folder changes, and the documents in that folder get the small T that marks them as document templates.

3. **Click the Add menu.**

   The document templates now appear on the list.

Changing the Default New Document Type

When you add a new document to a folder by selecting the folder — or a file in it — and pressing Return, or by clicking the Add button in the toolbar (covered Chapter 2), Scrivener adds a new file based on the default document type for that folder. For a standard folder in your manuscript, it's a text document. For the Characters folder (in the Novel project template), it's a document based on the Character Sketch template. And for the Places folder, it's a document based on the Setting Sketch template.

But what if you have a folder that you want to quickly and easily populate with forms from a template you've created? You can change the default document type for a folder by following these steps:

1. **Select the folder for which you want to designate a new default subdocument type.**

2. **Choose Documents⇨Default New Subdocument Type.**

3. **Select the desired template from the submenu that appears.**

   To change the default new subdocument to a text document, rather than a document based on a template, choose Text.

Part VI

Getting the Most Out of Scrivener

In this part . . .

If this book were an Everlasting Gobstopper with each new layer introducing you to another fascinating feature of Scrivener, this part would be the tangy, sweet center full of fabulous extras.

You can get the scoop on quick and easy searching, using collections to pull files together in new ways, saving versions of your documents, tracking revisions, and backing up your work.

Chapter 17

Searching High and Low

. . . .

In This Chapter

▶ Using Project Search

▶ Replacing words in a project

▶ Working with Document Find and Replace

▶ Searching by format type

▶ Adding bookmarks for easy navigation

. . . .

*E*ven if you've broken up your manuscript into sections with logical names and metadata tags, you still might have a need to search your project at some point. Whether you want to find all documents that mention gray squirrels, every instance of the name Josephine, or all yellow-highlighted text, you can do it.

Scrivener offers several options for searching and replacing. Project Search runs through every item in the Binder and returns a list of all matching items in the sidebar. Project Replace allows you to replace words across the entire project. Document Find and Replace is restricted to the document you're working on, and the Find by Formatting option searches the whole project for the desired format (for example, highlighter color, text color, or annotations). Finally, bookmarks let you mark places within the text so that you can navigate to them quickly.

This chapter covers all these methods.

Working with Project Search

The quickest way to start searching through your project files is with the Project Search. Scrivener uses the criteria you enter to sift through the entire project file (even the Trash folder) for documents that match.

You can specify what to search (for example, Title, Text, Notes, Synopsis, and so on), how to apply the search phrase (such as Exact Phrase, All Words, Any Word, or Whole Word), and other options to further limit the pool of searchable documents.

To select elements on the list, just keep going back into the menu and selecting or deselecting options until you have the search set up the way you want it.

Searching a project

For a quick no-frills search of your project, enter the word(s) you're looking for into the Search text box in the Scrivener toolbar (shown in Figure 17-1). The grayed out text tells you what type of search will run. The default is All (Exact Phrase), but that changes if you choose different options.

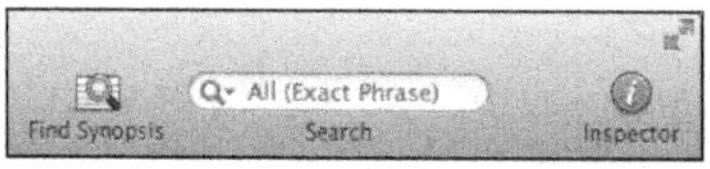

Figure 17-1:
The Search text box on the toolbar.

Exact Phrase means the exact letters or words in the exact order you specify. If the word you type is part of a larger word — the way *dent* is also part of *accident* — the larger words generate a result, too.

Follow these steps to run a basic search of everything in your project for an exact phrase:

1. **Click in the Search text box.**

2. **Type the desired search word(s).**

   While you type, the Binder turns into a Search Results list that displays all items that meet your criteria.

3. **To view a document in the Editor, select it in the Search Results list.**

   You're free to edit the document without losing the list.

   As shown in Figure 17-2, where I searched for every item containing the word **bob**, instances of the search phrase are highlighted.

   Sometimes, you don't see a highlight within the text of a document in the Search Results list. In those cases, check the Label and Status values, keywords, title, and document notes in the Inspector (covered in Part II) for a match.

Don't want to scroll through the document looking for highlights? Use Document Find (covered in the "Using Document Find" section, later in this chapter) to search the file. The Document Find window comes preloaded with the search string from the Search text box.

4. **Click the X at the bottom of the sidebar to close the Results list.**

   You can also click the X in the Search text box on the toolbar.

   The Search text box clears, and the Binder reappears.

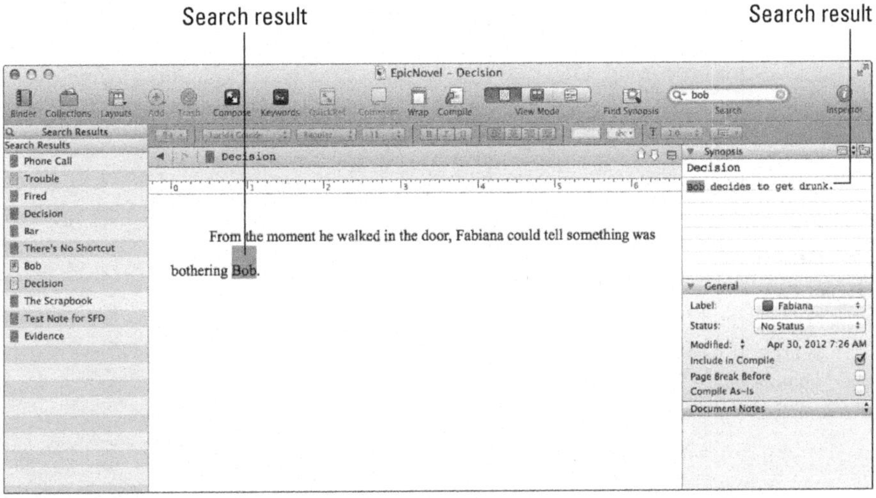

Search result   Search result

Figure 17-2: Search results for **bob**.

Choosing which elements to search

Sometimes, a search produces too many results — such as when you want to find the search term only if it's in the document notes. The Search menu lets you choose exactly what to search. Follow these steps to use it:

1. **Click the magnifying glass icon in the Search text box.**

   The Search drop-down list appears, as shown in Figure 17-3. The Search In section at the top provides a list of elements that you can search.

2. **Choose the desired element from the list.**

3. **(Optional) To add an additional element on the Mac, click the magnifying glass again, and then press the Option key while selecting another item from the list.**

4. **Type the desired word(s) in the Search text box.**

   The Search Results list displays documents that contain the desired word(s) in the element that you chose in Step 2 (and Step 3, if applicable).

5. **To close the Search Results list, click the X button in the Search text box.**

   You can also click the X at the bottom of the results list.

So, if you're looking for **Bob** and you chose to search Label, the Search Results list returns all documents that have Bob as the Label value.

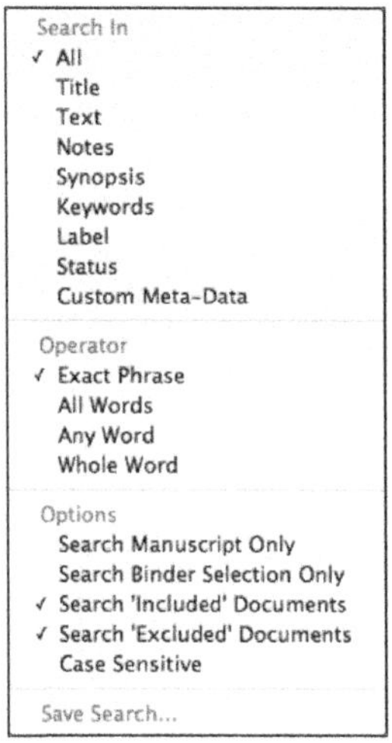

```
Search In
✓ All
  Title
  Text
  Notes
  Synopsis
  Keywords
  Label
  Status
  Custom Meta-Data

Operator
✓ Exact Phrase
  All Words
  Any Word
  Whole Word

Options
  Search Manuscript Only
  Search Binder Selection Only
✓ Search 'Included' Documents
✓ Search 'Excluded' Documents
  Case Sensitive

Save Search...
```

Figure 17-3:
The Project
Search
menu.

Limiting the search results

In addition to choosing the elements to search in, you can change how the search phrase is used.

For example, if you perform an Exact Phrase search for **asteroid belt**, you get only instances in which those two words are adjacent to each other. If you want to see documents that contain both words, but not necessarily appearing together, you need a different type of search.

Luckily, Scrivener offers other options in the Operator category:

✓ **All Words:** The All Words search returns documents that contain all the words entered in the Search text box, regardless of their location or proximity to each other. With this type of search, if a document contains only one of the criteria words, that document doesn't appear in the results.

- **Any Word:** The Any Word search finds documents that contain one or more of the specified words. So **bar fight** would return documents with just *bar,* just *fight,* and both *bar* and *fight* somewhere in them.

- **Whole Word:** In the section "Searching a project," earlier in this chapter, I did an Exact Phrase search for **bob**. The problem is that I might get results for words such as *bobbed, Bobby,* and *bobbin,* too. The Whole Word search eliminates that problem. It returns only documents in which the word you type appears by itself, not as part of a larger word.

  In Windows, the Whole Words search returns documents that contain any of the search words in the text box (much like Any Word), but only matches the complete words, not parts of words.

Examining other search options

The Options section of the Search menu (refer to Figure 17-3) lets you further limit the pool of searchable documents, and also allows you to run a case-sensitive search.

In this section of the Search drop-down list, you can choose more than one option by simply opening the menu again to make another selection. Here's what each of the choices does:

- **Search Manuscript Only:** Limits the search to only those files in the Manuscript (Draft) folder.

  This option is named based on the title of your draft folder, so if you're using a project template other than Novel, this option might display Screenplay, Draft, or something other than Manuscript.

  This option can't be selected in conjunction with Search Binder Selection Only.

- **Search Binder Selection Only:** Limits the search to files that you've selected in the Binder.

  You can't select this option in conjunction with Search Manuscript Only.

- **Search 'Included' Documents:** Limits the search to items that have the Include in Compile option checked in the Inspector.

- **Search 'Excluded' Documents:** Limits the search to items that have the Include in Compile option deselected.

- **Case Sensitive:** Want to search for **Bob**, not **bob**? Use the Case Sensitive search option. You can add this option, regardless of which elements you're searching and which type of word search you're performing (Exact, All, Any, or Whole).

Searching Synopses

For a quick search of only the Synopses, choose Edit⇨Find⇨Find Synopsis (or click the Find Synopsis button on the toolbar, shown in Figure 17-1). In the Synopsis Finder window that opens, enter the characters you're looking for in the Search text box at the top (which has a magnifying glass in it). The Synopsis Finder looks for exact matches of the text you enter (although it's not case sensitive).

The top half of the Synopsis Finder window lists all matching documents followed by a portion of the Synopsis text. Select a document in the list to display its Synopsis in the lower portion of the window. Click the red X button to close the window.

Wondering about the Save Search option at the bottom of the Search drop-down list? That option is covered in Chapter 18.

Your choice to search for included documents, excluded documents, or both, affects the results. Your Compile settings also affect the results, so if you just exported a partial manuscript and didn't change the Compile settings back to include the whole manuscript, you may not get the results you were expecting. (I cover compiling in Chapter 12.)

To close the Search Results list, click the X button in the Search text box or at the bottom of the Results list.

Using Project Replace

Did your editor decide she hates the name Bob? Did your manuscript setting move from Key West to Paris? If the idea of changing hundreds of instances of a word makes you cringe, relax. Making the change is painless with Project Replace.

Project Replace provides a global way to find and replace all instances of a word or words (except words where they appear in keywords, covered in Chapter 5, and Label and Status values, described in Chapter 4).

Follow these steps to use Project Replace:

1. **Choose Edit⇨Find⇨Project Replace.**

   The Project Replace window appears, as shown in Figure 17-4. Many of the options available in Project Search also appear here. (See the section "Working with Project Search," earlier in this chapter, for information on that search.)

   Changes made via Project Replace can't be undone. Consider creating a backup of the project before making substantial changes. Backups are covered in Chapter 21.

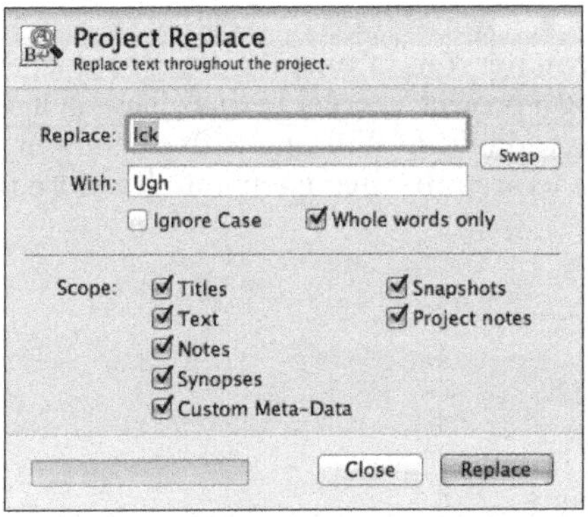

Project Replace
Replace text throughout the project.

Replace: | Ick |
Swap

With: | Ugh |

☐ Ignore Case   ☑ Whole words only

Scope: ☑ Titles   ☑ Snapshots
         ☑ Text   ☑ Project notes
         ☑ Notes
         ☑ Synopses
         ☑ Custom Meta-Data

[   ]   Close   Replace

Figure 17-4:
The Project
Replace
window.

2. **In the Replace text box, type the word that you want to replace.**

   If your editor hates the name Bob and wants you to change it to Abishek, you would type **Bob** here.

3. **In the With text box, type the new word.**

   Continuing with the example from Step 2, you would type **Abishek** here.

4. **If you don't care about the letter case, select Ignore Case.**

   In the example with the names, you'd want to uncheck Ignore Case to make sure that you don't change `continued to bob in the water` to `continued to Abishek in the water`.

5. **Select Whole Words Only to avoid changing words that contain the Replace word within them.**

   For example, you wouldn't want to change *bobbed* to *Abishekbed*.

6. **In the Scope section, choose the elements of a document on which you want to perform the replace.**

Deselect any item to which you don't want to apply the change.

7. **Click Replace.**

As shown in Figure 17-5, the progress bar at the bottom of the window shows the progress of the operation and displays a final count of how many documents were changed.

8. **Click Close to close the window.**

If you want to reverse the Project Replace you just ran, click the Swap button in the Project Replace window, and then click the Replace button.

Does Project Replace make you nervous? Consider using Project Search (refer to the section "Searching a project," earlier in this chapter) in conjunction with Document Replace (covered in the "Working with Document Replace" section, later in this chapter) to step through each match before replacing it.

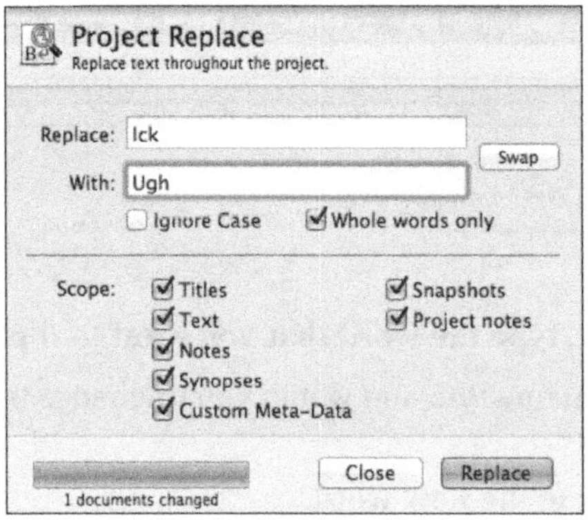

Figure 17-5:
Project
Replace
results.

Project Replace
Replace text throughout the project.

Replace: Ick

With: Ugh   Swap

☐ Ignore Case   ☑ Whole words only

Scope: ☑ Titles   ☑ Snapshots
        ☑ Text   ☑ Project notes
        ☑ Notes
        ☑ Synopses
        ☑ Custom Meta-Data

Close   Replace

1 documents changed

Running Document Find and Replace

Document Find and Document Replace work much like Project Search and Project Replace, but they narrow the search to a single document or Scrivenings session. (Check out the sections "Working with Project Search" and "Using Project Replace," both earlier in this chapter.)

Using Document Find

Document Find searches within the document(s) active in the Editor pane. It's especially handy if you've done a Project Search and the document you're looking at has a lot of highlighted results or is really long. Instead of scrolling through looking for highlights, you can perform a Document Find and have it step through the results one at a time.

Document Find even automatically loads the search string from the current Search text box in the toolbar. So you can run Project Search, select a document from the Results list, and then run Document Find to locate the text within that document.

Follow these steps to conduct a Document Find search:

1. **Select the document(s) that you want to view in the Editor.**

   If you select multiple documents and they appear in the Corkboard or Outliner, choose View⇨Scrivenings to return to the Editor.

2. **Choose Edit⇨Find⇨Find.**

   Alternatively, you can press ⌘+F (Ctrl+F in Windows).

   The Find window appears, as shown in Figure 17-6.

3. **Type the word(s) that you want to search for in the Find text box.**

   If you've run a Project Search, the text box is prefilled from that search.

4. **In the Find Options section, select Ignore Case if you don't care about the letter case.**

   If the case matters, deselect this option.

5. **Click the drop-down list below Ignore Case and make a selection.**

   What you choose changes how the Find looks for text matches:

   • *Contains:* Finds any text that contains the letters entered in the Find text box.

   • *Starts With:* Highlights only text that starts with the letters entered in the Find text box.

   • *Whole Word:* Finds text that matches the word in the Find text box, but not text that contains the letters as part of a larger word.

     For example, if the search text is **ed**, the Whole Word option returns *ed* or *Ed*, but not *bed*, *Edward*, or *redder*.

   • *Ends With:* Matches only words that end with the letters entered in the Find text box.

6. **Click Next.**

Scrivener moves to the first match. As shown in Figure 17-6, Scrivener highlights the match.

7. **Continue to click Next until you locate the instance of the search term you were looking for.**

If you click Next and don't see anything, you may have to move the Find window out of the way. If there's no match, Scrivener makes an error noise and displays Not Found in the space below the Replace text box.

Mac users, if you press Return instead of clicking Next, the Find panel finds the next match (if any) and then closes. To run the search again (or run your last Project Search for the document) without opening the Find window, press ⌘+G.

8. **Click the red X button to close the Find window.**

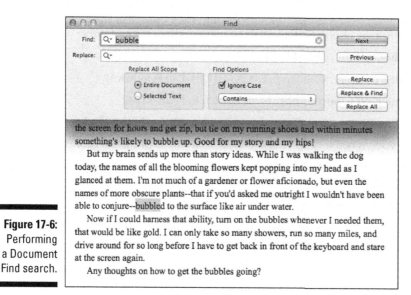

Figure 17-6:
Performing
a Document
Find search.

Viewing recent searches

A magnifying glass icon appears in the Find and Replace text boxes of the Document Find window. As detailed in Figure 17-7, clicking the magnifying glass provides a list of Recent Searches and Recent Replacements, respectively.

Here's how to work with this drop-down list:

✔ Click a word on the list to insert it into the text box.

✔ Clear the list by choosing Clear Recent Searches or Clear Recent Replacements from the appropriate list.

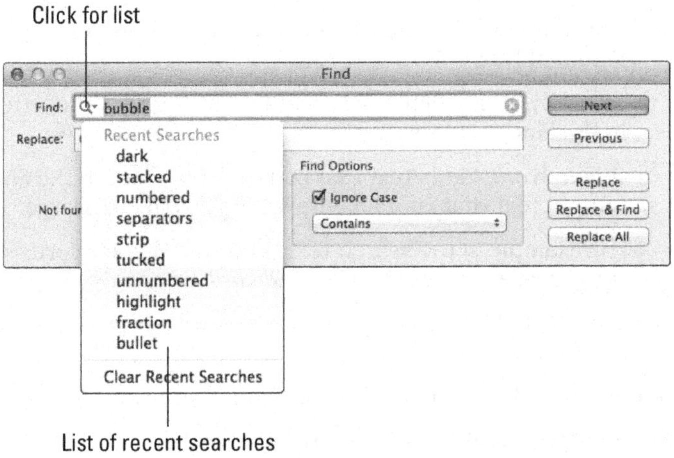

Click for list

Figure 17-7:
A list of recent searches.

List of recent searches

Working with Document Replace

To replace all instances of a word, but only within the document(s) you're viewing in the Editor, use the Document Replace option. Follow these steps:

1. **Select the document(s) that you want to view in the Editor.**

2. **Choose Edit⇨Find⇨Find.**

   The Find window appears (refer to Figure 17-6).

3. **Type the word(s) that you want to search for in the Find text box.**

4. **Type the word(s) with which you want to replace the Find word in the Replace text box.**

5. **In the Replace All Scope section, select either the Entire Document radio button or the Selected Text radio button.**

   Entire Document replaces all instances within the document(s) being viewed in the Editor. Selected Text replaces only matches found in text that you select within the Editor.

6. **In the Find Options section, select Ignore Case to replace all instances, regardless of case.**

   Otherwise, leave this option unchecked.

7. **Make a selection from the Contains drop-down list to change how the Find looks for text matches.**

   Here are your options:

   - *Contains:* Finds any text that contains the letters entered in the Find text box.

   - *Starts With:* Highlights only text that starts with the letters entered in the Find text box.

   - *Whole Word:* Finds text that matches the word in the Find text box, but not text that contains the letters as part of a larger word.

     For example, if the search text is **ed**, the Whole Word option returns *ed* or *Ed,* but not *bed, Edward,* or *redder.*

   - *Ends With:* Matches only words that end with the letters entered in the Find text box.

8. **Click the Next button to find a match that you want to replace.**

9. **Click Replace, Replace & Find, or Replace All.**

   If you click Replace before finding a match, Scrivener inserts the replacement text wherever your cursor is.

   The three Replace alternatives behave differently:

   - *Replace:* Inserts the replacement word at the cursor's location in the document. Because you clicked Next in Step 8, the highlighted match is overwritten.

   - *Replace & Find:* Replaces the current instance and finds the next match.

   - *Replace All:* To replace all instances of the matching text in your document, skip Step 8 and simply choose Replace All.

10. **Close the Find window by clicking the red X button.**

To approve each match before replacing it, start by clicking the Next button. For each match that you want to replace, click the Replace & Find button. If you get to a match that you don't want to replace, click the Next button to move to the next match without making a replacement.

Finding by Format

In addition to searching for text, you can search by format. If you've been highlighting certain parts of your manuscript in different colors — say, blue for emotion and yellow for setting and description — and now you want to find all the blue-highlighted text, Find by Formatting is the answer.

In addition to highlighted text, you can also search for comments and footnotes, inline annotations, inline footnotes, revision color, colored text, links, text with preserved style, and character format.

Follow these steps to search by format:

1. **Choose Edit⇨Find⇨Find by Formatting.**

   The Formatting Finder window appears, as shown in Figure 17-8.

2. **Click the Find drop-down list, and then select an option from the types of formatting available to search.**

   When you change the formatting type, the options at the bottom of the window change.

3. **To limit your search to specific text, enter the text in the Containing Text text box.**

   If you leave the text box blank, Scrivener finds all instances of the specified formatting.

4. **Click the Search In drop-down list, and then choose to search all documents in the project or only those selected in the Binder.**

5. **Specify the special options that appear below the Search In drop-down list, if applicable.**

   Several formats have extra options:

   - *Highlighted Text:* Offers a Limit Search to Color check box. Selecting this option limits the search to the color you choose. (To choose the color, click the Color box and select a color from the Colors window that appears.) If not selected, the search finds all highlighted text of any color.

   - *Comments & Footnotes:* The Type drop-down list lets you choose to search for linked Footnotes, Comments, or both.

- *Inline Annotations:* The drop-down list provides options for searching by color. Any Color finds all inline annotations, regardless of color. Limit Search to Color lets you choose the desired color to find from the Color box. Exclude from Search leaves out the selected color when matching results.

- *Revision Color:* The drop-down list lets you specify the revision color to search for.

- *Colored Text:* Offers a Limit Search to Color check box. Selecting this option limits the search to the color you choose from the Color box. If it's not selected, the search finds all text of any color.

  If you search for colored text — not limited to a specific color — and get a match that appears to be normal text, it may be colored black. Text that has black applied is different from regular text (which has no color formatting applied, even though it appears black). To remove the color, right-click the selected text and choose Text Color⇨Remove Color from the contextual menu that appears.

- *Links:* Provides options to search for All links, Web/File (external) links, or Scrivener (internal) links (which are links embedded in the text, not references; I cover references in Chapter 5).

- *Character Format:* Lets you search by text format, including Bold, Italic, Underline, Strikethrough, and Keep with Next (which ensures that a paragraph is kept on the same page as the one that follows it).

6. **Click Next to find the first match.**

   You can continue to click Next until you've cycled through all matches or found the one you were looking for.

7. **Close the Formatting Finder window by clicking the red X button.**

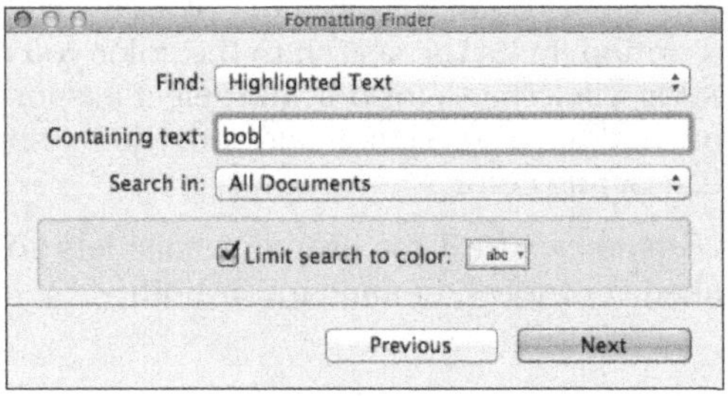

Figure 17-8:
Searching
by format.

> Formatting Finder
>
> Find: Highlighted Text
> Containing text: bob
> Search in: All Documents
>
> ☑ Limit search to color: abc
>
> Previous | Next

Marking the Spot with Bookmarks

Want to mark a spot within your manuscript to make it easy to find again? Try a bookmark. A *bookmark* is basically an inline annotation starting with an asterisk and a space that marks a place in your text for easy navigation.

Adding a bookmark

Follow these steps to add a bookmark to a document:

1. **Place your cursor in the paragraph that you want to mark.**

2. **Choose Edit⇨Insert⇨Bookmark Annotation.**

   Or you can press Shift+⌘+B.

   The marker is inserted at the front of the current paragraph, as shown in Figure 17-9. By default, Scrivener uses the first few words of the line to label the bookmark in the Bookmarks list (see the "Navigating to bookmarks" section, later in this chapter, for more about this list), but you can override that behavior by adding a space after the asterisk and text to create a custom label, as shown in Figure 17-10. In this instance, TNR3 is the bookmark label.

TIP

You can also add a bookmark by placing an inline annotation containing an asterisk followed by a space at the beginning of a paragraph. If desired, add the custom label after the space.

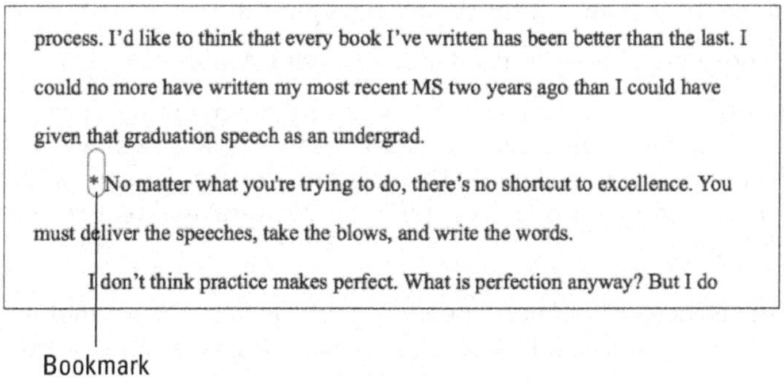

Figure 17-9:
A bookmark
inserted into
the text.

> process. I'd like to think that every book I've written has been better than the last. I
>
> could no more have written my most recent MS two years ago than I could have
>
> given that graduation speech as an undergrad.
>
>   * No matter what you're trying to do, there's no shortcut to excellence. You
>
> must deliver the speeches, take the blows, and write the words.
>
>   I don't think practice makes perfect. What is perfection anyway? But I do

Bookmark

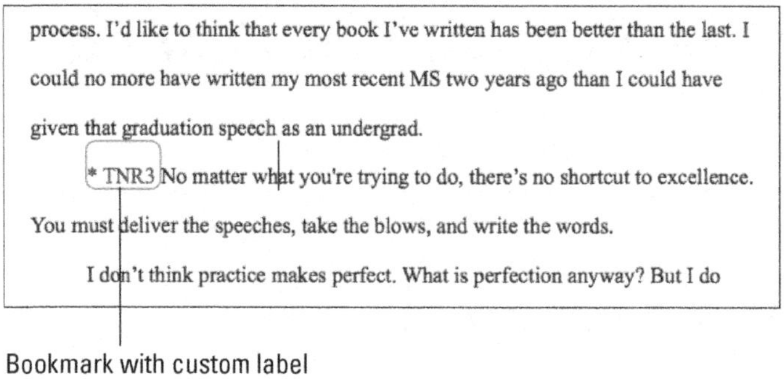

Figure 17-10:
A bookmark
with a
custom
label.

> process. I'd like to think that every book I've written has been better than the last. I
>
> could no more have written my most recent MS two years ago than I could have
>
> given that graduation speech as an undergrad.
>
>   * TNR3 No matter what you're trying to do, there's no shortcut to excellence.
>
> You must deliver the speeches, take the blows, and write the words.
>
>   I don't think practice makes perfect. What is perfection anyway? But I do

Bookmark with custom label

Removing a bookmark is as simple as deleting the annotation from the document.

Adding a bookmark header

A *bookmark header* is a special kind of bookmark that helps you keep your bookmarks organized. It works just like a bookmark but creates a hierarchical heading in the Bookmarks list for easier reading. (See the following section for details on the Bookmarks list.)

All bookmarks that fall after a header are considered children until the next bookmark header appears.

Add a bookmark header by following these steps:

1. **Place the cursor within the paragraph that you want to mark.**

2. **Choose Edit⇨Insert⇨Bookmark Header Annotation.**

    The bookmark appears at the front of the current paragraph as an annotation with two asterisks followed by a space, as shown in Figure 17-11. Just like with a bookmark, the first few words are used as the label, but you can add your own by typing the desired label text after the asterisks and space.

You can also add a bookmark header by placing an inline annotation that contains two asterisks followed by a space at the beginning of a paragraph.

Bookmark header with a custom label

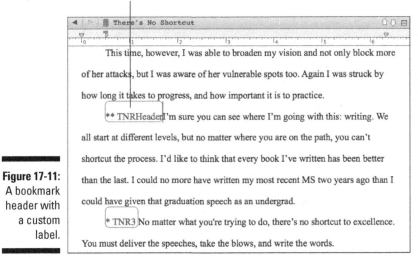

Figure 17-11:
A bookmark
header with
a custom
label.

Navigating to bookmarks

After you embed the bookmarks in your document, you can navigate to them in two ways. (Only those bookmarks in the current document or Scrivenings session are accessible.)

The following methods let you navigate to a bookmark:

✔ **Click the Document icon in the Header bar, choose Bookmarks from the menu that appears, and select the desired bookmark.** In Figure 17-12, the bookmark header and bookmark created in the preceding sections are displayed in a hierarchical list.

✔ **Choose View⇨Text Bookmarks, and then choose the desired bookmark from the submenu that appears.** After you choose a bookmark from the submenu, Scrivener jumps to the bookmarked paragraph.

Inline annotations that appear on a line by themselves also appear in the Bookmarks list, whether they contain an asterisk or not.

Click for Header Bar menu

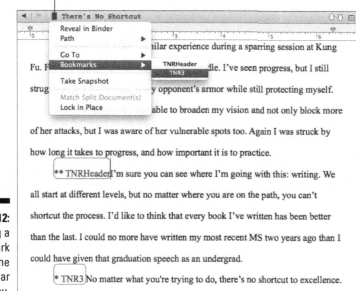

Figure 17-12:
Choosing a
bookmark
from the
Header Bar
menu.

Chapter 18

Creating Collections for Quick Access to Related Files

. . . .

In This Chapter

▶ Working with the two types of collections

▶ Changing a saved search collection to a standard collection

▶ Changing a collection's name

▶ Deleting a collection

▶ Using collections as containers

▶ Viewing the Label and Status values in the Collections list

. . . .

ollections in Scrivener aren't for displaying that stockpile of ceramic elephants or your stash of half-smoked cigars from famous people. But the idea is similar. They're a way to pull together files that are related in some way from various parts of your manuscript. You choose the relationship, whether it's based on search criteria, storyline, setting, Status, or some other thread understood only by you.

A collection is a *flat list* of files — meaning the files aren't organized hierarchically like they are in the Binder — that you can pull from anywhere in the project, in or out of the Manuscript (Draft) folder.

This chapter covers each type of collection in detail.

Looking at the Types of Collections

Created at the project level, a collection isn't available to all projects; however, you can save your collections as part of a project template for future use. (See Chapter 15 for more on project templates.)

After you create a collection, you can simply select all the files in the resulting list and view them in Scrivenings, Corkboard, or Outliner mode.

You can use two types of collections:

- **Standard collection:** You create this collection manually by adding and removing files to create a custom list. For example, a standard collection could be a list of your first three chapters to use as a compile source for exporting a partial manuscript (see Chapters 12 and 13 for more on compiling). Or you can make a collection list of all scenes that follow a particular subplot within your storyline. You can even use a standard collection to try out an experimental scene order.

- **Search collection:** A project search that you save for future use so that it isn't overwritten when you run another project search. For example, if you track your document status, you can create a collection of all files marked To Do. Or you might build a collection that lists all documents written in a specific point of view.

  Scrivener automatically creates a search collection called Search Results when you run a Project Search (covered in Chapter 17). You can't rename or delete the Search Results collection, and it always holds the most recent query and results.

Working with Standard Collections

Want to try out a new scene order without committing? Or maybe you want to set up a collection of files to quickly compile a partial manuscript. In that case, you need a standard collection.

Creating a standard collection

After you create a standard collection, that collection is *static,* which means the contents don't change unless you add or remove files manually, even if the original collection was created from the results of a search.

Follow these steps to create a standard collection:

1. **Select all the files that you want to include in the collection.**

   You can either manually select the files in the Binder or run a Project Search and select the files from the Results list, as shown in Figure 18-1.

2. **Click the Collections button in the toolbar (see Figure 18-1).**

Alternatively, you can choose View➪Collections➪Show Collections.

The Collections pane appears in the left sidebar above the Binder (or Search Results if you ran a project search), as shown in Figure 18-1.

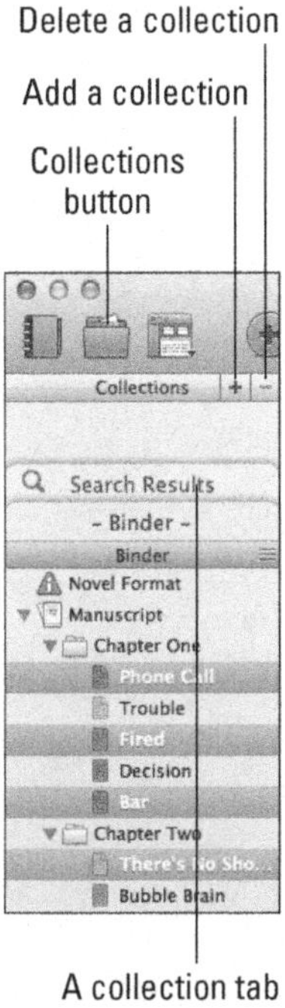

Delete a collection

Add a collection

Collections button

Figure 18-1:
The Collections pane.

A collection tab

3. **Click the Add a Collection button to add a new collection from the selected items.**

   A new tab appears in the Collections pane, ready to be named, as shown in Figure 18-2. The tab and the collection list below it are colored (the color is picked at random each time you create a collection).

4. **Type the desired name for the collection in the highlighted tab, and then press Return.**

   The collection is now set. If you can't see it, you may need to scroll up in the Collections pane. You can also resize the Collections pane to make more tabs visible.

5. **Click the X at the bottom of the collection list to return to the Binder.**

   If the Collections pane is visible, another option is to click the Binder tab.

6. **To close the Collections pane, as well, click the Collections button in the toolbar.**

   Or you can choose View➪Collections➪Hide Collections.

Color box

Close Collection
File List

Figure 18-2:
A new
collection
created
from the
selected
files.

Adding an item to a standard collection

If you forget a file when you create the collection, or write a new document later and want to add it after the fact, you can add a new file in two ways: by using a contextual menu or by dragging and dropping.

If you add the same file twice, it isn't duplicated, so if you're not sure whether the file is already in the collection, select that file. If it's already there, Scrivener just ignores your attempt to add it again.

Adding by menu

Follow these steps to add a file to an existing collection via the contextual menu:

1. **Select the desired file(s) in the Binder.**

2. **Right-click the file(s).**

3. **Choose Add to Collection from the contextual menu that appears, and then choose the desired collection from the submenu, as shown in Figure 18-3.**

    The selection is added to the chosen collection.

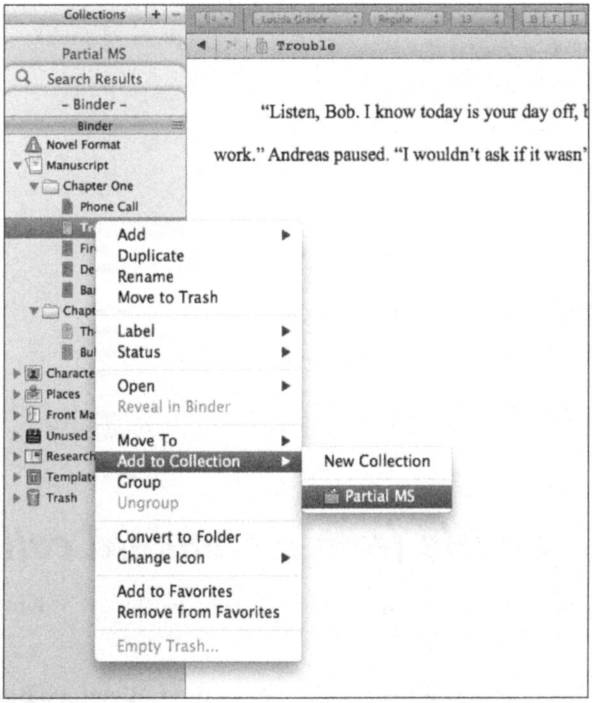

Figure 18-3:
Adding to a collection via contextual menu.

Adding by drag and drop

You can also drag the desired files and drop them onto the collection. To make it easy, follow these steps:

1. **If the Collections pane doesn't appear in the sidebar, click the Collections button in the toolbar.**

The Collections pane appears.

2. **Click the Binder tab to view the Binder below the Collections pane, as shown in Figure 18-4.**

3. **Drag the desired file from the Binder and drop it onto the tab of the collection to which you want to add it.**

Wait for the blue box to appear around the correct tab before dropping the file.

The file is added to the collection.

To add more than one file, select the desired files first, and then drag them all onto the tab for the desired collection.

Drop file here

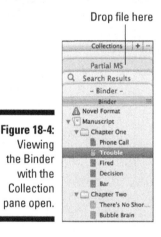

Figure 18-4:
Viewing
the Binder
with the
Collection
pane open.

Removing a file from a standard collection

If for some reason a file no longer belongs in a collection, removing it is as simple as following these steps:

1. **If the Collections pane isn't visible, click the Collections button in the toolbar to view it.**

2. **Click the tab for the desired collection.**

The list of files within the collection appears, as shown in Figure 18-5. The collection gets its own header, colored to match.

3. **Select the file(s) that you want to remove.**

4. **Click the Remove Item button.**

   Alternatively, you can press the Delete key (Windows users, press Shift+Delete).

   The selection is removed from the collection (not from the project).

5. **Click the Binder tab to view the Binder but leave the Collections pane open.**

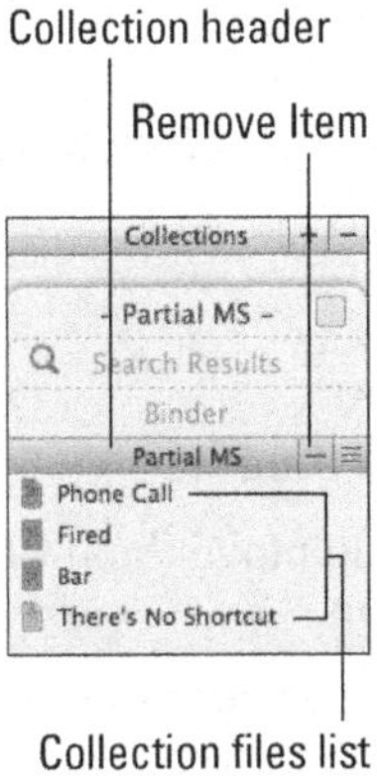

Collection header

Remove Item

Figure 18-5: Removing files from a standard collection.

Collection files list

Reorganizing a standard collection

Because a collection is a flat list of files, you can move the files into any order you want, without affecting their position within the Binder. For that reason, it can be a great way to play with new scene arrangements, create a different compile order, or change the order in which you work on files that need to be written or revised.

To rearrange files in a collection, follow these steps:

1. **Click the Collections button in the toolbar to view the collections, if necessary.**

   The Collections pane appears.

2. **Select the tab of the desired collection.**

   The list of files appears below the Collections pane.

3. **Drag and drop the desired files in their new positions.**

Moving reordered collection items back to the Binder

What if you've moved your documents around in a standard collection and decide the order is perfect for your manuscript? No need to rearrange the items in the Binder to match, you can simply move the items from the collection into the Binder to overwrite the old arrangement.

Just follow these steps:

1. **If necessary, click the Collections button in the toolbar to view the Collections pane.**

2. **Select the desired collection's tab.**

   The collection's file list appears.

3. **Select the files that you want to move to the Binder.**

   The files still appear in the collection after you move them to the Binder. You're really just moving their Binder location.

4. **Drag the files to the Binder tab and, after the Binder opens, drop the files in the desired location.**

   You can also right-click the selected files in the collection, choose Move To from the contextual menu that appears, and then select a new location from the submenu.

   The original files move to the new location in the Binder.

Changing the collection color

Scrivener automatically assigns a color to each collection you create, but if you're not happy with the choice, you can change it by following these steps:

1. **If the Collections pane isn't visible, click the Collections button in the toolbar to open it.**

2. **Click the tab for the desired collection.**

3. **Double-click the Color box to the right of the collection name in the tab (refer to Figure 18-2).**

   The Colors window opens. Windows users get a color menu.

4. **Choose the desired color from the Colors window (or menu).**

   The collection color changes to match your choice.

5. **Close the Colors window by clicking the red X button.**

   The Windows color menu closes automatically after you select a color.

Creating a Search Collection

If you run a particular Project Search regularly, you can save time by saving it as a search collection. Search collections are dynamic, which means that every time you select the collection, it runs the query and updates the file list with the most current results. Because the results are automatically updated based on the criteria, you can't manually add, remove, or reorder files in a search collection.

Why might you use a search collection? Well, say you want to start each day running a search for documents with a Status of To Do so that you know where to start working. Or maybe you only want to work on scenes written from Bob's point of view. A saved search collection is perfect.

Not a fan of inline annotations but still want to flag certain spots in your manuscript for follow-up? You could insert **ZZZ** in those places, and then run a saved search to find the relevant files when you're ready to work on those parts.

Follow these steps to create a saved search collection:

1. **Run a project search, as outlined in Chapter 17.**

2. **Click the magnifying glass in the Search bar, as shown in Figure 18-6, and choose Save Search from the drop-down list that appears.**

   A window appears, prompting you for the name of the saved search.

   Is the Save Search option on the menu grayed out? Check the Options section of the Search menu and make sure Search Binder Selection Only isn't selected. A Binder selection is a temporary state that can't be saved.

Figure 18-6:
Creating
a saved
search
collection.

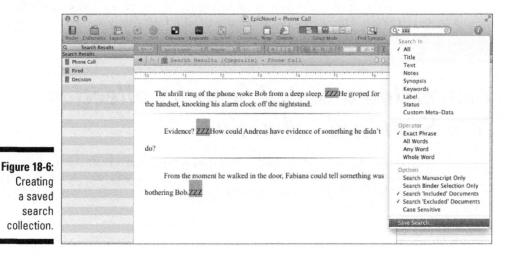

3. **Enter the desired collection name in the New Saved Search Collection text box.**

   The saved search becomes a tab in the Collection pane, as shown in Figure 18-7. I called mine ZZZ Search.

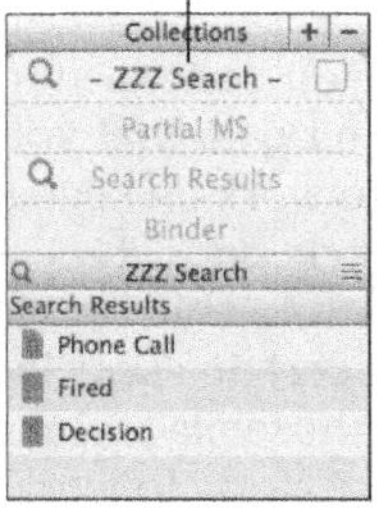

Saved Search
collection tab

Figure 18-7:
A saved
search
collection.

Working with the Search Results Collection

The search results collection stores the most recent Project Search criteria and results. To rerun your most recent project search, follow these steps:

1. **If the Collections pane isn't visible, click the Collections button in the toolbar.**

2. **Click the Search Results tab.**

   The most recent project search is run again, and the results appear in the list. The Search bar is populated with the criteria and settings used so that you can adjust them for a new search, if desired.

Converting a Saved Search Collection to a Standard Collection

If you want to freeze the results of a saved search, convert the collection to a standard collection. You lose the search criteria, but you don't have to worry about the file list changing automatically.

Convert the saved search collection by following these steps:

1. **If necessary, click the Collections button in the toolbar to view the Collections pane.**

2. **Select the tab of the saved search collection.**

3. **Choose View➪Collections➪Convert to Standard Collection.**

   The search criteria are removed and no longer populate the Search bar when you select the collection.

Renaming a Collection

If you change your mind about the name of a standard or saved search collection, it's simple to rename it. Just follow these steps:

1. **If the Collections pane isn't visible, click the Collections button in the toolbar to view it.**

2. **Double-click the name of the collection that you want to rename.**

   The name is highlighted, ready to overwrite.

3. **Type the new name or edit the existing one.**

4. **Press Return.**

   The name is updated.

Removing a Collection

If you no longer want a standard or saved search collection that you created, you can remove it by following these steps:

1. **If the Collections pane isn't visible, click the Collections button in the toolbar to view it.**

2. **Select the tab of the collection that you want to remove.**

3. **Click the Delete Collection button in the Collections header (refer to Figure 18–1).**

   A warning window appears to remind you the action can't be undone.

4. **Click OK.**

   The selected collection is removed.

Viewing a Collection as a Container

After you create a collection, you can work with it in a Scrivenings session, the Corkboard, or the Outliner, just like any other container.

To select a collection as a container, follow these steps:

1. **If the Collections pane isn't visible, click the Collections button in the toolbar to view it.**

2. **Select the tab of the collection that you want to view.**

3. **Click the collection header (refer to Figure 18-5).**

   Windows users, Shift-click to select the files in the collection.

   The files appear in Composite mode in whichever container view you used last.

4. **From the View menu, choose the desired view mode.**

   Or you can click the appropriate Group View mode button on the toolbar.

Showing the Label and Status Columns in the Collections List

For search results and saved search collections, the Label and Status values appear in the individual collection header. If you can't see them, try dragging the right edge of the collections pane to make it wider. Then, you can resize the Label and Status columns by dragging the bars between the column headers.

If the Label and Status columns aren't visible, follow these steps to display them:

1. **If necessary, click the Collections button in the toolbar to view it.**

2. **Select the tab of your search results collection or one of your saved searches.**

3. **Right-click the Search Results bar just below the collection header.**

   As shown in Figure 18-8, a small contextual menu appears.

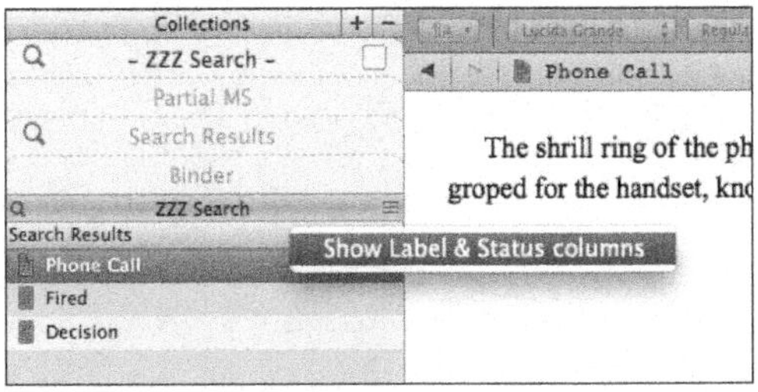

Figure 18-8:
The Search
Results
header's
contextual
menu.

4. **Click Show Label & Status Columns, if it appears.**

   If the menu shows Hide Label & Status Columns, they're already turned on. Drag the edge of the Collection pane to the right to further expand its width to view the columns.

   The Label and Status columns appear in the list. With these columns displayed, you can change the values for a file and sort the list by clicking the desired column header, as shown in Figure 18-9.

   The sort is denoted by the small triangle in the header. If the point is up, the sort is ascending; point down is a descending sort. Click the header to toggle between the two sorts.

To remove the Label and Status columns, right-click the Search Results bar and choose Hide Label & Status Columns from the contextual menu that appears.

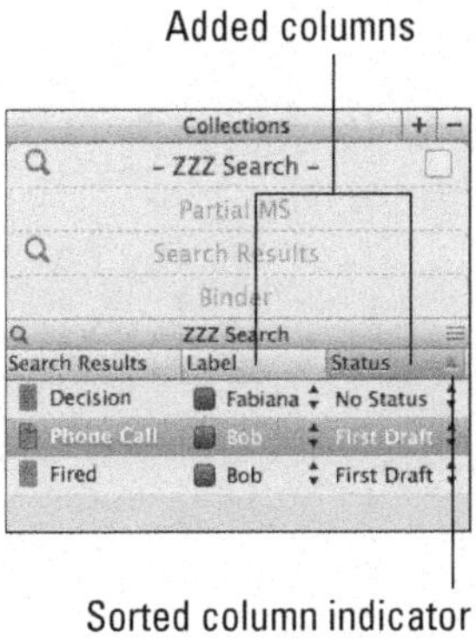

Added columns

Figure 18-9:
Viewing and
sorting by
Label and
Status.

Sorted column indicator

Chapter 19

Saving Versions of Your Files with Snapshots

*A*ny time you're making significant — or even not-so-significant — changes to a document, it's good practice to keep a copy of the old version. You could make a copy and store it in an Old Versions folder, but that can also get unwieldy. Scrivener has a more elegant tool: snapshots.

A *snapshot* is a copy of a document that's frozen in time and stored for future reference, as if you took a photo of it with your camera so that you could refer back later — but better, because it's stored right in the document itself and easily accessible if you want to copy from, compare to, or roll back to the older version. In addition to the text, snapshots store annotations, comments, and footnotes, which not only lets you revisit your comments, but also offers you a way to take notes on a version before making the copy, if desired.

This chapter leads you through everything you need to know to make snapshots a useful part of your writing process.

Creating a Snapshot

Snapshots are really meant for saving versions of individual documents, rather than the entire project or many files at the same time (see Chapter 21 for information on backing up your project). That said, you can apply the following steps to more than one document at a time by simply selecting multiple files. To create a snapshot, follow these steps:

1. **Select the desired item(s) in the Binder, Corkboard, or Outliner.**

2. **Choose Documents⇨Snapshots⇨Take Snapshots of Selected Documents.**

   If a single item is selected in Windows, or if your cursor is in the Editor on the Mac, the submenu option is Take Snapshot.

   Alternatively, you can press ⌘+5 (Ctrl+5 for Windows).

   If your sound is turned on, you hear what sounds like a camera shutter.

   As shown in Figure 19-1, the icon for the selected document now has a folded corner, an indicator that it has one or more associated snapshots. In addition, the Snapshots button in the Inspector panel contains an asterisk to denote content.

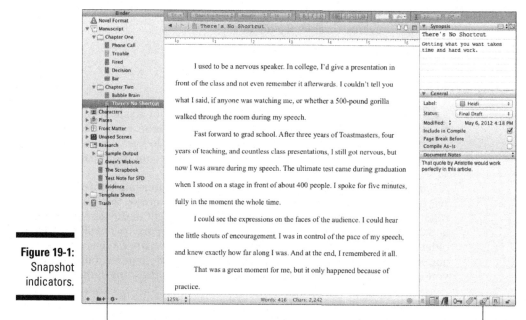

Figure 19-1:
Snapshot
indicators.

Folded corner   Asterisk in the Snapshots button

Viewing Snapshots in the Sidebar

After you take a snapshot (as described in the preceding section), you probably want to go look at it. Just click the Snapshots button at the bottom of the Inspector pane to bring up the list.

You can also choose Documents➪Snapshots➪Show Snapshots to open the Inspector directly to the Snapshots pane. This option is especially handy if you like to work while keeping the Inspector hidden.

Figure 19-2 shows the Snapshots pane. The snapshots are listed by date and time. When you select a snapshot in the list, you can view its text in the lower portion of the pane. In this area, you can select and copy text, if desired.

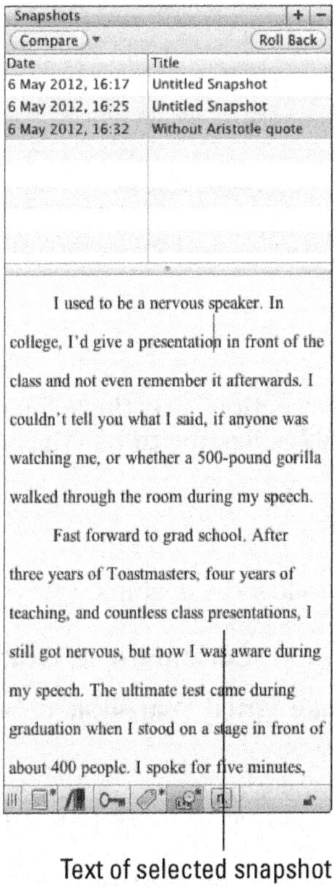

Figure 19-2:
The
Snapshots
pane.

Text of selected snapshot

Creating Titled Snapshots

If you're just taking snapshots at regular intervals for peace of mind, you might not want to title them, but if you're making major revisions, a title can help you sort through your versions quickly.

Consider using something meaningful to help you understand which version of your document the snapshot represents. For example, if you're changing the opening scene of your manuscript from a bar fight to a wedding, you might name the snapshot of the old version Bar Fight Version.

In the titled snapshot shown in Figure 19-3, the title makes it clear that the earlier version doesn't include the quote that I added after taking the snapshot.

Titled snapshot

Figure 19-3:
A titled
snapshot.

You can title snapshots in two ways:

- ✔ Take the snapshot, as outlined in the section "Creating a Snapshot," earlier in this chapter, and then double-click the title in the Snapshots pane and type a new name.
- ✔ Name the snapshot when you take it.

To name the snapshot when you take it, follow these steps:

1. **Select the desired item(s) in the Binder, Corkboard, or Outliner.**

2. **Choose Documents➪Snapshots➪Take Titled Snapshots of Selected Documents.**

   When a single file is selected in Windows, or if your cursor is in the Editor on the Mac, the submenu option is Take Snapshot with Title.

   A window appears, prompting you for the title. If you've chosen more than one item, the same title is applied to all of them, which can be handy if you want to give them all the same version number or designation before making major changes to a section of your project.

3. **Type the desired title in the Snapshot Title text box.**

Sorting Snapshots

By default, snapshots are sorted by Date (date and time) in ascending order, but you can sort by Date in descending order or by Title in either order.

To sort by a column, click in the column header. A small triangle appears. Click again to change the sort order. A triangle pointing up denotes ascending order (A–Z), pointing down indicates descending order (Z–A).

Comparing Snapshots

Not only can you view the text of snapshots to review and pilfer from your old versions, you can compare a snapshot to the current version of your document.

Viewing comparisons in the sidebar

You can view the differences between a snapshot and the current version of the document in the Snapshots pane by following these steps:

1. **If needed, open the Snapshots pane in the Inspector by clicking the Snapshots button.**

2. **From the list of snapshots, select the one that you want to compare.**

3. **Click the Compare button, which changes to Original when clicked.**

   The text differences are highlighted in the lower portion of the right sidebar, as shown in Figure 19-4. Red struck-through text shows deleted words (those that aren't in the current version of the document), and blue underlined text shows what's been added (text that exists in the current document but not the snapshot).

4. **To view the snapshot text without markups, click Original.**

To compare two snapshots to each other, ⌘-click to select both of them in the Snapshots pane. The differences are highlighted in the lower portion of the Snapshots pane.

Deleted text

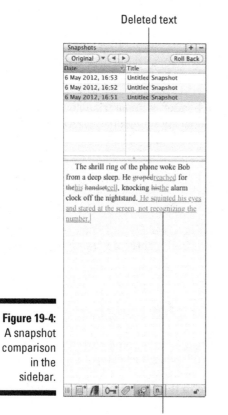

Figure 19-4:
A snapshot
comparison
in the
sidebar.

Added text

Viewing comparisons in a split screen without markups

If you don't like the small format of the Snapshots pane, you can compare your current document and the snapshot in Split Screen mode. This method doesn't highlight changes, it merely puts the snapshot in an Editor pane, where you can view or copy text. Follow these steps to open a snapshot in Split Screen mode:

1. **Click the Snapshots button to open the Snapshots pane in the Inspector, if necessary.**

2. **Click the Split toggle button to split the Editor pane.**

   For more on using Split Screen mode, see Chapter 6.

3. **Drag the desired snapshot from the list in the Snapshots pane to the Header bar of one of the Editors.**

   As shown in Figure 19-5, the snapshot text appears in the Editor, but without the markups to show the changes.

   Want to view a second snapshot rather than the current document? Simply drag another snapshot to the other Editor pane's Header bar.

   You can't make changes to a snapshot, even when it's in the Editor.

4. **Click the Split toggle button in the header of the current document to return to a single Editor.**

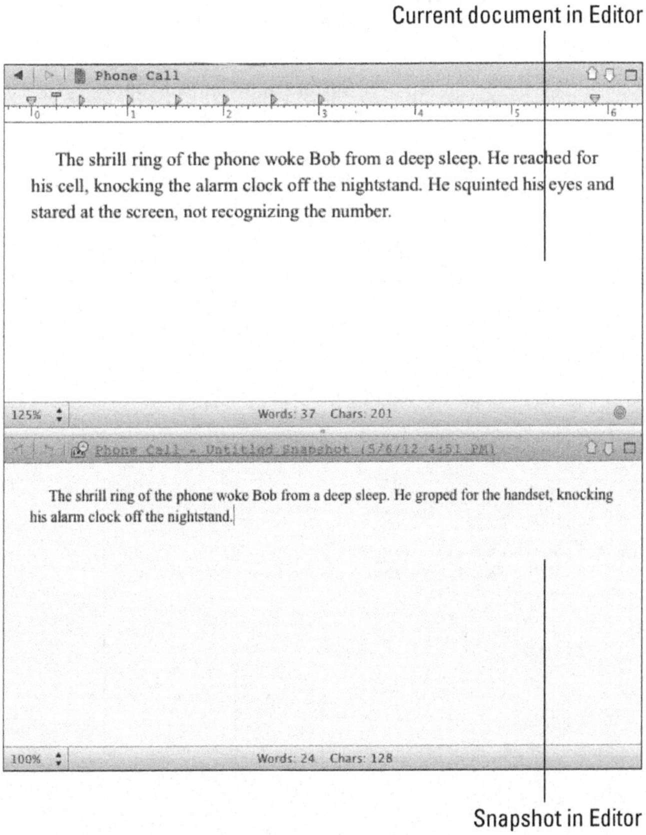

Current document in Editor

Phone Call

The shrill ring of the phone woke Bob from a deep sleep. He reached for his cell, knocking the alarm clock off the nightstand. He squinted his eyes and stared at the screen, not recognizing the number.

125%   Words: 37   Chars: 201

Phone Call – Untitled Snapshot (5/6/12 4:51 PM)

The shrill ring of the phone woke Bob from a deep sleep. He groped for the handset, knocking his alarm clock off the nightstand.

Figure 19-5: A Split Screen comparison without markups.

100%   Words: 24   Chars: 128

Snapshot in Editor

Viewing comparisons in a split screen with markups

To clearly see the changes you've made when viewing a snapshot in Split Screen mode, follow these steps:

1. **If it's not already, open the Snapshots pane in the Inspector by clicking the Snapshots button.**

2. **Click the Split toggle button to split the Editor pane.**

3. **Hold down the Option key while dragging the desired snapshot to the header of one of the Editor panes.**

   The snapshot appears in the Editor with differences from the current document highlighted, as shown in Figure 19-6. Remember, you can't edit a snapshot, even in the Editor pane.

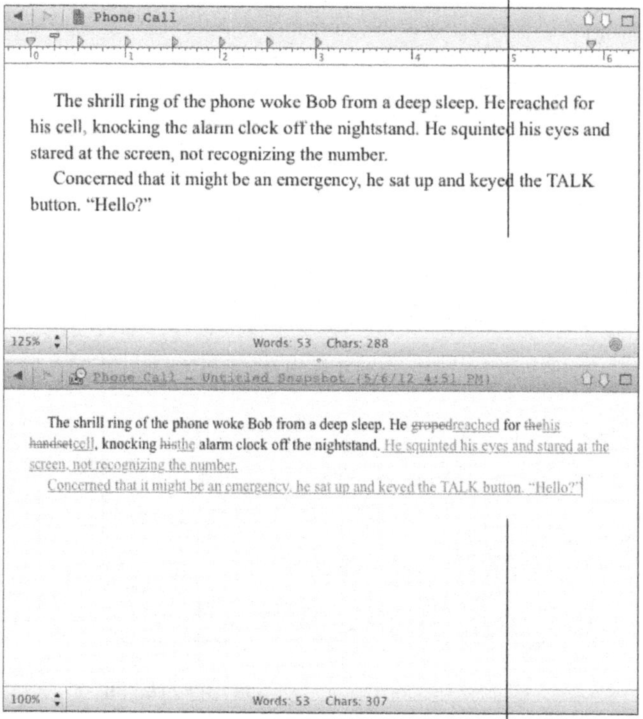

Current document in Editor

Figure 19-6: A Split Screen comparison with changes highlighted.

Snapshot with markups in Editor

You can view a second snapshot comparison by dragging another snapshot to the other Editor pane's header bar. The markups in each pane show the differences between the snapshot and the current document.

4. Click the Split toggle button in the header of the current document pane to return to single Editor view.

Changing Compare settings

When comparing a snapshot to the current version of your document, you can adjust how the markup appears. Click the arrow next to the Compare button to open a drop-down list, as shown in Figure 19-7.

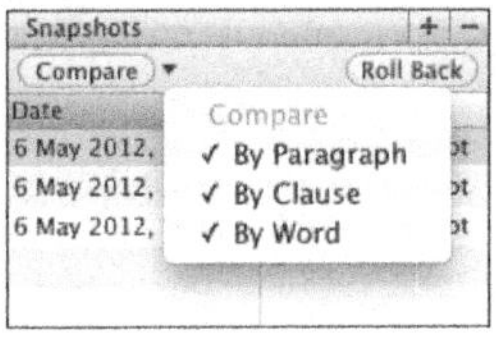

Figure 19-7:
The
Compare
Options
drop-down
list.

When more than one option is selected — the default is all three — Scrivener runs through the comparison process at the broadest level first, then moves to the next level of detail. However, you can choose to focus your comparison at only one or two levels:

- **By Paragraph:** This is the highest-level view. If only this option is selected, Scrivener makes markups at the paragraph level only. That means if you deleted a word from a paragraph in the current version, the markup shows the entire paragraph as deleted, and then the current paragraph as a new addition, as displayed in Figure 19-8.

  This option is useful if you've made a lot of edits since the snapshot was taken, and the word or clause level is too hard to read.

- **By Clause:** Choosing this option means that markups are shown at the clause level or sentence level. So, if a word has been added or deleted in the current version, the whole clause is shown as modified. Figure 19-9 shows an example of comparisons at the clause level, using the same snapshot and current document as in Figure 19-8.

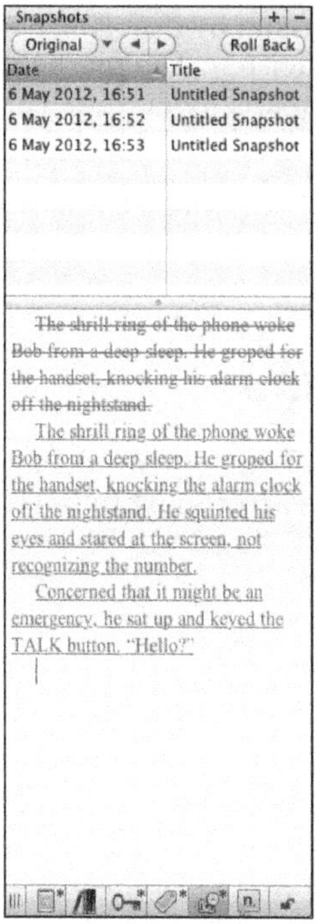

Figure 19-8:
Comparison
by
paragraph.

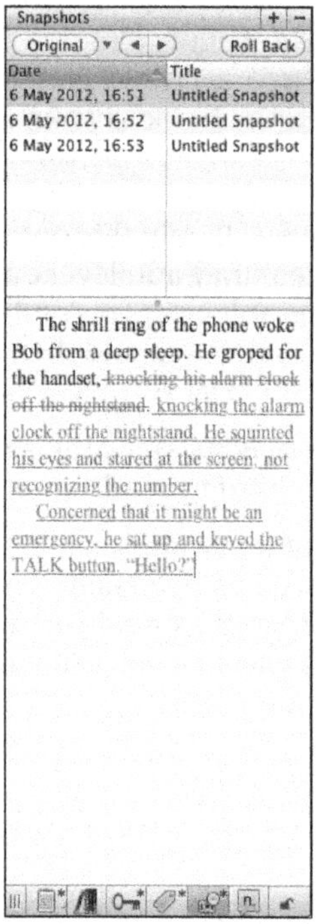

Figure 19-9:
Comparison
by clause.

If word-by-word analysis is too messy but the paragraph level doesn't provide enough detail, choose this option.

✔ **By Word:** Choosing this option forces the markups to go word by word, showing exactly which words were deleted or added to the document, as depicted in Figure 19-10. Again, the example in Figure 19-10 uses the same snapshot and current document for comparison as in Figures 19-8 and 19-9. Entire sentences, clauses or paragraphs are highlighted only if they're entirely new or were wholly deleted.

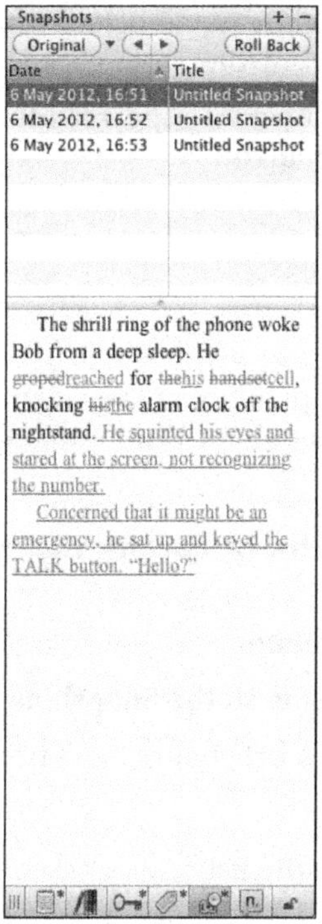

Figure 19-10:
Comparison
by word.

Rolling Back to a Previous Document Version

Say you've been cruising along with revisions, and at some point decide the new version of your document is horrible and you want to go back to what you had before. Snapshots make it easy to do just that by following these steps:

1. **If the Snapshots pane isn't visible in the Inspector, click the Snapshots button.**

2. **(Optional) Using the Take Snapshot button, take a snapshot of your current document.**

   Or you can use one of the other methods outlined in this chapter.

   I highly recommend this step in case you change your mind again later. I know, writers *never* change their minds, but humor me. Thank you.

3. **Select the snapshot of the version to which you want to roll back.**

4. **Click the Roll Back button.**

   To make sure you followed my advice in Step 2, Scrivener asks whether you want to take a snapshot of the current version before rolling back. If you didn't do it yet and want to, click Yes. Otherwise, click No.

   The snapshot version you chose to roll back to appears in the Editor pane as the current version of your document.

Deleting a Snapshot

Although there's no real need to delete a snapshot, you can clean up your list if it's bothering you or if you took two snapshots of the same version by mistake. Follow these steps:

1. **Open the Snapshots pane in the Inspector by clicking the Snapshots button.**

2. **Select the snapshot that you want to delete.**

3. **Click the Delete Selected Snapshot button in the Snapshots header.**

   A window appears, warning you that this procedure can't be undone.

4. **Click OK.**

   The selected snapshot is removed from the list.

Setting Up Automatic Snapshots

If you want save the day's changes after each writing session, the Automatic Snapshots feature is for you. You can set up Scrivener to automatically take a snapshot of all changed documents every time you manually save your project.

Follow the steps below to automate snapshots:

1. **Choose Scrivener⇨Preferences.**

   The Preferences window appears.

2. **Click the General button at the top of the window to view the General options.**

3. **In the Saving section, select the Take Snapshots of Changed Text Documents on Manual Save check box.**

Now, whenever you manually save the project — either by choosing File⇨Save or pressing ⌘+S — Scrivener takes a snapshot called Untitled (Save) for each changed text document.

Chapter 20

Tracking Your Revisions

*H*ow would you like a way to visually represent your revisions right in the text, and even keep track of multiple levels of revisions at the same time? You can with Scrivener's revision marking feature.

The revision tools let you track added and deleted text with colors coded for each round of revisions, up to five.

Before you rush ahead, keep a few things in mind. Marking revisions is not a full-featured change-tracking tool that lets you toggle between the marked up and final versions. (However, you can compare file versions with snapshots, covered in Chapter 19.) And when you delete or overwrite text, it disappears just like in a standard writing session, although there is a way to mark text for deletion instead.

Essentially, Revision mode is a simplified way to change the text color to match revision levels.

That said, if you want an organized way of applying text colors to keep track of your edits or another user's changes, this chapter takes you through the process.

Marking Text

When the Revision mode is on, all new text added is in the selected revision color until you turn it off.

To turn on Revision mode, choose Format⇨Revision Mode, and then choose the desired revision level/color from the submenu that appears, as shown in Figure 20-1.

A small window appears to let you know you're about to enter Revision mode. Click OK to continue. The cursor changes color to match the selected revision level color and to remind you that you're in Revision mode.

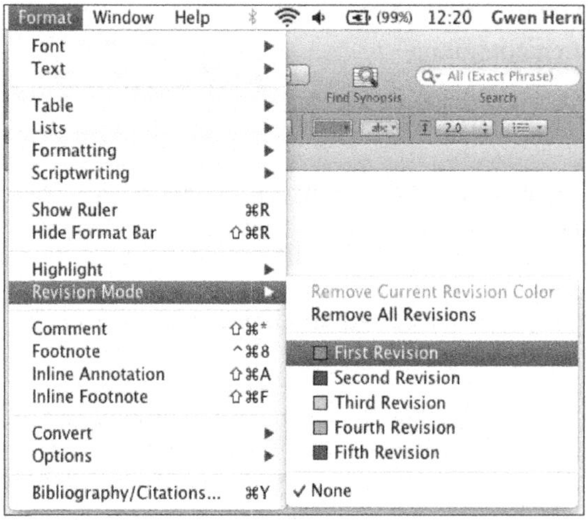
Format
Window
Help
12:20
Gwen Hern
Font
Text
Table
Lists
Formatting
Scriptwriting
Show Ruler ⌘R
Hide Format Bar ⇧⌘R
Highlight
Revision Mode
Comment ⇧⌘*
Footnote ^⌘8
Inline Annotation ⇧⌘A
Inline Footnote ⇧⌘F
Convert
Options
Bibliography/Citations... ⌘Y
Remove Current Revision Color
Remove All Revisions
First Revision
Second Revision
Third Revision
Fourth Revision
Fifth Revision
✓ None

Figure 20-1: The Revision Mode submenu.

All text you add until you exit Revision mode is in the selected color. In Figure 20-2, I chose First Revision, so the new text shows up red.

If you copy and paste text, instead of typing it in, the text doesn't get marked. To get around this omission, choose Edit⇨Paste and Match Style rather than the standard Paste command. Just be aware that Paste and Match Style drops formatting such as italics and bold.

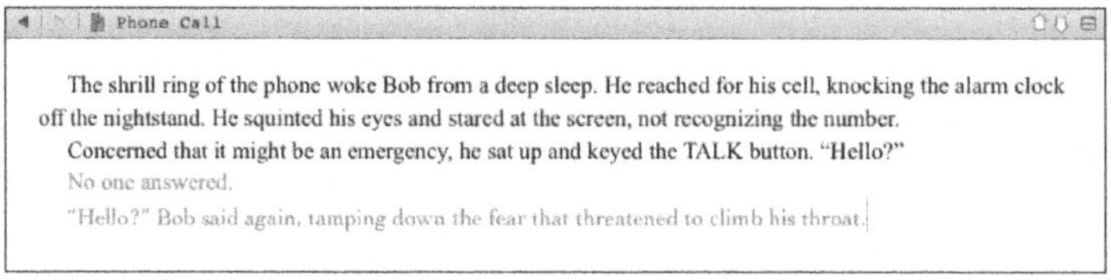
Phone Call
The shrill ring of the phone woke Bob from a deep sleep. He reached for his cell, knocking the alarm clock off the nightstand. He squinted his eyes and stared at the screen, not recognizing the number.
Concerned that it might be an emergency, he sat up and keyed the TALK button. "Hello?"
No one answered.
"Hello?" Bob said again, tamping down the fear that threatened to climb his throat.

Figure 20-2: Added text marked in Revision mode.

If you want to turn off Revision mode, choose Format➪Revision Mode, and then choose the current revision level from the submenu that appears or choose None. (The current revision level is designated with a checkmark.)

Marking text with a new level

When you're done with one round of edits but don't want to get rid of the color denoting your previous changes, you can move to a new level — and color — of revisions. Choose Format➪Revision Mode, and then choose a different revision level from the submenu that appears. The cursor changes to match the color of the level you chose.

Any text you add now appears in the new color, as shown in Figure 20-3. In the last sentence, where I replaced the last three words with `suffocate him` — don't judge! — you can't tell what was there before. For that reason, it's still a good idea to take a snapshot before you make any changes to a document. (I cover snapshots in Chapter 19.)

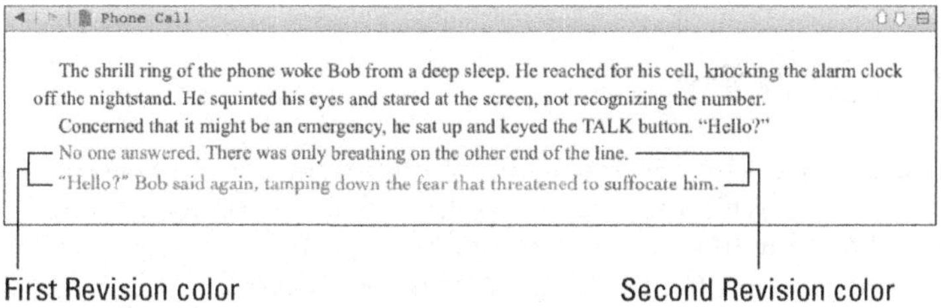

Figure 20-3: An additional level of revisions.

First Revision color   Second Revision color

Marking existing text

If you changed text before you remembered to turn on revision marking, or you pasted in text without using Paste and Match Style, you can go back and mark it up. Just select the text to mark, and then choose Format➪Revision Mode➪Mark Revised. The text changes to the current revision level color.

Marking text for deletion

Revision mode doesn't keep track of deleted text, but you can mark the text for deletion by applying strikethrough formatting while in Revision mode. Select the text that you want to mark for deletion, and then choose Format➪Font➪Strikethrough.

A line is drawn through the text, colored to match the current revision level, as shown in Figure 20-4. Only the line is colored to match, not the text, which makes sense when you consider that the text might be in one revision color, and the strikethrough in another, as is the case in the second sentence marked for deletion in Figure 20-4.

You can leave strikethrough-formatted text in your project but omit it when you export your manuscript. The "Compiling with Marked Revisions" section, later in this chapter, talks about handling revisions during the Compile process.

Marked for deletion

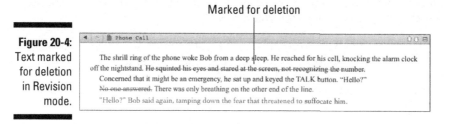

Figure 20-4:
Text marked
for deletion
in Revision
mode.

Finding Revisions

Scrivener's Find by Formatting function provides the option to search by revision level, which lets you step through each change to decide whether you're happy with it or ready to delete it. (You can discover more about Find by Formatting in Chapter 17.) Follow these steps:

1. **Choose Edit➪Find➪Find by Formatting.**

   The Formatting Finder window opens.

2. **In the Find drop-down list, select Revision Color.**

3. **If you're looking for a revision with specific text in it, enter the text into the Containing Text text box.**

   Otherwise, leave this text box blank.

4. **From the Search In drop-down list, select whether you want to go through All Documents or Selected Documents (those selected in the Binder).**

5. **In the drop-down list at the bottom of the window, select which revision color you want to find.**

6. **Click Next.**

Scrivener highlights the next instance of that revision color in your project, as shown in Figure 20-5 (where I searched all documents for Second Revision). Continue to click Next until you've cycled through all the desired revisions.

Any other text in your project that uses the same color as the revision level is also highlighted.

7. **Click the red X button to close the Formatting Finder window when you're done.**

Matching revisions are highlighted

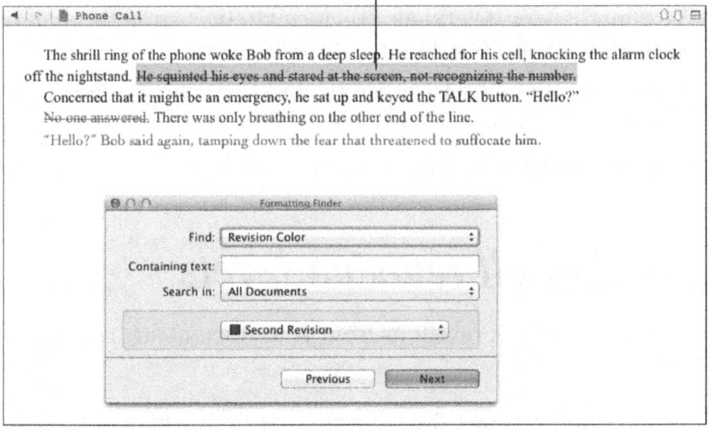

Figure 20-5:
Finding text
by revision
level.

Removing Revisions

When you're done working with the revision colors, you can remove them from the text one color at a time or all at the same time.

Removal applies only to the document(s) being viewed in the Editor, so to affect the entire manuscript, select the Manuscript (Draft) folder and go to View⇨Scrivenings.

Removing revisions by color

If you're done working with a specific level of revisions and you're ready to make the changes permanent — meaning change them back to regular text — you can remove the revisions in only that color by following these steps:

1. **Select the desired document(s) to work with in the Binder.**

2. **Click in the Editor pane to activate it.**

3. **If you're not in Revision mode already, choose Format➪Revision Mode, and choose the color/level that you want to remove from the submenu that appears.**

   The cursor changes color to indicate that you're in Revision mode.

4. **Choose Format➪Revision Mode➪Remove Current Revision Color.**

   All text in that revision color changes to regular text.

   In fact, because revision marking is really just applying text colors, any text in the same color as the Revision mode you're removing reverts to regular text, even if the color was not applied via Revision mode.

   Text marked for deletion is still formatted as strikethrough text, rather than actually deleted, but it returns to black.

5. **Choose Format➪Revision Mode, and then choose the color/level that you were working with or choose None.**

   Revision mode is toggled off.

Removing all revision levels

To remove all levels of revisions from your document(s) at one time, follow these steps:

1. **In the Binder, select the document(s) from which you want to remove revision colors.**

2. **Click in the Editor pane to activate it.**

3. **Choose Format➪Revision Mode➪Remove All Revisions.**

   All revision markings, regardless of color, are removed. Text marked for deletion still has strikethrough formatting applied, it just appears in the standard text color.

Changing Revision Mode Colors

Not a fan of the default revision color scheme used by Scrivener? In that case, you can modify the colors to suit your taste — but keep a couple of things in mind before doing so:

   ✓ **If you change the colors used, any previously applied revision markings are no longer associated with that revision level.** So, if you change First Revision from red to yellow, red text isn't converted to regular text when you remove revisions, nor can you find that text by using the Revision Color setting in the Formatting Finder (although you can search for Colored Text, instead). Refer to the "Finding Revisions" section, earlier in this chapter, for more on the Formatting Finder.

✓ **If you're using Revision Mode with a partner who also uses Scrivener and you change your colors, the revision features don't work properly when you exchange projects.** You must either both use the standard colors or both choose exactly the same set of colors.

To ensure you and your writing partner are using the same palette, you can share your Revision mode colors — and all other preferences. Choose Scrivener➪Preferences to open the Preferences window. From any tab, click the Manage button at the bottom of the window and choose Save All Preferences from the pop-up menu that appears. If desired, change the filename in the Save As text box. Choose a location from the list at the left, and then click Save.

To load saved preferences, click the Manage button and choose Load All Preferences from the pop-up menu that appears. In the Open window, navigate to the file in the list on the left, and then click Open. Scrivener updates with the preferences from the file.

✓ **When you change the colors, you're changing the palette at the Scrivener level, not the project level.** So, all projects use the new color scheme.

If you still want to change the colors, follow these steps:

1. **Choose Scrivener➪Preferences.**

2. **Click the Appearance button in the window that appears.**

3. **In the left half of the Customizable Colors pane, select Revision Colors.**

4. **In the right half of the pane, choose the revision level that you want to change.**

5. **Click the Color box on the far right and select the desired color from the Colors window that appears.**

6. **Repeat Steps 2 through 5 for each level that you want to change.**

7. **Close the Preferences window by clicking the red X button.**

To change back to the default color, follow the preceding steps, but in Step 5, click the Use Default Color button.

Compiling with Marked Revisions

If you want to leave your revision colors and struck-through text in your project but don't want them to appear in your exported file (see Part IV of this book for more on exporting), you can use a couple of Compile options for most output types:

✓ **To remove text that's marked for deletion from the final output, go to the Transformations tab in the Compile window and select Delete Struck-Through Text.** This option actually strips out the text, deleting it from the output, but not from your project. It's a great way to see how your final manuscript would read without the text, without actually getting rid of it.

✓ **Remove all revision colors by going to the Transformations tab in the Compile window and selecting Remove Text Color.** This option leaves all text as written but removes the color from the output. It also removes text color from other text, even if it wasn't colored through the revision process.

If you have text marked for deletion, it appears with strikethrough formatting unless you also select the Delete Struck-Through Text option.

Chapter 21

Protecting Your Work with Automatic and Manual Backups

. . . .

In This Chapter

▶ Figuring out how and why to use backups

▶ Changing the automatic backup preferences

▶ Turning off automatic backup for a project

▶ Creating a backup file manually

▶ Opening a backup file

. . . .

I've dropped my laptop onto a hard tile floor and scratched the hard drive, had a water bottle leak onto a three-day-old laptop when my tote bag fell over in the car, and had a hard drive go bad within two weeks of buying the computer.

The moral of the story? Things happen. Kids, animals, viruses, natural disasters, spilled coffee, thieves, and manufacturing defects. The worst-case scenario is that you lose everything, but if you're backing up your important files — and all your writing is important — then a damaged computer can be nothing more than a nuisance.

I'll take the nuisance any day.

Follow the strategies in this chapter to mitigate the effects of your next disaster.

Understanding the Importance of Backups

You have several things to consider when coming up with a backup plan:

- **I'm not just talking about your Scrivener files.** Seriously consider backing up anything and everything you wouldn't want to lose: photos, saved e-mails, important documents, resumes and job histories, tax returns, electronic receipts, and everything you've ever written.

- **I recommend both a local and offsite backup method.** A flash drive works great for your writing projects, but it doesn't do you any good if it's turned to goo in a fire right along with your computer, or snatched with your laptop from your hotel room. An external hard drive might be able to store everything, but it's subject to natural disasters and theft, as well.

- **Use local options, but look into something offsite, too.** Check your Internet service provider to see whether they offer storage with your account. If not, you have plenty of online sites to choose from. Ask around, do some research, and think about what you need from a site before spending any money.

- **Have an easily accessible backup of your writing project.** Create this backup, in addition to a regular, large-scale backup of all your files (both on- and offsite). I use a flash drive most of the time, but you could use a CD, DVD, external hard drive, online file-drop service, another computer in your house, or a floppy disk (if you're old school). Some people even e-mail themselves their project at the end of each day!

Luckily, Scrivener provides options to automate the process, so you have no excuse not to back up your work.

Setting Up Automatic Backup Preferences

Scrivener is set up to save your project to your hard drive two seconds after user activity stops. So, every time you stop typing or working with a menu, Scrivener saves the project. It also automatically backs up each project to your hard drive upon closing, maintaining five versions. Although you're unlikely to lose any work if your power goes out or you encounter a fatal error, you could very well lose your work if the hard drive starts smoking and the data can't be recovered.

Never fear, automatic backup is here. Before I get into how to set it up, keep the following in mind:

- ✔ **You can choose only one location for all Scrivener file backups.** If you're like me and you keep your projects organized into nice hierarchical folders, it might annoy you that your backups can't be organized in a similar way. Just remember that all backups are in the same place, and you'll be fine.

- ✔ **If you want to backup your project to more than one location — which I highly recommend anyway — you have to find a way to schedule one of the backups to run on its own or remember to do it manually.** This is where the companies that provide backup software come in handy. You can include your Scrivener files in the list of those to backup offsite automatically, then use the Scrivener backup feature for your local drive. Or backup automatically to a file-drop site and perform a manual flash-drive backup.

- ✔ **Automatic backup settings apply to all projects.** This not only includes the location, but all the other settings, as well. You may override this behavior by excluding a project from automatic backup, if desired. See the following section for more information.

- ✔ **The drive you plan to use must be visible as a folder when you set up and perform backups.** If you're using a flash drive, external drive, or online file-drop service, make sure it's connected before setting up the backup preferences.

Follow these steps to set up the backup preferences:

1. **Choose Scrivener⇨Preferences.**

   For Windows users, choose Tools⇨Options.

   The Preferences window appears.

2. **Select the Backup tab.**

   The Backup Options window appears, as shown in Figure 21-1. The options may be initially grayed out (which shows they're unavailable) until you complete Step 3.

3. **If it's not already, select Turn on Automatic Backups.**

   The Backup options become active.

4. **Select the desired backup trigger.**

   These options aren't mutually exclusive; you can choose more than one:

   - *Back Up on Project Open:* Saves a backup when you open the project to ensure that you have one before you start making changes. If you had several projects open when you last closed Scrivener, it may take a few minutes to start up because it saves a backup for each file while it opens.

Figure 21-1:
Automatic
backup
options.

Backup

General Appearance Corkboard Compose Navigation Editor Formatting Corrections Import/Export Backup

☑ Turn on automatic backups
☐ Back up on project open
☐ Back up on project close
☑ Back up with each manual save

☑ Compress automatic backups as zip files (slower)
☐ Use date in backup file names
☑ Only keep 5 ⇕ most recent backups

Backup location: /Volumes/GwenH   [Choose...]
                  [Open backup folder...]

[Manage... ▼]   [Defaults]

WARNING!

I don't recommend using this option by itself because if you close your project down at night and something happens before you open it the next morning, you lose a whole day's work.

• *Back Up on Project Close:* Choosing this option saves a backup when you close the project, regardless of whether you close the project individually or quit Scrivener.

If you have several projects open in Scrivener and then close Scrivener with this option set, it may take a while to actually shut down because it has to perform backups for each file first.

This option is best if you close your project after each writing session or each day.

• *Back Up with Each Manual Save:* This choice creates a backup every time you choose File➪Save or its shortcut (⌘+S [Mac] or Ctrl+S [Windows]).

I love this option because I can force a backup just by saving my file, so I don't have to wait all day if I've made a lot of changes. This option also works well for me because I tend to not close my projects or Scrivener for days at a time.

The downside is that this option requires you to initiate the backup, so it's good to use it in conjunction with one of the other choices, just to be safe. It can also slow you down if you manually save your project frequently out of habit, especially if the project file is large.

TIP

If you want to be able to create a backup on command but don't want it to happen every time you manually save your project, you can use the Back Up Now option covered in the "Forcing a Manual Backup" section, later in this chapter.

5. **Select Compress Automatic Backups as Zip Files.**

   This option does slow down the backup process, but it creates smaller files that are less likely to become corrupted. Zipped files work much better for Internet transfer, so if you're using a file-drop service or online storage, definitely choose to zip the files.

6. **If desired, select Use Date in Backup File Names.**

   This option inserts the date right into the name of the backed up file.

7. **Specify how many versions you want to keep before deleting.**

   The default is five. Too many versions will fill up your storage device, but sometimes it's good to be able to go back to an earlier version. Think about how often your file gets backed up and how many versions you want to be able to access.

   I recommend keeping at least two versions so that you can go back to a previous version, if necessary, but anything more than five backups starts to eat up space on your backup drive.

8. **Next to the Backup Location text box, click Choose.**

   A file window appears.

9. **Select the location where you want Scrivener to store your backup files.**

   If you get an error message that the backup volume isn't available, go into your file system (Finder or Windows Explorer) and make sure it's connected. Sometimes online storage sites get disconnected after you restart your computer, and you have to re-establish the link.

   If you're using a flash drive and it doesn't show, it may have been ejected without being removed from the computer. Try removing it and plugging it in again. For an external drive, ensure that it's plugged in and turned on.

10. **Click the red X button to close the Preferences window.**

    On a Windows PC, click OK.

Excluding a Project from Automatic Backup

At some point, you may have a project that you want to exclude from Scrivener's automatic backup settings. Maybe it's so large that it takes too long to back up. You really notice this lag when you're backing up when closing the project and have several projects to shut down. A large project can also slow you down if you have Scrivener set so that it creates a backup when you manually save.

Other reasons include not wanting that file backed up to the same location or not wanting to back up the project at all if it's something that you'll delete right away (such as a practice project).

Whatever your reasons, you can exclude a project from the automated Scrivener backup easily. Just open the project you want to exclude, and then choose File⇨Back Up⇨Exclude from Automatic Backups.

Be sure to have another backup method in place so that you don't lose your work.

To include a project in automatic backups again, simply remove the check mark from Exclude from Automatic Backups in the File⇨Backup submenu.

Forcing a Manual Backup

Want to quickly back up your project right now, but don't have — or don't want — the preferences set up to create a backup on project save? Choose File⇨Back Up⇨Back Up Now. A backup is immediately created in the location specified in Backup preferences. Backups created this way are treated just like automatic backups and are replaced by newer backup files when the version limit set up in Backup preferences is reached.

However, if you want to back up the file to another location, follow these steps:

1. **Choose File⇨Back Up⇨Back Up To.**

   A Save window appears.

2. **(Optional) Enter a new filename in the Back Up To text box.**

   You can also simply keep the provided filename.

3. **From the file list on the left, choose the location.**

   If you don't see the full window of location options, click the expansion button to the right of the Back Up To text box. (Windows users, click Browse.)

4. **For best performance, make sure Backup as a Zip File is selected.**

5. **Click Save.**

   Windows users, click OK.

A backup of the project is saved with the name and to the location you chose.

Backups created this way aren't automatically deleted, regardless of the number of versions you chose to keep in the Backup preferences, so Back Up To is a good option when you want to keep a backup of a specific version of your project.

Restoring a Project from a Backup File

Having all these project backup files doesn't do you any good if you don't know how to use them when needed.

Follow these steps to open a project from a backup file:

1. **Locate the file in Finder or Windows Explorer.**

   Automatically backed up files are called *ProjectName*`.bak.scriv` if uncompressed, or *ProjectName*`.bak.zip` if compressed.

   To locate the backup files easily, choose Scrivener⇨Preferences (Windows users, choose Tools⇨Options), and then select the Backup tab to view the Backup settings and click the Open Backup Folder button. (The backup drive must be connected for this process to work.)

2. **(Optional) Make a copy of the backup file and move it to the folder in which you keep your writing projects.**

   Copying the file ensures you're not working on the file in the backup folder, which could cause problems with other backup files. It also prevents you from losing that version of the backup.

3. **If using a compressed file with the `.zip` extension, double-click the file.**

   On a Windows PC, right-click the file and choose Extract.

   The Archive Utility runs, unzipping the file. After it finishes, you have the original `.zip` file and the uncompressed `.scriv` file.

   If necessary, remove the `.bak` portion from the name to make it clear that it's a working file. Be sure to rename the original project file (that you're replacing with the backup) to something like `OLD_`*filename*`.scriv` to avoid confusion.

4. **Open the restored project file by double-clicking it, and then get back to work!**

What if you don't want to roll back to the old version of your project, but you need to restore one or two documents? No problem. Follow the preceding steps to open the backup file, but rename the backup rather than your current project. With both projects open at the same time, you can drag the old versions of the files you need from one Binder to the other, creating a copy in the current project.

Part VII
The Part of Tens

"Shouldn't we just contact Scrivener Technical Support?"

In this part . . .

In this part, I throw in the things that I didn't get to mention elsewhere in the book. But don't be fooled: These aren't the worthless crumbs, they're gold.

You can find ten nifty things you can do in Scrivener and ten ways to get help beyond this book.

Chapter 22

Ten Awesome Features That Didn't Fit Anywhere Else

*I*f I covered absolutely everything that Scrivener can do, this book would be better for bench-pressing than reading, so I had to pare it down. But a few of the nifty tools I wanted to share with you wouldn't fit neatly into any of the other chapters.

This chapter gives you ten of my favorites.

Showing Invisible Characters

Just like your favorite word processor, Scrivener has a way to reveal those hidden codes for elements such as tabs, paragraph breaks, spaces, and page breaks.

Not sure what's up with your formatting? Choose Format⇨Options⇨Show Invisibles to check. The invisible characters appear in blue. To turn them off, choose Format⇨Options⇨Hide Invisibles.

Copying Files between Projects

Have a document, research file, or image in another project, but you want it in this one, too? Dead easy.

Just open both Scrivener projects — after you open one, choose File➪Open and choose the other. Then, move or resize one window so that you can see both Binders and drag the file — or files if you've selected more than one — from one Binder to the other.

Scrivener copies the documents into the Binder where you drop them.

Taking Notes with the Scratch Pad

The Scratch Pad is a tool that lets you jot down notes that don't apply to a particular project. If you later decide that they belong in a particular project, you can import the notes to the Binder.

But even better, you can use the Scratch Pad when your project's not even open (as long as Scrivener's running)!

Here's how it all works:

- ✔ **Opening the Scratch Pad:** To open the Scratch Pad from within Scrivener, choose Window➪Show Scratch Pad (or Tools➪Scratch Pad in Windows).

  The Scratch Pad window appears. This window floats above all other programs, which makes it good as a reference tool or to enter notes while viewing a web page or other document.

  The top half of the window is a list of all the notes you've stored. When you first open it, your note is called Untitled Note. Double-click to change the name. Click the plus sign (+) button at the bottom-left to add a new note. Do your writing in the bottom pane.

- ✔ **Sending a note to a project:** When you're ready to send a note to a project, select it from the list, click the Send to Project drop-down list at the bottom (called Send File to Scrivener in Windows), and then choose from your open projects.

- ✔ **Deleting a note:** Delete a note by selecting it and pressing the Delete key (Shift+Delete on Windows), or clicking the Delete button (which looks like a circle with a diagonal line through it). Click OK to close the window.

✔ **Opening the Scratch Pad when Scrivener is minimized:** This is a Mac-only option. To open the Scratch Pad when Scrivener isn't visible, right-click the Scrivener icon in the Dock and choose Scratch Pad.

Looking at the Editor in Page View

To make the Editor appear more like a printed page, including document edges and margins, choose View⇨Page View⇨Show Page View.

Want to see two pages side by side? After you turn on Page view, choose View⇨Page View⇨Two Pages Across.

Just remember, Page view isn't necessarily an accurate representation of how pages will print; it's merely a visual preference. The final layout of your output depends on your compile settings (see Part IV for details on compiling).

To turn off Page view, choose View⇨Page View⇨Hide Page View.

For scriptwriters who tend to compile based on the settings in the Editor, Page View is especially handy because it can provide a page count that's fairly close to the final output. To set it up, after you turn on Page View, choose View⇨Page View⇨Use Printed Page Size. The Editor footer displays the estimated page number and total pages for the document(s) being viewed in the Editor, based on the page size and margin settings available by choosing File⇨Page Setup (select Scrivener from the Settings drop-down list to change the margins).

Appending Text to a Document

If you have a chunk of text in one document that you want to add to the bottom of another — but you don't want to merge the two documents, as outlined in Chapter 2 — follow these steps:

1. **Select the desired text in the Editor.**

2. **Choose Edit⇨Append Selection to Document.**

3. **From the submenu that appears, choose the file to which you want to append the text.**

   The text is copied from the current document and added at the end of the document you selected.

In the submenu, you can also select New, rather than an existing file. If you do, a window appears, prompting you to choose a Binder location and a title, and then creates a new file that contains the selected text after you click OK. It also adds an internal reference (covered in Chapter 5) between the current document and the new one.

Append Selection to Document is also available from the contextual menu that appears when you right-click a selection of text.

Creating Links between Documents in a Project

You can create links from one document to another that appear just like web-page hyperlinks — but they jump you to a document.

Inserting a link with a title

To create a link to a document right within the current text, click in the desired location. Then, choose Edit⇨Scrivener Link (or right-click in the Editor), and choose the document to which you want to link from the submenu that appears.

The linked document title appears as a hyperlink within the current document.

Converting existing text to a link

To add a link to a specific selection of text, instead of using the linked document title, select the desired text, choose Edit⇨Scrivener Link, and then choose the document to which you want to link from the submenu that appears.

The selected text becomes a hyperlink that takes you to the linked document when clicked.

Removing a link

To remove a link with a title, you can simply select and delete the link from the text. If you converted text to a link, you probably don't want to delete the text, but merely remove the hyperlink.

To remove the hyperlink without removing the linked text, select the text in the Editor, and then choose Edit⇨Unlink. To remove multiple links in a document, select a range of text that includes all the links, and then choose Edit⇨Unlink.

Be careful, though — Unlink removes all hyperlinks, not just Scrivener links.

Changing link behavior

You can either open links in the current Editor, a second split Editor (listed as Other Editor), or a QuickReference panel. To determine the behavior, follow these steps:

1. **Choose Scrivener⇨Preferences.**

2. **Click the Navigation button at the top of the window.**

    The Navigation options appear.

3. **Select the desired location from the Open Clicked Scrivener Links In drop-down list.**

Inserting a Table of Contents

Want to include a table of contents (TOC) in your project? Just follow these steps:

1. **Add a new text document in the Binder by clicking the Add button in the toolbar.**

    Alternatively, choose Project⇨New Text.

    Skip to Step 2 if you're planning to insert the TOC within an existing document.

2. **In the Binder, select the desired documents that you want include in the TOC.**

    You must select all items that you want to include. (Choosing a folder doesn't include its subdocuments.)

    To expand all items in the Binder for easy selection, click in the Binder, and then choose View⇨Outline⇨Expand All.

3. **Choose Edit⇨Copy Special⇨Copy Documents as TOC.**

4. **Select the document in which you want to insert the TOC.**

5. **Click in the Editor to position the cursor at the desired location within the document, and then choose Edit⇨Paste.**

The list of selected Binder items is pasted into the document, along with placeholder tags (covered in Chapter 12) that automatically insert the page number when the project is compiled by using the Print, PDF, or RTF output type (for more on compiling, see Part IV).

You can click the page tags to view the linked document. How the document opens depends on the Navigation settings, which are covered in the preceding section.

Sorting Paragraphs

It's a snap to put a selection of paragraphs in alphabetical order, either ascending or descending. Just select two or more paragraphs (lines of text followed by a paragraph break — a hard return), choose Edit⇨Sort Paragraphs, and choose Ascending (A–Z) or Descending (Z–A) from the submenu that appears.

Note: This option doesn't work for rows within a table. To sort table rows, click in the column that you want to sort by, and then choose Format⇨Table⇨Sort Rows Ascending or Sort Rows Descending (depending on how you want to sort).

Making Duplicates of Binder Items

The Duplicate feature lets you make an exact copy of an item, including all its settings, contents, and metadata. You may want to make a duplicate if you want a copy of a scene before you revise it — although I recommend taking a snapshot, instead (see Chapter 19). Alternatively, you can use duplicates if you want to create a series of folders that have the same properties so that you can use them for a new project or project template.

You can choose to duplicate an item by itself or copy the item and all its subdocuments.

Duplicate with subdocuments

When you duplicate with subdocuments, Scrivener makes a complete copy of the item and all the items it contains, so if you duplicate a folder, all the documents inside that folder are copied, too.

To use Duplicate, in the Binder, select the item that you want to copy, and then choose Documents➪Duplicate➪With Subdocuments and Unique Title (in Windows, the option is simply With Subdocuments).

On the Mac, this option creates a new file with the same name, but the word copy appended to the end. In Windows, the new file appears with the name ready to edit.

To duplicate with subdocuments, you can also right-click a file in the Binder and choose Duplicate from the contextual menu that appears, or press Command+D (Control+D in Windows). The item and any subdocuments are copied.

Duplicate without subdocuments

Choosing to duplicate without subdocuments doesn't copy subdocuments or provide a distinguishing title for the new file. To use it, in the Binder, select the item that you want to copy, and then choose Documents➪ Duplicate➪Without Subdocuments.

On the Mac, this option creates a new file with the same name. On Windows, the new file appears with the name ready to edit.

Naming Names

Ever have trouble thinking of a character name? Need a name for your baby or your new Betta fish? Try the name generator. Just choose Edit➪Writing Tools➪Name Generator (Tools➪Writing Tools➪Name Generator in Windows).

In the Name Generator window that appears, use the slider to determine how many names you want (Windows users, enter the number in the # of Names to Generate text box), and then click Generate Names.

For more options, Mac users can click the gear button to choose gender, ethnic persuasion, and other nifty tricks such as alliterative names (think Walt Whitman, Galileo Galilee, Marilyn Monroe). Windows users have access to additional options in the right half of the window, and also in the tabs along the top of the window.

Chapter 23

Ten Ways to Get More Help

I hope this book is a resource you'll use until it falls apart. But if you want to know something I haven't covered, or you need some extra help, you don't have to just muddle through. This chapter provides ten more ways to find answers.

Getting Interactive with the Tutorial

If you haven't browsed the Help menu lately, you're missing out on some valuable resources. One of the best places to start is the interactive tutorial that walks you step-by-step through Scrivener's main features. The tutorial provides a good introduction to get you up and running in no time.

Get started by choosing Help⇨Interactive Tutorial. You can also access the tutorial by choosing File⇨New Project in the Getting Started tab.

Using the User Manual

The Scrivener manual is the complete, definitive guide to everything you ever wanted to know about Scrivener. Yes, it's a bit technical at times — by necessity — but it's searchable and has a helpful table of contents. When you want the nitty-gritty details, or the complete list of options for a feature, the User Manual is your man(ual).

Choose Help⇨Scrivener Manual to dig in. The manual is also available by choosing File⇨New Project in the Getting Started tab.

Letting the Template Be Your Guide

When you choose any project template other than Blank, the template comes preloaded with a guide. That guide appears at the very top of the Binder, above the Manuscript (Draft) folder, and contains all sorts of information about how the template is set up, how to use it, how to change it, and the compile settings.

If you're not sure about something mentioned in the template guide, look it up in this book!

Watching Online Video Tutorials

In addition to the interactive tutorial mentioned in the section "Getting Interactive with the Tutorial," earlier in this chapter, those awesome folks at Literature & Latte continue to create helpful online videos that take you step-by-step through a Scrivener topic. Access the videos at http://literatureandlatte.com/videos.php or by choosing Help⟹Video Tutorials.

Finding Your Answers in the Forum

Chances are, if you have a question, someone else has already asked it. If they did, you can probably find it in the Scrivener support forum. And if they didn't, you can ask the question yourself and get an answer from one of the super-knowledgeable forum moderators — the same folks at Literature & Latte who respond to technical support requests and help build the program — or a helpful user.

In addition to technical support, the forums also include announcements about new releases and beta versions, a place to share your wishes for new features, tips from other users, a place to report bugs, and even some forums for fun and procrastination.

Check out the forums — gladiator-free — at http://literatureand latte.com/forum or by choosing Help⟹User Forums.

Searching for Answers on the FAQ page

For a quick search of frequently asked questions (FAQs), check out the Scrivener Knowledge Base at `https://scrivener.tenderapp.com/help/kb`.

Checking Out the Scrivener Support Page

Got a problem with your Scrivener purchase? Want to load the software onto more than one personal computer (the license allows for use on multiple computers in your home that have the same operating system), but it's not working? Can't find your serial number to activate the program?

The Support page has helpful links for all these issues and more. Check it out at `http://literatureandlatte.com/support.php` or by choosing Help⇨Support.

E-Mailing Technical Support

If you've gone through all the suggestions in the preceding sections and still can't find the answer you need, as a last resort, you can e-mail technical support.

Just make sure you've exhausted your other options. These guys are friendly and smart, and won't growl like a bear poked with a stick, but they are busy making Scrivener so amazing it'll take over the world. Personally, I like to leave them to it.

You can make their job easier — and your experience better — by giving them a concise but detailed description of your issue, what you were doing when it happened (if applicable), and any other helpful information you can think of (such as the version of operating system you're using).

For help via e-mail, send a message to one of these addresses:

- **For Mac:** `mac.support@literatureandlatte.com`
- **For Windows:** `windows.support@literatureandlatte.com`

Revving the Search Engine

Want to know how others are using Scrivener to craft screenplays, create comics, plot their stories, or write a thesis? Head over to your favorite search engine and enter your query.

Scrivener has fans all over the world who use the program in interesting and unexpected ways — and they blog about it. You might be amazed at what you can find out.

Schmoozing

Writer's groups offer camaraderie and understanding for those of us who often work our craft in solitude. But beyond the fellowship of kindred spirits, many groups offer their own e-mail loops — similar to a discussion board or distribution list — that are devoted to topics such as Scrivener and other technical aspects of writing. If not, maybe you can start one.

There's a group for just about every type of writer out there. Search the web for *writer's organizations* or *writer's associations*, ask your librarian about local meetings of writers, or check out one of these groups:

- **Romance Writers of America:** www.rwa.org
- **International Thriller Writers:** http://thrillerwriters.org
- **Sisters in Crime:** www.sistersincrime.org
- **Mystery Writers of America:** www.mysterywriters.org
- **Science Fiction and Fantasy Writers of America:** www.sfwa.org
- **American Christian Fiction Writers:** www.acfw.com
- **Horror Writers Association:** www.horror.org
- **Society of Children's Book Writers and Illustrators:** www.scbwi.org
- **American Screenwriters Association:** www.americanscreenwriters.com
- **American Society of Journalists and Authors:** www.asja.org

The National Novel Writing Month (NaNoWriMo) site offers forums to its participants, including one on writing technology that has a Scrivener thread going, at: http://new.nanowrimo.org/en/forums/nano-technology.

Index

• D •

Notes

Notes

Notes

Making Everything Easier!™

GADGETS

978-1-1180-2444-7   978-1-1180-3671-6   978-1-1180-2445-4

MAC OS X LION

978-1-1180-2205-4   978-1-1180-2206-1   978-1-1180-2772-1

PROGRAMMING LANGUAGES

978-0-470-37173-2   978-0-470-92996-4   978-0-470-52275-2

Amazing Android Apps For Dummies
978-0-470-93629-0

AutoCAD 2012 For Dummies
978-1-118-02440-9

BlackBerry PlayBook For Dummies
978-1-118-01698-5

Blender For Dummies, 2nd Edition
978-0-470-58446-0

Creating Web Pages All-in-One For
Dummies, 4th Edition
978-0-470-64032-6

Digital SLR Cameras and Photography
For Dummies, 4th Edition
978-1-118-14489-3

Facebook For Dummies, 4th Edition
978-1-118-09562-1

HTML, XHTML & CSS For Dummies,
7th Edition
978-0-470-91659-9

iPad 2 For Dummies, 3rd Edition
978-1-118-17679-5

Laptops and Tablets For Seniors For
Dummies, 2nd Edition
978-1-118-09596-6

Mac Application Development
For Dummies
978-1-118-03222-0

Macs For Dummies, 11th Edition
978-0-470-87868-2

Nikon D5100 For Dummies
978-1-118-11819-1

QuickBooks 2012 For Dummies
978-1-118-09120-3

Samsung Galaxy Tab 10.1
For Dummies
978-1-118-22833-3

Twitter Marketing For Dummies,
2nd Edition
978-0-470-93057-1

WordPress Web Design For Dummies
978-0-470-93503-3

Windows Phone 7 Application
Development For Dummies
978-1-118-02175-0

Making Everything Easier! ™

The ultimate beginner guide to the groundbreaking music service, Spotify!

978-1-1199-5234-3